ROYAL ORDERS

HUGO VICKERS

ROYAL ORDERS

BOXTREE

To my aunt, Margaret Vickers, with love

First published in Great Britain in 1994 by Boxtree Limited, Broadwall House, 21 Broadwall, London SE1 9PL

Copyright © Hugo Vickers 1994

The right of Hugo Vickers to be identified as Author of this work has been asserted by him in accordance with the Copyright, Designs and Patents Act 1988

1 3 5 7 9 10 8 6 4 2

Designed by Robert Updegraff
Printed in Great Britain by Bath Press Colourbooks, Glasgow
ISBN 1 85283 510 9

A CIP catalogue entry is available from the British Library

HALF-TITLE: *The Knights of the Bath, 1953.*

FRONTISPIECE: *Her Majesty the Queen, fount of honour, with the Sultan of Oman*

CONTENTS

ABBREVIATIONS

The following abbreviations are used in this book:

AC   Companion of the Order of Australia
AD   Dame of the Order of Australia
ADC   Aide-de-Camp
AK   Knight of the Order of Australia
AM   member of the Order of Australia; Albert Medal
AO   Officer of the Order of Australia
BEM   British Empire Medal
Bt   Baronet
CB   Companion of the Order of the Bath
CBE   Commander of the Order of the British Empire
CC   Companion of the Order of Canada
CH   Companion of Honour
CI   Imperial Order of the Crown of India
CIE   Companion of the Order of the Indian Empire
CM   Member of the Order of Canada
CMG   Companion of the Order of St Michael and St George
CMM   Commander of the Order of Military Merit
CSI   Companion of the Order of the Star of India
CVO   Commander of the Royal Victorian Order
DBE   Dame Commander of the Order of the British Empire
DCB   Dame Commander of the Order of the Bath
DCMG   Dame Commander of the Order of St Michael and St George
DCVO   Dame Commander of the Royal Victorian Order
DSO   Distinguished Service Order
DStJ   Dame of Grace/Justice, Most Venerable Order of the Hospital of St John of Jerusalem
ERD   Emergency Reserve Decoration (Army)
FRS   Fellow of the Royal Society
GBE   Knight/Dame Grand Cross of the Order of the British Empire
GC   George Cross
GCB   Knight/Dame Grand Cross of the Order of the Bath
GCH   Knight Grand Cross of the Order of Hanover
GCIE   Knight Grand Commander of the Order of the Indian Empire
GCMG   Knight/Dame Grand Cross of the Order of St Michael and St George
GCSI   Knight Grand Commander of the Order of the Star of India

GCStJ   Bailiff/Dame Grand Cross of the Most Venerable Order of the Hospital of St John of Jerusalem
GCVO   Knight/Dame Grand Cross of the Royal Victorian Order
ISO   Imperial Service Order
KB   Knight Companion of the Order of the Bath
KBE   Knight Commander of the Order of the British Empire
KCB   Knight Commander of the Order of the Bath
KCIE   Knight Commander of the Order of the Indian Empire
KCMG   Knight Commander of the Order of St Michael and St George
KCSI   Knight Commander of the Order of the Star of India
KCVO   Knight Commander of the Royal Victorian Order
KG   Knight of the Garter
KP   Knight of St Patrick
KStJ   Knight of the Most Venerable Order of the Hospital of St John of Jerusalem
KT   Knight of the Thistle
LVO   Lieutenant of the Royal Victorian Chain
MBE   Member of the British Empire
MC   Military Cross
MM   Military Medal
MMM   Member of the Order of Military Merit
MVO   Member of the Royal Victorian Order
OBE   Officer of the Order of the British Empire
OC   Officer of the Order of Canada
OM   Order of Merit
OMM   Officer of the Order of Military Merit
ONZ   Order of New Zealand
PC   Privy Counsellor
QGM   Queen's Gallantry Medal
QSM   Queen's Service Medal
QSO   Companion of The Queen's Service Order
RVM   Royal Victorian Medal
RVO   Royal Victorian Order
TD   Efficiency (Territorial) Decoration
VA   Lady of the Order of Victoria and Albert
VC   Victoria Cross

Acknowledgments

I am grateful to the help given me over the years in encouraging my interest in the subject of Orders. My first debt of gratitude must go to the late Roy Read, M.V.O., Virger of St George's Chapel, Windsor, who kindly answered a question about the location of Lord Palmerston's stall-plate in 1966, when I was 14, and unleashed a mass of similar questions put by me to that kind and patient man over the next three years. I feel particularly lucky that he encouraged my interest and allowed it to grow. Any young person is more than fortunate if such a thing happens.

The late General Sir Peter Gillett, Secretary of the Central Chancery of the Orders of Knighthood from 1968 to 1979, kindly agreed to come down to address the Eton College Heraldic and Genealogical Society of which I was honorary Secretary in the late 1960s. He brought with him a considerable quantity of Orders and stars, including the Garter collar of the late Earl of Radnor. His was one of the most interesting talks we had in the society, made the more special by the admitted anxiety of an official he brought with him from the Central Chancery, whose job it was to see that none of these valuable treasures disappeared on their outing from the stronghold of the Central Chancery.

General Gillett greatly fostered my interest in the subject by inviting me on a tour of the Central Chancery, showing me the records he kept, and the fantastic collection of stars, ribands and robes that were stored in their then office in Buckingham Gate. His kindness did not end there. He gave me a front row seat in the nave of Westminster Abbey to witness the installation service of the Prince of Wales as Great Master in May 1975.

Over the years, I have attended every Garter ceremony since 1965 (when I was 13), witnessed services of the Order of the Bath, St Michael and St George, the Royal Victorian Order and the Order of the British Empire. I have visited the chapels of the different Orders in London, and the seat of the Order of St Patrick in Dublin Castle and St Patrick's Cathedral. I have also visited the Thistle Chapel, in St Giles's Cathedral, Edinburgh. Some years ago I saw the collection of uniforms and Orders of the late Duke of Gloucester in the exhibition, *Soldier Royal*, at the Imperial War Museum. I spent two happy afternoons, looking at the late Duke of Windsor's Orders in the National Army Museum, Chelsea, and the late Lord and Lady Mountbatten's at Broadlands, in Romsey, Hampshire.

7

The genesis of this book therefore goes back many years but the possibility of publishing it only came to fruition in the last year thanks to the support and enthusiasm of my friend Michael Alcock at Boxtree. Rare amongst publishers he has allowed my enthusiasm to find its own outlets, encouraged me to create its concept in my own way, and as a result of this I have never enjoyed the process of writing a book more. I am also grateful to Kate Hill for her enthusiastic help.

Colonel Anthony Mather, the present Secretary of the Central Chancery, kindly allowed me to bombard him with questions, and helped me in my quest to check the accuracy of the lists of currently living Grand Crosses of the various Orders. Since my first visit to the Central Chancery some twenty-four years before, it was fascinating to find him poised over a computer on which the honoured are now stored, and equally pleasing to find the old volumes of records still being kept, daily, up to date. I am also grateful to Mr Jeremy Bagwell Purefoy for answering a barrage of questions.

I enjoyed a stimulating conversation with Lord Charteris of Amisfield on the Garter, Thistle and Commonwealth Orders. I am grateful, too, to Lt-Colonel Sir John Johnston, former Comptroller of the Lord Chamberlain's Office, for his interest in this book and for several sources and stories that would otherwise have eluded me.

Sir Edward Ford has been Secretary and Registrar of the Order of Merit since 1975. I enjoyed a long talk with him not only about the Order of Merit but about the other Orders too. Having worked in the Royal Household since 1946 he was somewhat more than an expert on all of them. Kenneth Rose was also a mine of information.

I am grateful to Charles Anson, Press Secretary to H.M. The Queen, Miss Penny Russell-Smith, Assistant Press Secretary to H.M. The Queen, Major Nicholas Barne, Private Secretary to H.R.H. The Duke of Gloucester, Rear Admiral Sir John Garnier, Private Secretary to H.R.H. Princess Alexandra, The Hon. Lady Ogilvy, and to the office of H.R.H. The Duke of Kent for information about the Orders held by Members of the Royal Family; and to Francesca Alden, Deputy Curator of the Museum and Library of the Order of St John, who kindly perused records dating back over one hundred years

I am also grateful to Mr Douglas Sturkey, Secretary of the Order of Australia and to Mr Gordon Lewis, Director, Honours, Rideau Hall, Canada, for help with the Australian and Canadian honours system, to Mr Steve Ruelberg, of California, for information on the Indian princes, and also to my friends, Mr and Mrs Richard Dumbrille, who sent me wonderful information about the Order of Canada and the other Canadian decorations.

I would also like to thank my cousin, Elizabeth Vickers, Christie's and Spink's for their help with photographs for this book.

Finally I thank Mrs Bronwen Sutton, who helped me marshal the Knights and Dames Grand Cross into order and transcribed a great deal of other information into my text.

Introduction

The need to give recognition for service is long established, and strange customs have evoled concerning the methods whereby some people are elevated over others. Today it seems almost anachronistic to talk of giving someone the Garter, the Thistle or indeed the Bath. And yet these Orders are as keenly sought now as ever they were in medieval times. And it is extraordinary that when countries like Canada disassociate themselves from the British honours system they soon find they are inventing their own orders and so the system continues.

We are used to receiving, or seeing others receive prizes, whether at school or in the Olympic Games. Little children troop up to have their hands shaken by a lady in a petal hat. There is the victor, hot from the race, standing on a plinth while some worthy figure hangs a ribbon and badge around his or her neck.

The Orders discussed in this book are those in the gift of the Queen or those given by the Queen on the recommendation of the Prime Minister. The Order of the Garter is of course the most famous and the most prestigious and dates back to 1348. In its long history there have been many intrigues and dramas, some of which are not so far back in time. In Scotland there is the Thistle, reserved in the olden days for landed Scottish peers but now given to a varied crowd of worthy recipients as long as they have some Scottish ancestry. The Irish order, the Order of St Patrick, was always a somewhat strange affair, and has sadly played but a small part in the history of this century.

The Order of Merit, on the other hand, thrives, and amongst its 160 members are found perhaps the most fascinating group of achievers in the fields of science, medicine, the arts, literature and even politics, despite the original hope that politicians be excluded. The Order of the Bath has developed, too, into an Order in the one part military (naval and air force), and the other civil (distinguished civil servants and others). A fine Order with a beautiful chapel in Westminster Abbey, the Order of the Bath has its own magnificence.

The Order of St Michael and St George is the diplomat's Order, given to ambassadors and Foreign Office figures. Founded in 1818, it too thrives. Perhaps more interesting still is the Royal Victorian Order, the personal gift of the Sovereign. Acute observers should have spotted the strange fact that Sir Anthony Blunt, K.C.V.O., was not advanced to G.C.V.O. on retirement and drawn from this important conclusions as to what was known, at the Palace, about his spying activities. Separate from it, but a charming invention of King Edward VII, is the rarely given Royal Victorian Chain.

The Order of the Companions of Honour is a kind of lesser Order of Merit, which in the course of its history has included some of the most interesting men of the twentieth century, particularly in the cultural field. The Order of the British Empire, the outdated title of which has caused such problems to recipients in the Antipodes, is, of course, the most widely given of all the Orders.

But the story does not end at this point. There are still many survivors of the Imperial Service Order, recently killed by John Major in his curiously muddling onslaught on the honours system. There exist a few old holders of the various Indian orders – the Star of India, the Indian Empire, and the Crown of India. There is the totally defunct Order of Victoria and Albert and there are the holders and indeed the slightly surprising non-holders of the various Royal Family Orders.

The Order of St John of Jerusalem exists in a class of its own, with its emphasis on charity. And then there are the Commonwealth Orders, so ill understood in this country – the substitute Orders created virtually the moment those countries rejected British honours.

However anachronistic the honours system may be, it is a system that has evolved over the centuries to its present form. There have been times in the history of Britain when the system has been misused by prime ministers. There have been men who have acquired orders and who have gone down in history as rogues and villains. Some have been stripped of their knighthoods, such as Sir Anthony Blunt, the spy, and Sir Jack Lyons, the businessman involved in the Guinness affair. And yet it is a better system than that of bribery. Without honours, the rewards have to be financial. A much decorated man, Lord Mountbatten, decried the Foreign Office's refusal of his acceptance of an Ethiopian Order from Haile Selassie. Instead there was an exchange of gifts, which meant that Mountbatten had to give something himself. The honour would have been a one-way thing.

It is relatively cheap to give a man a badge on a ribbon and some letters to place after his name, and in order to obtain such distinctions, wealthy businessmen have donated vast sums to charity and consequently to the benefit of the less fortunate.

No one is forced to accept an honour, and there are some citizens to whom such things are anathema. But once you join an Order you are one of a club. And like all clubs there are rules and responsibilities attached. If you belong to an Order, you must not bring it into disrepute, and if involved in public scandal, you risk expulsion or may feel the need to resign your honour. Should you go to prison, the loss of an Order is as good as automatic, witness the loss of Lester Piggott's O.B.E. when he went inside for a tax infringement. Every now and again there have been curious revolts within an Order, as for example when in 1965 numerous irritated holders of the M.B.E. sent their medals back in protest of the awards of M.B.E. given to the Beatles.

Sir Anthony Blunt, whose K.C.V.O. was stripped from him in 1979.

Since March 1993 the whole question of honours has been placed under further scrutiny by the changes that John Major wants to impose on the honours system. Our present Prime Minister began by declaring that he hoped for a classless society. He then announced the splendid appointment of Denis Thatcher as a baronet – an hereditary Knight. He wants more royal investitures, which will impose a huge additional burden on the Queen, or on members of her family who may now have to deputise for her from time to time. He has killed off various minor awards, and he has told us that honours will in no sense be automatic. In these days when people chop and change their jobs so regularly, I still maintain that long service is a great quality. And I also believe that certain positions, like that of senior ambassador representing this country abroad or of field marshal, automatically merit some kind of recognition *per se*. To deny a knighthood to the Lord Mayor of London is a disgrace.

High court judges are still knighted automatically because it was pointed out that there would be a dirth of them if this did not happen.

Sir Dighton Probyn, V.C., wearing the collar of the Bath, and three British stars, the G.C.B., the G.C.V.O., and the G.C.S.I. The other star is Danish. A modest man, his handsome beard conceals the medal of the Victoria Cross.

The termination of the British Empire Medal (B.E.M.) was one recent move. Now all ranks of the army are eligible for the M.B.E.. This sounds sensible but there are certain people who would easily have qualified for the B.E.M. but not really an M.B.E., given what others have had to do to earn it. The result is they get nothing at all.

In conclusion, the Queen's role has become more difficult and the Armed Services have suffered considerably by the new plans.

Mr Major also announced that we could all now recommend the worthy for honours, but there was nothing to prevent us from so doing in the past. Evidently Downing Street was deluged with nominations following his announcement.

I would urge the retention and gradual evolution of the honours system, and would hope that it could fill the gap that might otherwise be filled with bribes. We do not want a situation such as occurs in South America. Mountbatten told a terrible tale of a cattleman attempting to put five million pesas in cash into the bank. The manager refused to take it, so the man sat up over his cash with a shotgun. In the night he shot two intruders – the bank manager and the chief of police. Honours create respectability and the quest for them can bring healthy revenue to deserving causes. Anything is better than corruption.

Mr William Woolf, writing in *The Times*, had a point when he said: 'Now that Mr Major seems about to deprive some of our most senior civil servants of their non-monetary rewards, may we assume that he will take immediate balancing steps to bring their pay into line with that of the private sector?'[1] He feared a rush from public service to the city.

Also in this book, the question of royal honours is treated in inverse fashion, from the point of view of the members of the Royal Family themselves, what they wear and how they wear them. This section is in two parts: the present Royal Family, and those who were around in the early part of the century, but who are now deceased.

Many of the Orders keep the spirit of unity alive amongst the recipients by holding a ceremony. The best known of these is the annual Garter ceremony at Windsor Castle. The Knights of the Thistle, the Bath, the Royal Victorian Order and the British Empire meet less regularly, while the Order of St Michael and St George has an almost annual service at St Paul's Cathedral.

It is an accepted fact that the British are the best at running such ceremonies. This is due to the calm nature of the British character, their love of detail, precision and timing, and above all the fact that they rehearse each ceremony to the point of tedium in order that things should be all right on the day. I was once present at a rehearsal for the Royal Victorian Order Service in St George's Chapel, Windsor, the afternoon before the service in April 1983. I wrote some notes at the time:

> It was a lengthy but rather fascinating rehearsal. Everyone was in mufti and was being marched in and out according to the dry weather and wet weather programme. All the Royals had representatives there – some had sent important ones, others not.
>
> The Military Knights were in suits with bowler hats under their arms. They sat patiently in their stalls for ages as the General (Sir Peter Gillett) gave them the nod when to stand up or sit down.
>
> The Yeomen of the Guard marched with their pikes but again in mufti. While on the day itself they look like Tudor figures, in mufti with their bright red or orange shirts and handle-bar moustaches they look like any pub bore, reminiscing and soaking on the bar-stool of the local. The Gentlemen-at-Arms look more distinguished.
>
> The Knights and Dames Grand Cross wore robes and no collars. It was fun to see brown shoes and brown suits peeping out from under these robes. They were a distinguished bunch of men, the Governor of Fiji (a black face in the procession), one or two Knights of the Garter, people like Lord Cobbold, the dapper old Sir Allan Adair, the Duchesses of Abercorn and Grafton, and a rather doddery Lord Adeane.
>
> Of the Knights, Lord Gladwyn and Sir John Russell didn't bother to turn up. Old hands like Lord Charteris and Sir Martin Gilliat sat contentedly in their stalls. My job [as a lay steward] was to give an arm to anyone who needed help on the way up into the stalls. Later they reckoned it wasn't necessary for me to be there.
>
> But I was needed as they came down, particularly by one elderly knight. The Knights tended to step on the long, flowing robes of the Order, either on their own,

or more often on each other's. They sometimes stood on the tassels. This knight was the only one who needed an arm down and then he set off into the centre of the aisle, out of my care of him. Suddenly, alas, he failed to see the step by the Royal Vault and down he went, rolling in the aisle like a puppy who wanted his tummy tickled. He wasn't hurt because he was wrapped up in the heavy robes, and it was as though he was wound up in a curtain. But he looked so undignified and that was the worst. However, he was rescued and set off in pursuit of the procession. On future progresses he was all right*.

One aspect of the proceedings which I enjoyed was the way that the old courtiers bowed to the ladies-in-waiting representing the Queen and Queen Mother, but not to the rather scruffy secretaries sent by the Gloucesters. Sir Martin Gilliat[†] made jokes at the end of the ceremony, behaving like a schoolboy: 'May we be excused, Sir?' etc., and he left the chapel with eyes blinking.[2]

Needless to say, the ceremony next day passed without a hitch, entirely thanks to the exertions of the participants the day before and the zealous briefings by the Secretary of the Central Chancery[§].

Likewise our honours are held in high esteem overseas. The reason that foreign heads of state love to give out so many honours when they come here, is that they like to receive our Orders in return. Funnily enough it is easier to pick up a G.C.V.O. if you are an important courtier accompanying a head of state than if you serve the British Sovereign for many years.

Queen Elizabeth I did not like British subjects accepting foreign Orders, and apparently expressed her disapproval by announcing that she 'did not like her dogs to wear any collar but her own'. George III followed this theme by declaring that he 'liked his sheep to be marked with his own mark'.[3] In 1873 a debate took place in the House of Lords about honours, during which Britons were discouraged from being allowed to accept foreign honours, Lord Granville maintaining that if they were allowed to have them, it would encourage Britons to intrigue at foreign courts, large and small, for honours that were not worth a brass farthing.

It cannot be certain that some future government will not sweep away the honours system at a stroke, but they would be unwise to do so. As in Australia, New Zealand and Canada, they will find the need to recognize faithful service and acts of valour and new ways of so doing will soon form. The chances of these new methods having any of the prestige or mystique of the present Orders are not strong.

Meanwhile the Orders flourish and this book seeks to explain why.

HUGO VICKERS
February 1994

---

*   The next day the Queen said to him: 'I hear you took a tumble'.
[†]   Private Secretary to Queen Elizabeth the Queen Mother until his death in 1993.
[§]   I cannot resist adding that the Dowager Duchess of Abercorn dropped her spectacles as she left her stall. I was in my appointed place and managed to rescue them before the next G.C.V.O., Sir Allan Adair, had a chance to plant his foot on them.

* CHAPTER ONE *

THE PRESENT ROYAL FAMILY

The Queen is the fount of all honour. This section deals with the orders and decorations with which the Royal Family are adorned on state occasions.

HER MAJESTY THE QUEEN
(born 1926)

ER MAJESTY THE QUEEN is Sovereign of all the British Orders and Commonwealth Orders where she is head of state. The Order of the Garter, the Thistle, the Order of Merit and the Royal Victorian Order are her personal gift. All other Orders are given in her name on the advice of the Prime Minister.

In practice the Queen wears the insignia of very few Orders. On state occasions, when she is in full evening dress, she normally wears the riband and star of the Order of the Garter, with the Royal Family Orders of her grandfather, King George V, and her father, King George VI.

In Commonwealth countries, she wears the appropriate Orders: in Australia, the Order of Australia; in Canada, the Order of Canada and the Order of Military Merit; and in New Zealand, the Order of New Zealand, and the Queen's Service Order.

When in Scotland, the Queen wears the riband and star of the Order of the Thistle.

At her coronation, she wore the collar of the Order of the Garter over her robes, but no star or riband. This is also how she is dressed for the state opening of Parliament.

The Queen has taken part in services of the Order of the Garter, Thistle, Bath, St Michael and St George, Royal Victorian Order and the Order of the British Empire. On these occasions she wears the robe of the Order with the appropriate collar, except that for some reason, she attends the Royal Victorian Order service in day clothes, and does not then wear even the star of the Order. At Garter ceremonies she wears her father's Garter robes, and sits under his banner in St George's Chapel. Her

The Queen's state portrait by Sir James Gunn. She wears the collar of the Order of the Garter.

15

robe differs from those of the other Knights by having an actual star on the left shoulder, instead of the normal badge, and a long train, borne by two pages of honour. In a memorable scene in the documentary, *Elizabeth R*, the Queen mused on the curious style of the Garter robes: 'I wonder who invented these robes. They are not really very practical. They couldn't have been very practical in the days when somebody wore clothes like this, I don't think.'[1]   The Queen admitted to the portrait painter, Andrew Festing, that the robes were 'certainly warm on a June day plodding down. It's always very lucky we plod downhill and not uphill.'[2]

There have been gatherings of the Order of Merit, but there is no Sovereign's badge of that Order.

In the days when the Queen used to wear uniform at the Birthday Parade, she would wear the riband and star of the Garter, or, if the colour of the Scots Guards was being trooped, the riband and star of the Thistle. On these occasions only, she wore the badge of the Order of the Crown of India as a medal, with the following other medals:

1939–1945 Defence medal
1939–1945 war medal
King George V Silver Jubilee Medal 1935
King George VI Coronation Medal 1937
Canadian Forces Decoration (Silver)

The Queen was appointed a Dame Grand Cross of the Order of St John of Jerusalem in 1947, and held an investiture of the Order at Buckingham Palace in 1971, at which she wore the Sovereign's mantle.

The Queen also holds a great number of foreign Orders and decorations:

The Order of the Elephant (1947) Denmark
Grand Cordon of the Order of Al Kamal (1948) Egypt
Grand Cross of the Legion of Honour (1948) France
Order of Ojaswi Rajanya (1949) Nepal
Grand Cross of the Order of St Olga and St Sophia (1950) Greece
Grand Cross of the Order of the Netherlands Lion (1950)
Order of the Seraphim (1953) Sweden, (Collar of the Order 1975)
Gold Collar of the Order of Manuel Amador Guerrero (1953) Panama
Collar of the Order of Qeladet El-Hussein Ibn Ali (1953) Jordan, (Sash and Badge of the Order, 1984)
Grand Collar of the Order of Idris I (1954) Libya
Collar of the Order of the Seal of Solomon (1954) Ethiopia
Grand Cross with Collar of the Order of St Olav (1955) Norway
Riband of the Three Orders: Christ, Aviz and St James (1955) Portugal
Grand Order of the Hashimi with Collar (1956) Iraq
Grand Cross with Collar of the Order of Merit of the Republic (1958) Italy
Grand Cross Special Class with Star of the Order of Merit of the Federal Republic of Germany (1958)

Grand Cross with Brilliants of the Order of the Sun of Peru (1960)
Order of Pakistan, First Class (1960)
Collar of the Order of San Martin (1960) Argentina
Order of the Royal House of Chakri with Collar (1960) Thailand
Mahendra Chain (1961) Nepal
Grand Collar of the Order of Independence of Tunisia (1961)
Collar of the Order of the White Rose of Finland (1961)
Grand Cross of the Order of the Lion of Senegal (1961)
Grand Cordon of the Order of the Pioneers of the Republic (1961) Liberia, (Collar
    of the Order, 1979)
Grand Cross of the Order of the Ivory Coast (1962)
Order of the Chrysanthemum with Collar (1962) Japan
Grand Band of the Order of the Star of Africa (1962) Liberia
Grand Cross of the Order of Valour of Cameroon (1963) Cameroon Republic
Grand Cordon of the Order of Leopold (1963) Belgium
Grand Cross of the Order of the Redeemer (1963) Greece
Grand Cross with Collar of the Order of the Falcon (1963) Iceland
Chain of Honour (1964) Sudan
Collar of the Order of Merit (1965) Chile
Grand Cordon of the Austrian Order of Merit (1966)
Grand Collar of the Order of the Southern Cross (1968) Brazil
Grand Cross of the National Order of The Niger (1969) Nigeria
Order of Al-Nahayyan, First Class (1969) Abu Dhabi
Grand Cross of the Equatorial Star (1970) Gabon
Order of the Supreme Sun (1971) Afghanistan
Grand Cross of the Order of the Gold Lion (1972) Luxembourg
Order of the Great Yugoslav Star (1972)
Order of the Crown (1972) Malaysia
Order of Temasek (1972) Singapore
Family Order, First Class (1972) Brunei
Order of Ghaazi (1972) Maldives
Order of the Golden Heart (1972) Kenya
Collar of the National Order of the Aztec Eagle (1973) Mexico
Grand Cordon of the Order of the Leopard (1973) Zaire
Star of Indonesia, First Class (1974)
Grand Commander of the Order of the Republic of Gambia (1974)
Collar of the Order of the Nile (1975) Egypt
Grand Collar of the Order of St James (1978) Portugal
Necklace of Mubarak Al Kabir (1979) Kuwait
Order of the Khalifiyyeh Necklace (1979) Bahrain
Collar of the Order of King Abdul Aziz (1979) Saudi Arabia
Collar of the Order of Independence (1979) Qatar
Order of Oman, First Class (1979)
Order of the Lion of Malawi, First Class (1979)

Presidential Order of Botswana (1979)

Grand Cordon of the Order of the Republic of Tunisia (1980)

Collar of the Order of Mohammed (1980) Morocco

Order of Al Said (1982) Oman

Order of the Solomon Islands, First Class (1982)

Dominica Award of Honour (1985)

Trinity Cross Medal of the Order of the Trinity (Gold) (1985) Trinidad and Tobago

Collar of the Order of Charles III (1986) Spain

Order of Mugunghwa (1986) Republic of Korea

Order of the Golden Fleece (1988) Spain

Grand Cordon of the Federal Republic (1989) Nigeria

Chain of the Federation of the United Arab Emirates (1989)

Order of Merit of the Republic of Poland (1991)

Royal Family Order of the Crown of Brunei (1992)

Military Order of the Tower and Sword for Valour, Loyalty and Merit (1993)
Portugal.

The wearing of foreign Orders presents many problems, and if worn over the wrong shoulder, the wearer does not have time to change when the mistake is realised. When the Queen wore the Order of the Royal House of Chakri (Thailand) the wrong way in Bangkok in the spring of 1972, the error was recorded in formal photographs, and she attended a state banquet thus adorned.

Her Majesty was given the Star of the Socialist Republic, 1st class by President Ceausescu of Romania on his State Visit to Britain in the summer of 1978, but returned it in December 1989.

The King of Spain's State Visit to Britain 1986. From left to right, the Duke of Edinburgh, Queen Sofia, the Queen, King Juan Carlos at the Spanish Embassy. On this occasion the Queen wore the Spanish Order of Charles III, while King Juan Carlos wears the Royal Victorian Chain round his neck.

LEFT: *Prince Philip
as Marshal of the
R.A.F. with the
same array as
opposite, but minus
the G.B.E. star.*

H.R.H. THE DUKE OF EDINBURGH
(born 1921)

The Duke of Edinburgh has remained relatively undecorated at his own request. He is K.G. (1947), K.T. (1952), O.M. (1968)*, and G.B.E. (1953), of which he also serves as Grand Master. Interestingly, he is not a G.C.B. despite being an Admiral of the Fleet, Field Marshal, and Marshal of the Royal Air Force. He is a Companion of the Order of Australia (1988), and has the Q.S.O. in New Zealand, and regularly wears its medal as the first of his set. He also has the New Zealand Commemorative medal (1990).

It is fair to say that the Duke does not take a great interest in Orders etc., but he is meticulous when he wears them, and for the state banquet at Windsor for the late King Olav of Norway, he went to the Royal Library and borrowed an Order of St Olav, surrounded by a Garter.† Such charming gestures tend to pass unnoticed in the reporting of such events.

ABOVE: *Prince
Philip in the
uniform of Colonel
of Grenadier
Guards, with
Garter, Thistle and
G.B.E. stars, Garter
riband, and the
Order of Merit from
his collar. His first
medal is the Queen's
Service Order, New
Zealand.*

* Though holding the highest rank in all three services, the Duke is in the civil division of the Order of Merit.
† It is a little known fact that Knights of the Garter are allowed to encircle foreign stars with the Garter, and at Windsor a number of such stars exist in the Royal Collection, including the Danish Order of the Elephant, and the Russian Order of the Black Eagle, dating from the 19th century.

Prince Philip in the uniform of Admiral of the Fleet, wearing the riband and star of the Legion of Honour, on the occasion of the 1976 State Visit of President Valery Giscard d'Estaing of France. Also in the picture, Madame Giscard and the Queen. The wands are held by the Lord Chamberlain (the late Lord Maclean, K.T.) and the Lord Steward (the late Duke of Northumberland, K.G.).

The Duke also has a great number of foreign Orders:

Grand Cross of the Order of the Redeemer (pre-1947) Greece
Grand Cross of the order of the Phoenix (pre-1947) Greece
Grand Cross with Swords of the Order of George I (pre-1947) Greece
Order of St George and St Constantine, First class with Swords (pre-1947) Greece
Order of the Elephant (1947) Denmark
Grand Cross of the Order of St Charles (1951) Monaco
Grand Cross of the Order of St Olav (1952) Norway
Grand Cross of the Order of Manuel Amador Guerrero (1953) Panama
Collar of the Order of the Queen of Sheba (1954) Ethiopia
Order of the Seraphim (1954) Sweden
Grand Cross of the Order of the Tower and the Sword (1955) Portugal
Order of King Feisal I, First Class (1956) Iraq
Grand Cross of the Legion of Honour (1957) France
Grand Cross of the Order of Merit, First Class (1958) Federal Republic of Germany
Grand Cross of the Order of Merit (1958) Italy

Grand Cross of the Order of the Netherlands Lion (1958)
Order of Ojaswi Rajanya (1960) Nepal
Grand Band of the Order of the Star of Africa (1961) Liberia
Grand Cross of the Order of Boyaca (1962) Colombia
Grand Cross of the Order of National Merit (1962) Ecuador
Grand Cross with Brilliants of the Order of the Sun of Peru (1962)
Grand Cross of the Order of the Condor of the Andes (1962) Bolivia
Chain of the Order of Merit (1962) Chile
Collar of the National Order of Merit (1962) Paraguay
Grand Cross of the Order of the Southern Cross (1962) Brazil
Grand Cross of the Order of San Martin (1962) Argentina
Grand Cordon of the Order of Leopold (1963) Belgium*
Order of the Brilliant Star of Zanzibar, First Class (1963)
Grand Cross of the Order of the Falcon (1964) Iceland
Collar of the Order of the Aztec Eagle (1964) Mexico
Order of the Republic of Sudan, First Class (1964)
Order of the Renaissance, First Class (1966) Jordan
Grand Cordon of the Austrian Order of Merit (1966)
Grand Commander of the Order of Maritime Merit (1968) USA
Grand Cross of the Order Rio Branco (1968) Brazil
Grand Cross of the Order of the White Rose of Finland (1969)
Medal of the Order of Dogwood (1971) Canada
Grand Cordon of the Order of the Chrysanthemum (1971) Japan
Order of the Superior Sun (1971) Afghanistan
Family Order (1972) Brunei
Grand Cross of the Order of the Gold Lion (1972) Luxembourg
Order of Izzuddin (1972) Maldives
Order of Temasek (1972) Singapore
Order of the Great Yugoslav Star (1972)
Grand Collar of the Order of Prince Henry the Navigator (1973) Portugal
Grand Cordon of the Order of the Leopard (military) (1973) Zaire
Commander of the Order of the Golden Ark (1979) Netherlands
Order of Oman, First Class (military) (1979)
Collar of the Order of Independence (1979) Qatar
Order of Mohamed, First Class (1980) Morocco
Grand Cross of the Order of Charles III (1986) Spain
Grand Ribbon of Merit (1991) Poland Silver Jubilee Medal (1992) Brunei

* The Duke was meant to wear the Leopold at King Baudouin's state funeral in Brussels in 1993. Unfortunately
he wore the Leopard of Zaire by mistake.

HER MAJESTY QUEEN ELIZABETH
THE QUEEN MOTHER
(born 1900)

*A Norman
Parkinson portrait
of Queen Elizabeth
the Queen Mother,
wearing the riband
and star of the
Order of the
Garter, and the
Royal Family
Orders of the Queen
and George VI.*

Queen Elizabeth The Queen Mother has the most important British Orders – the Garter (1936), the Thistle (1937), the Crown of India (1931), the Royal Victorian Chain (1937) – and she is Grand Master of the Royal Victorian Order (appointed 1 February 1937). She is also a Dame Grand Cross of the Order of the British Empire (27 June 1926).

Normally Her Majesty wears the riband and star of the Garter, with the Royal Family Orders of her husband, King George VI, and the present Queen. (In the past she has worn the Royal Family Order of George V, and the Order of the Crown of India, but does so no longer.)

At services of the Royal Victorian Order, the Queen Mother has worn the ladies' badge of the Royal Victorian Chain. She was photographed by Norman Parkinson in 1975, wearing the collar of the Royal Victorian Order, the reason for so doing being apparently a whim of the moment.

At the present Queen's coronation, the Queen Mother followed the practice of Queen Mary in 1937, and wore the Garter riband and star, rather than the collar. At the appropriate services, she has often worn the robes of the Garter (wearing those made for Queen Alexandra, which are very dark blue, with a little collar at the neck, and a train that is borne by a page), and occasionally the robes of the Thistle.

For many years, the Queen Mother has made it her practice not to accept foreign Orders of any kind, mainly because she has not been on any state visits herself. Nevertheless she does have the following, and has occasionally had to wear one of these at the state banquet of a visiting sovereign:

> Grand Cross of the Order of St Sava of Servia (1923)[*]
> Grand Cordon of Lernor Ala (1928) Afghanistan
> Grand Cross of the Legion of Honour (1938) France
> Red Cross Medal, First Class (1938) France
> Grand Cross of the Order of the Crown of Romania (1938)
> Grand Cross of the Order of St Olga and St Sophia (1938) Greece
> Military Cross (1942) Norway
> Red Cross medal (1945) France
> Order of Ojaswi Rajanya (1946) Nepal
> Grand Cross of the Order of the Netherlands Lion (1950)
> Grand Cross of the Order of the Sun of Peru (1960)
> Grand Cross of the Most Excellent Order of Independence of Tunisia (1961)[†]

The Queen Mother used to hold the Order of the Sacred Crown of Japan, but gave it up during the war. She did not wear it or any other Japanese Order at the state banquet for Emperor Hirohito in 1971.

---

[*]   given when the Duke of York stood sponsor to the future King Peter of Yugoslavia.
[†]   The Queen Mother visited the ruins of Carthage in Tunisia in 1961.

H.R.H. THE PRINCE OF WALES
(born 1948)

The Prince of Wales is not as highly decorated as his predecessors, reflecting the present Queen's attitude to honours. He became a Knight of the Garter in 1958 automatically on becoming Prince of Wales, and was installed in 1968. He was appointed Knight Grand Cross of the Order of the Bath, and Great Master of the Order in succession to the late Duke of Gloucester in 1975.* He was appointed a Knight of the Thistle in Silver Jubilee Year. He has no other British Orders of any kind.

He is one of the very few Knights of Australia, and has the Queen's Service Order (New Zealand).

The Prince wears five medals when in full dress uniform (and a great deal more as miniatures when in evening dress):

The Queen's Service Order (New Zealand)
Queen Elizabeth II Coronation medal 1953
Queen Elizabeth II Silver Jubilee medal 1977
The Canadian Forces Decoration medal 1991
The New Zealand Commemorative medal

The Prince has many foreign Orders:

Grand Cross of the Order of the White Rose of Finland (1969)
Grand Cordon of the Order of the Chrysanthemum (1971) Japan
Grand Cross of the Order of the House of Orange (1972) The Netherlands
Grand Cross of the Order of the Oak Crown (1972) Luxembourg
Order of the Elephant (1974) Denmark
Order of the Seraphim (1975) Sweden
Coronation Medal (1975) Nepal
Order of Ojaswi Rajanya (1975) Nepal
Order of the Star of Ghana (1977)
Grand Cross of the Order of St Olav (1978) Norway
Grand Cross of the Order of the Southern Cross (1978) Brazil
Collar of the Republic (1981) Egypt
Grand Cross of the Order of Orange Nassau (1982) The Netherlands
Grand Cross of the Legion of Honour (1984) France
Order of the Lion of Malawi, First Class (1985)
Grand Cordon of the Khalifeyyeh Order of Bahrain (1986)
Collar of Merit of the Qatari Order (1986) Qatar
Grand Cross of the Order of Charles III (1986) Spain

---

*   At his installation in Westminster Abbey in 1975, the Prince wore his Welsh Guards uniform under the robes. He had just returned from a cold spell in the Arctic where, because shaving was impossible, he had grown a beard. Beards are not permitted in military dress. He shaved off most of the beard in the morning, but left a moustache. This disappeared later in the day before he returned to the Royal Navy, where moustaches are forbidden. Thus this was the only occasion when Prince Charles appeared in public with a moustache.

Grand Cordon of the Order of Merit (1986) Saudi Arabia
The Amari Order of Ahmed Al Fateh (1986) Bahrein
The Amari Order of Mubarak The Great (1993) Kuwait

These orders were either given when foreign heads of state visited Britain or when
Prince Charles toured their country. In 1992, the Prince wore his Elephant from the
wrong shoulder, when attending the Silver Wedding celebrations of Queen Margrethe
and Prince Henrik (as can be seen in the appropriate edition of *Hello* magazine).

ABOVE: *The
Prince of Wales
taking the salute at
an Armistice Day
service in Paris in
1988. He wears
the uniform of
Colonel, Welsh
Guards, and the
star of the Grand
Cross of the Legion
of Honour.*

LEFT: *The Prince of
Wales in naval
uniform, with the
star of the Garter,
and the neck badge
of the Bath. His
first medal is the
Q.S.O. of New
Zealand.*

H.R.H. THE PRINCESS OF WALES
(born 1961)

The Princess of Wales was given the Royal Family Order shortly after her marriage, and wore it for the first time at the 1981 state opening of Parliament. At the state banquet given by President Evren of Turkey at Claridge's in July 1988, the Princess wore a blue dress that completely exposed the left shoulder. On that occasion she wore her Royal Family Order on the right shoulder, which may or may not have been popular.

Besides the Royal Family Order, the Princess has not been given any English Orders. It was her quiet ambition to become a Lady of the Garter one day, and while this is not likely to happen now, it is not impossible that her son might give it to her, when he becomes King in the fullness of time.

The Princess was occasionally given a foreign Order:

The Order of Al Kamal (1981) Egypt.
Grand Cross of the Order of the House of Orange (1982) The Netherlands

The Princess of Wales with her Royal Family Order at a banquet for President Cossiga of Italy in 1990. He wears the riband of the Order of the Bath, the Queen's habitual gift to visiting Presidents.

26

H.R.H. THE DUKE OF YORK
(born 1960)

The Duke of York has only been made a C.V.O. (1985), on his 25th birthday, a curious choice of the Queen's, since it is such a very low grade in an Order. He would have been a Knight of the Garter and Thistle by now, had he lived half a century earlier. The Duke also has the Queen's Silver Jubilee Medal, the Falklands Medal (1982), and the New Zealand Commemorative Medal.

He has one foreign Order: the Grand Cross of the Order of St Olav of Norway, given to him on the occasion of the state visit of King Olav of Norway in April 1988.

The Duke of York, wearing the C.V.O. from his neck, and his three medals.

H.R.H. THE DUCHESS OF YORK
(born 1959)

The Duchess of York has no British Orders, nor any overseas ones. She has not been given the Queen's Royal Family Order.

Prince Edward in his C.V.O. and with his medals.

H.R.H. THE PRINCE EDWARD
(born 1964)

Like his brother, the Duke of York, Prince Edward is merely a C.V.O.. This he was given in 1989 on his 25th birthday. He also has the Queen's Silver Jubilee Medal, and the New Zealand Commemorative Medal.

On 16 November 1993 Prince Edward received the medal of the Ministry of Education, Youth, and Sport of the Czech Republic.

The Princess Royal in uniform, wearing the riband and star of the G.C.V.O., the star of the Order of St John, and two medals, the Coronation medal, and Silver Jubilee medal.

H.R.H. THE PRINCESS ROYAL
(born 1950)

The Princess Royal received the Grand Cross of the Royal Victorian Order on her 24th birthday (15 August 1974) following an attempt to kidnap her in the Mall in London on 22 March 1974. The attempt was unsuccessful, though as the Queen commented to Lord Mountbatten at the time: 'If the man had succeeded in abducting Anne, she would have given him a hell of a time while in captivity!'[3] At one time, the Princess favoured wearing the miniature medal of the G.C.V.O. when in evening dress, rather than the riband and star.

The Princess is also a Dame of Justice of the Order of St John (1971). She was given the Queen's Royal Family Order in 1969, at which time a badge was made for her.

The Princess Royal has the following foreign orders:
Grand Gold Cross of the Austrian Order of Merit (1969)
Grand Cross of the Order of the White Rose of Finland (1969)
Order of the Precious Crown, First Class (1971) Japan

The Princess Royal at the Lech Walesa banquet at the Guildhall. She wears the riband and star of the G.C.V.O. and the Queen's Royal Family Order.

Distinguished Service Order (1972) Singapore
Family Order (1972) Brunei
Grand Cross of the Order of the House of Orange (1972) Netherlands
Grand Cross of the Order of the Oak Crown (1972) Luxembourg
Order of the Yugoslav Flag (1972)
Grand Cross of the Order of Merit of the Federal Republic of Germany, First Class (1972)
Riband of the Order of the Aztec Eagle (1973) Mexico

Captain Mark Phillips was given a C.V.O. following the kidnap attempt in the Mall in 1974. He is also a Personal A.D.C. to the Queen.

Commander Timothy Laurence, Princess Anne's second husband, was appointed an M.V.O. following his retirement as Equerry to the Queen in 1989.

H.R.H. THE PRINCESS MARGARET,
COUNTESS OF SNOWDON
(born 1930)

Princess Margaret is a C.I., G.C.V.O. and has the Royal Victorian Chain. She was appointed a Dame of Justice of the Order of St John (1948) and promoted Dame Grand Cross (1956). She was almost the last recipient of the Order of the Crown of India in 1947.* She is the only lady still to wear it from time to time in public. She was given the Grand Cross of the Royal Victorian Order on 1 June 1953, just before the coronation. And on the occasion of her 60th birthday, 20 August 1990, she was given the Royal Victorian Chain by the Queen at Balmoral.

Princess Margaret, wearing the riband of the G.C.V.O. and the Queen's Royal Family Order, with those of her father and grandfather, partially concealed. Today she no longer wears the riband, preferring the Royal Victorian Chain.

*   The late Lady Clydesmuir was appointed in 1948.

Princess Margaret has the Royal Family Orders of King George V, King George VI, and the Queen, and she usually wears all three of them when in full evening dress.

Until she received the Royal Victorian Chain, it was Princess Margaret's habit to wear the riband and star of G.C.V.O., the C.I. and the three Royal Family Orders. Now she sometimes wears just the Royal Victorian Chain, or she wears five shoulder badges, the Chain, the C.I. and three Royal Family Orders. There would seem to be no actual reason why she could not wear the G.C.V.O. riband too, except that is the same as the bow over which the Royal Victorian Chain is spread.*

At services of the Royal Victorian Order, Princess Margaret now wears both the Star of G.C.V.O. and her Royal Victorian Chain. It is possible that she will succeed the Queen Mother as Grand Master of the Royal Victorian Order.

Princess Margaret does not seem to be a great devotee of Orders, having often appeared at state functions without her Orders, though she does appear to be proud of her Royal Victorian Chain.

Princess Margaret also has certain foreign Orders:

Grand Cross of the Order of the Netherlands Lion (1948)
Order of the Brilliant Star of Zanzibar, First Class (1956)
Grand Cross of the Order of the Crown of Belgium (1960)
Order of the Crown, Lion and Spear of Toro Kingdom (1965) Uganda
Order of the Precious Crown, First Class (1971) Japan
Grand Cross, 1st class, Order of Merit (1972) Federal Republic of Germany

The Earl of Snowdon received a G.C.V.O. following the investiture of the Prince of Wales at Caernarvon Castle in 1969, which he arranged as Constable of the castle. He occasionally wears the riband and star of the G.C.V.O., but even as a member of the Royal Family, he was not particularly interested in these things. He attended the 1969 opening of Parliament without wearing the Order's collar over his parliamentary robes, which he should have done. Nor does he attend the services of the Royal Victorian Order at Windsor Castle. By dint of having been appointed to the Order so young, he is now quite a senior G.C.V.O..

He picked up the following foreign orders when married to Princess Margaret:

Grand Officer of the Order of Leopold II (1961) Belgium
Grand Cross of the Order of the Crown (1963) Belgium

---

* H.M. Queen Margrethe of Denmark wore both the Royal Victorian Chain and G.C.V.O. during her state visit to Britain in 1974, as did Queen Beatrix of the Netherlands on her state visit in 1982.

H.R.H. PRINCESS ALICE, DUCHESS OF GLOUCESTER
(born 1901)

Princess Alice, Duchess of Gloucester, the Queen's aunt, is the first lady ever to have been given the Grand Cross of the Order of the Bath (on 2 April 1975). As a descendant of John, Duke of Montagu, the Order's first Great Master in 1725, and the widow of another Great Master, the Duke of Gloucester, this was an appropriate appointment. Princess Alice was invested with the insignia of the Order on 23 April 1975 at Windsor Castle, following the quincentenary service at St George's Chapel. At Prince Charles's installation in May 1975, Princess Alice took her place in the procession, walking alone, behind the robed Grand Crosses, and she has taken part in all the services of the Order since then. Princess Alice was not installed as such, though she occupies one of the stalls half way down the south side of the Henry VII Chapel. She remains the only British lady so honoured. Princess Alice was depicted in the robes of the Order of the Bath on the jacket of her memoirs, published in 1983.

Princess Alice, Duchess of Gloucester, wearing the riband of Dame Grand Cross of the Order of the Bath.

Besides being G.C.B., Princess Alice is C.I., G.C.V.O., G.B.E. and G.C.St.J.. She was given the Order of the Crown of India in 1937 and the G.B.E. on 11 May (the day before the coronation) by King George VI, and the Grand Cross of the Royal Victorian Order on 1 January 1948 at the time of the silver wedding of the King and Queen. She became a Dame Grand Cross of the Order of St John on 17 July 1936. She also has the Royal Family Orders of King George V, King George VI and the present Queen. In full evening dress she used to wear the riband and star of the Royal Victorian Order, with the Crown of India, and the three Royal Family Orders. After 1975, she wore the red riband of the Order of the Bath, with a lady's star of the Order.

Now aged 92, Princess Alice no longer goes out in the evening, so her fine display of Orders are not worn. She gave up attending State Banquets in 1987.

Princess Alice has taken part in the various services of the Order of the British Empire, wearing the robes of the Order, and she was present at the Cathedral in May 1988. She also attends the services of the Royal Victorian Order, wearing the star, and was last present at such a service in 1991. Princess Alice also has a few foreign Orders:

Star and Badge of Grand Cross of the Order of the Crown (1938) Roumania
Grand Cordon of Al Kamal (1950) Egypt
Badge and Star of the Order of the Queen of Sheba (1958) Ethiopia

In her memoirs she recounts the strange tale of being given the badge and star of the Order of the Queen of Sheba on a visit to Ethiopia in 1958. She knew that an Order was on its way, but there was no sign of it and she was in the process of dressing for the state banquet when the Emperor's Chamberlain announced himself. The Duchess was alarmed to discover that he had every intention of decorating her with the Order in person, and something of a struggle had to be put forward to prevent him entering the bedchamber.

H.R.H. THE DUKE OF GLOUCESTER
(born 1944)

The Duke and Duchess of Gloucester, both wearing the G.C.V.O. The Duke also wears the star and neck badge of the Order of St John. The Duchess wears the Royal Family Order above her medals.

The Duke of Gloucester, first cousin of the Queen, eschewed royal duties until the death of his brother, Prince William, in 1972. Until then he was a practising architect and intended to build himself a home on the Isle of Dogs, and live a relatively bohemian life. But within days of his brother's death, he was living at Kensington Palace and running the estates at Barnwell. Today he and the Duchess undertake their normal share of royal duties and they live at Kensington Palace and Barnwell with Princess Alice.

The Duke was given a G.C.V.O. on 1 January 1974, shortly before he succeeded his father as 2nd Duke of Gloucester. The Duke wears the collar of that Order when attending the State Opening of Parliament – indeed in November 1993 he could be observed carrying the red box under his arm that contained the collar, on his arrival at the Palace of Westminster. He serves as Bailiff Grand Cross of the Order of St John of Jerusalem (appointed 26 February 1975) and undertakes numerous duties for that order. It seems likely that he will be made a Knight of the Garter on his 50th birthday, as was his cousin the Duke of Kent. The Duke wears the following medals:

G.C.V.O. (as miniature)
Order of St John
Coronation medal (1953)
Silver Jubilee medal (1977)
Solomons Islands Independence medal (1978)
St John Long Service medal
New Hebrides Independence medal (1980)

The Duke has the following foreign Orders:
Grand Cross of the Order of St Olav (1973) Norway
The Order of the Aztec Eagle, (1973) Mexico
Order of Trishakti Patta, (1975) Kathmandu
Royal Order of the Northern Star (1975) Sweden

H.R.H. THE DUCHESS OF GLOUCESTER
(born 1946)

The Duchess of Gloucester was given the Queen's Royal Family Order soon after her marriage, and was appointed a G.C.V.O. on 23 June 1989, after seventeen years in the Royal Family. She became a Dame of Justice of the Order of St John of Jerusalem on 26 February 1975.

The Duchess sometimes wears the stars of the Royal Victorian Order and of St John when in evening dress, with the riband of the Royal Victorian Order, her Royal Family Order and four medals beneath it. These are the G.C.V.O., the Order of St John, the Silver Jubilee medal (1977) and the Solomon Islands Independence medal (1978). The Duchess wore all the above at the State Opening of Parliament in November 1993.

H.R.H. The Duke of Kent

(born 1935)

The Duke of Kent is more decorated than his senior cousin, the Duke of Gloucester, and this is because he is older and has taken a fuller part in royal duties over the years. He began royal duties very young as there were so few active royals about at that time. Having succeeded to the dukedom at the age of six in 1942, he took a prominent position at the Queen's coronation and was one of the three royal dukes to do homage personally to the Queen. He is K.G., G.C.M.G., and G.C.V.O..

The Duke and Duchess of Kent. The Duke wears the Garter riband, and the stars of the Garter, G.C.M.G. and G.C.V.O. The Duchess wears the G.C.V.O. and the Royal Family Order.

He was made a Knight of the Garter in 1985 to mark his 50th birthday. The next year he was installed, and then the year after he was invested in the Garter Throne Room. The reason for this was a muddle at the College of Arms, Garter King of Arms of the time taking the erroneous line that the Royal princes admitted to the Order did not need to be invested. The Duke habitually takes his place in the Garter procession, walking behind the Knights Companion and before the Queen Mother and the Prince of Wales.

The Duke of Kent was appointed a Knight Grand Cross of the Order of St Michael and St George on 12 October 1967 and serves as the Order's Grand Master (in succession to Field Marshal Earl Alexander of Tunis). As the Order has a service every other year, this is an important commitment. He was made a G.C.V.O. on Christmas Day 1960. In June 1993 the Queen handed the Duke his baton as Field Marshal following the Birthday Parade,* and this he carried at the 1993 Service of Remembrance at the Cenotaph. Thus he is now as honoured as any of the cousins is likely to be.

The Duke wears the following medals when in uniform:

The United Nations Forces in Cyprus medal (1970)
King George VI Coronation medal (1937)
Queen Elizabeth II Coronation medal (1953)
Queen Elizabeth II Silver Jubilee Medal (1977)
Canadian Forces Decoration
Sierre Leone Independence medal (1961)
Guyana Independence medal (1966)

The Duke also has seven foreign Orders:

Order of St George and St Constantine of Greece, First Class (1957) Greece
Tri Shakti Patta, First Class (1960) Nepal
Grand Band of the Order of the Star of Africa (1962) Liberia
Order of the Renaissance, First Class (1966) Jordan
Grand Cross of the Order of St Olaf (1988) Norway
Grand Cross of the Order of the Legion of Honour, France
Independence Star, Afghanistan

* The Duke is one of the rare field marshals not to belong to the Order of the Bath.

H.R.H. THE DUCHESS OF KENT
(born 1933)

The Duchess of Kent was given the Queen's Royal Family Order soon after her marriage. But she had to wait until the Silver Jubilee celebrations, 9 June 1977, before receiving the Grand Cross of the Royal Victorian Order. At that time it appeared that she had been made to wait a very long time before being so honoured, but the Duchess of Gloucester also waited a similar length of time. In earlier times, the Duchess would certainly have received an Order soon after marriage.

H.R.H. PRINCE MICHAEL OF KENT
(born 1942)

Prince Michael was for many years something of an outsider as far as the Royal Family was concerned. Only when he married did he become a more prominent figure, taking part in a wide variety of royal duties. Nevertheless his royal engagements are not reported in the Court Circular.

To mark his 50th birthday in 1992, the Queen created him K.C.V.O., which was a mark of moderate respect, but in tune with her rather underplayed distribution of honours. The chances are that he will eventually be elevated to G.C.V.O. – possibly around the time of the Golden Jubilee.

H.R.H. PRINCESS MICHAEL OF KENT
(born 1945)

Princess Michael has no Orders, British or foreign. She does not have the Queen's Royal Family Order.

H.R.H. PRINCESS ALEXANDRA,
THE HON. LADY OGILVY
(born 1936)

Princess Alexandra in G.C.V.O. riband, her two Royal Family Orders and the Silver Jubilee medal.

Princess Alexandra was given the G.C.V.O. on Christmas Day 1960, which was also her 24th birthday. She also has the Royal Family Orders of King George VI (1951) and the present Queen. Princess Alexandra was very much a front line member of the Royal Family in the 1950s and 1960s when there were fewer of them to undertake royal duties. She was part of the team led by the Queen, the Queen Mother, Princess Margaret, the late Princess Royal, the Duchess of Gloucester (Princess Alice), and her mother, the late Duchess of Kent.

Princess Alexandra has a number of foreign orders:

The Order of the Aztec Eagle, 1st class (1959) Mexico
Grand Cross of the Order of the Sun (1959) Peru

Grand Cross of the Order of Merit (1959) Chile
Grand Cross of the Order of the Southern Cross (1959) Brazil
The Order of the Precious Crown, 1st class (1961) Japan
Grand Cross of the Order of the White Rose (1969) Finland
Grand Cross of the Order of the Oak Crown (1972) Luxembourg
Canadian Forces Decoration (1980)
Grand Cross of the Order of the House of Orange (1982) The Netherlands

The first four of these Orders the Princess received when touring Latin America with her mother, Princess Marina, in February and March 1959. In November 1961 the Princess paid a state visit to Japan, the first of the Royal Family to visit that country not only since the war, but since 1929 when the Duke of Gloucester was there. On that occasion Emperor Hirohito gave a banquet and asked permission to be allowed to wear his Garter star and this was granted. The Luxembourg and Netherlands Orders were given during state visits to Great Britain.

Princess Alexandra also wears her 1977 Silver Jubilee medal when in full evening dress.

The Hon. Sir Angus Ogilvy was appointed K.C.V.O. on 1 January 1989. At the time some felt that perhaps he should have received the same degree as his wife, but that is not the way of the present Queen. He would certainly have been a G.C.V.O. had he lived in earlier times. He has two foreign orders:

Grand Officer of the Order of the Lion (1969) Finland
Order of the Oak Crown (1972) Luxembourg.

THE OTHER ROYALS

The other members of the Royal Family are the Earl of Harewood, his brother, Hon. Gerald Lascelles (sons of the late Princess Royal, and thus first cousins of the Queen), the Duke of Fife (great-grandson of King Edward VII), Captain Alexander Ramsay of Mar (grandson of the Duke of Connaught) and his wife, Lady Saltoun, and Lady May Abel Smith (born 1906) (the last survivor of the old Royal Family, being Queen Mary's niece, a descendant of King George III through the Cambridges, and the great-grand-daughter of Queen Victoria, through her mother, the late Princess Alice, Countess of Athlone). They all have their share of coronation and Silver Jubilee Medals, but none of them have any royal Orders as such.*

The late King Olav V of Norway was a grandson of King Edward VII through his mother, Queen Maud. His son, King Harald is therefore a great-grandson, and he received a G.C.V.O. on the Queen's state visit to Norway in 1955. It is traditional for the Queen to give a G.C.V.O. to the Crown Prince on such a visit, even if he is very young. Thus there are quite a number of descendants of Queen Victoria, members of other Royal houses, who have been so honoured.

*   The Countess of Harewood, being Lord Harewood's second wife, was not received at court for some years. But she was given a Silver Jubilee Medal in 1977, and wore it at her first presentation to the Queen in Yorkshire that summer.

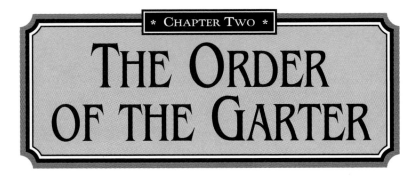

CHAPTER TWO

THE ORDER OF THE GARTER

WHEN A MAN IS CREATED a Knight of the Garter, a stall is assigned to him in St George's Chapel, his banner hangs above it for the rest of his life and his crest is placed on a helm above the stall. A half-drawn sword is affixed below this to symbolise the fact that every Knight of the Garter has his hand on his sword, ready to defend his Sovereign. The arms on the banner would have been worn by a medieval knight as a tabard over his armour. The crest on his helmet would have helped his companions identify him in the fray of battle. The mantling that now hangs splendidly from the helm in St George's Chapel was originally a cloth to protect the helmet from the heat of the sun or the rain.

When he is invested a Knight is given his star of chipped silver, and the Garter blue riband of the Order (worn from left shoulder to right hip), from which is appended the badge, the Lesser George. The dark blue velvet robe, lined with white satin and embroidered on the left side with the badge of the Order, is put about the Knight's shoulder. From this robe hangs the hood of red velvet, now attached to the robe on the right shoulder, and the robe is slit on the right side to free the Knight's sword arm for action.* The hat that accompanies the robe is of black (or very deep blue) velvet, adorned with white ostrich plumes, held in place by another small Garter badge.

Over the robe is placed the collar of the Order, Tudor roses surrounded by garters, held with interlocking gold pieces, and attached to the shoulders by white ribbons. Finally there is the Garter itself, with its motto 'Honi Soit Qui Mal Y Pense' attached on the left leg, just below the knee.

Normally the collar of the Garter and the ribbon are never worn together, though for some reason, perhaps to make himself look more splendid in the absence of other orders, Prince Charles wore both at his investiture as Prince of Wales at Caernarvon Castle in July 1969. Indeed, as we shall see, the occasional misuse of Garter regalia has caused some memorable exchanges in the past.

The 1967 Garter Procession winding its way down the hill at Windsor Castle, with the Queen and Prince Philip at the end of the procession. In front of them can be seen the Bishop of Winchester (the Prelate), the late Marquess of Salisbury, K.G. (the Chancellor), Garter King of Arms (Sir Anthony Wagner) and the Dean of Windsor (Register of the Order).

---

* The Prelate, the Bishop of Winchester, wears a robe without a slit. Being a man of the cloth he is not expected to fight.

*The badge of the
Order of the
Garter, with a
section of the collar,
from which hangs
the "George".*

THE HISTORY OF THE ORDER

Scholars will argue forever about the precise reasons for the founding of the Order of
the Garter, and the date of its foundation. Unfortunately the early annals are incom-
plete, so evidence is drawn from a number of conflicting sources. The accepted date of
foundation is 1348. The Order was founded by King Edward III, and we know that he
ordered twenty-four garters with the motto: 'Honi Soit Qui Mal Y Pense'. The King
saw the advantages of gathering round him the flower of European knighthood to
assist him in his incessant struggles with France. Indeed in St George's Chapel there is
a portrait of the king wearing the crown of England and with the crowns of Scotland
and France impaled on his sword. This portrait is displayed in the South Quire Aisle
of St George's Chapel.

The concept of King Arthur and the Round Table, with its attendant ceremonies and
jousting, was in the forefront of the King's mind. The emblem is said to have been inspired

by his dance with Joan, Countess of Salisbury. The Countess's garter slipped to the floor and the King retrieved it and tied it round his own leg. His courtiers were amused by this but the King admonished them: 'Shame on him who thinks badly of it' [*Honi Soit Qui Mal Y Pense*]. I will make of it ere long the most honourable garter that was ever worn.'* Garter historians maintain that the Garter was rather 'an emblem of the tie and union of warlike qualities'[1], or that 'the Princely Garter . . . as it is framed with a Buckle to fasten it closely to the leg, doth resemble the bond of inmost Society, and can be called nothing more aptly, than a Badge of Unity and Concord'[2]. The colour of the Garter, blue and gold, was again said to be inspired by the King's avaricious glances in the directions of France.

A Garter buckled round a Knight's left leg.

In January 1344 Edward III held a Feast of the Round Table at Windsor, and many scholars believe that the Order was founded then. Others favour 1348, and certainly the 600th anniversary of the Order was celebrated in 1948. St George's Day was first celebrated in 1344, while the College of St George was established in 1348. Edward III gathered his son, the Prince of Wales and the twenty-four so-called Founder Knights at Windsor in 1348. He was but 36 years old, and the other Knights, all of whom had served at the Battle of Crecy, were in their twenties or thirties. His son, better known as the Black Prince, was to the fore.

Whole volumes have been written on the history of the Order since then. Any precis of such a history, encompassing as it does the great men of each era (and missing or excluding some too) is bound to be unsatisfactory. But some highlights are worth recording, and the later composition of the Order will be analysed more fully.

The Order has certainly gone from strength to strength since the days of Edward III and the Black Prince. But some Knights fell by the wayside. There was the case of Enguerrand de Couci, Earl of Bedford, who was married to Isabella, daughter of Edward III. He was nominated in 1365, but resigned in 1377 on the accession of Richard II, declaring his allegiance to the King of France.

In the reign of Henry IV, the first foreign sovereigns were appointed, the Kings of Spain, Portugal and Denmark. In 1410 Henry, Lord Scrope of Masham, Lord Treasurer to Henry IV, was appointed. But he conspired against the King's successor, Henry V, and was beheaded in 1415. Out of deference to his status as a Garter Knight, he was drawn and beheaded, but not hanged.

King Henry VIII declared that 'The King and His Heirs should be for ever Sovereigns of the Order'. Interestingly Cardinal Wolsey was appointed Register of the Order in 1510. In 1519, a declaration was issued to the effect that no man of lower status than a baron or a Knight of the Garter was to wear any velvet, either crimson or blue. It has been suggested that this is the true origin of the expression 'blue-blooded'. Henry VIII instituted various other statutes to the Order to the effect that:

1. Only people of a certain class could be appointed to the Order.
2. Treason, religious differences, cowardice etc. would lead to degradation from the Order.
3. Knights were to wear their Garters, and also be present at ceremonies on St George's Day. If they failed to do so, there would be fines, possibly 'a Jewel for the Altar of the value of twenty marks of Troy silver'.

---

* Many scholars dispute this as the romantic inspiration of the great Order. One scholar went so far as to write: 'It is a vain and idle romance derogatory both to the Order and to its Founder.'

If a discrepancy was discovered, it was resolved. Thomas, 12th Lord Ros (later 1st Earl of Rutland), who had been present with Henry VIII at the Field of the Cloth of Gold, was invested with the Garter in 1525 but it was discovered that he had not actually received the accolade of knighthood. His insignia were removed from him, and he was called before the King. The Knights Companion were summoned and private business began. Lord Ros was knighted and then selected for the Garter, and duly invested and installed according to the statutes.

Now, too, Knights were not blotted out from the records when they were degraded from the Order. Instead, the phrase 'Out upon thee Traitor!' was placed in the margin of the register beside their names.

An interesting situation arose in the reign of Queen Mary between 1553 and 1558. Mary married Philip of Spain on 27 July 1554 and the royal pair were immediately pronounced joint Sovereigns. Philip was installed Knight of the Garter in August that year and led into the Sovereign's stall with Mary. Philip used to preside at chapter meetings alone, and his banner hung alongside his wife's over the Sovereign's stall. When Mary died in 1558, his banner was placed over a near-by stall, and in 1560 he returned the Sovereign's badge to Queen Elizabeth via an ambassador.

Charles I did much to enhance the honour of the Garter. Magnificent installations became customary and Knights elect proceeded to Windsor amongst a vast company of their splendidly apparelled and mounted attendants. Solemn services followed and when all the religious duties were concluded, a mighty banquet was invariably held in the Castle.

Inevitably the interregnum of Oliver Cromwell was a low spot in the Order's history. Beltz records:

> After Charles I's execution which had, according to all appearance sealed the
> doom of the monarchy, the Order of the Garter, one of the most revered of its
> institutions, was shorn for a long season of its wonted lustre. Amidst constant
> endeavours in several antecedent years to preserve the vessel of the state from an
> inevitable wreck, the affairs of the society its festive conventions and hallowed
> rites, were of necessity intermitted and the venerable castle and chapel, once the
> scene of splendid ceremonies and pious observances, were profaned by the occu-
> pation of a rude soldiery.[3]

King Charles II was installed as Charles, Duke of Cornwall, in 1638. During the Civil War and the difficult years between 1649 and the Restoration in 1660, Sir Edward Walker, Garter King of Arms, faithfully kept up the records of the Order in no small danger to himself. And when Charles II was restored, he installed some of the sixteen Knights who had been appointed in the intervening years, but not installed for obvious reasons.

William and Mary were also joint Sovereigns. It tended to be William who oversaw the various functions of the Order, but when he was out of the country in 1694, Queen Mary presided at various installations. Mary died in December that year, and at William's first chapter, he elected and installed William, Duke of Gloucester, son of Princess Anne, later Queen Anne. The Duke of Gloucester was one of the youngest

The Quire of St George's Chapel facing East. The banners of the Knights of the Garter hang above their stalls. On the left can be seen the lion of the late King Olav of Norway, and the chrysanthemum of the controversial Emperor Hirohito of Japan. The red banner with the white saltire and the rose (1st right) is that of the present Chancellor, the Marquess of Abergavenny.

Knights, being but 5 years old when he was created.* But William III, who installed him, had been appointed yet younger. He was a mere 2½ years old when appointed in 1653.

Queen Anne was the first Lady Sovereign to wear the Garter insignia regularly. It was in the reign of George I that there occurred the last traditional degradation of a Knight of the Garter: James, 2nd Duke of Ormonde, appointed in 1688, and serving as Lord Lieutenant of Ireland from 1703-1710, was degraded in 1716. He had been impeached in 1715 as a supporter of James Stuart, and for taking part in the Jacobite Rebellion of the same year. When degraded from the Order of the Garter, his achievements were thrown down by the heralds, kicked out of the quire and through the west door of the Chapel. Then Clarenceux King of Arms pulled his stall plate from his stall.

King George III added four extra Garter stalls to the quire of St George's Chapel, and extended membership of the Order to sons of the Sovereign, additional to the twenty-four Knights and the Prince of Wales. In 1805, the Order was further extended to include lineal descendants of George I, who may be elected. In 1821 George IV decreed that any such lineal descendants should be 'Extra Knights', if appointed.† Various foreign kings were also appointed, such as Emperor Alexander I of Russia, in 1813.

QUEEN VICTORIA

Queen Victoria greatly extended the use of the Garter as a gift to foreign kings and princes, and during the next reign there was a time when Edward VII had as many foreign Knights as English ones. Queen Victoria created 132 Garter Knights, of whom 51 were emperors, kings, sultans, princes, or in other ways married to members of her family. Amongst these there were some very famous names: Louis Philippe, King of the French; Emperor Napoleon III of the French; King Christian IX of Denmark; King Leopold II of the Belgians; Emperor Franz Josef of Austria; the future Kaiser Wilhelm of Germany; Emperor Alexander III of Russia; the Prince Imperial of Austria; and Emperor Nicholas II of Russia.

Amongst her English Knights we find many dukes and marquesses, but of the great men of the day, there were several prime ministers: the Earl of Aberdeen, who was given the Garter after his resignation following revelations about the conditions of the sick and wounded in the Crimean War; Viscount Palmerston, not always Queen Victoria's favourite; the Earl of Derby, a Whig who succeeded in bringing the East India Company to an end; Earl Russell (formerly Lord John Russell); Benjamin Disraeli, Earl of Beaconsfield, whom the Queen held in high esteem and who caused her to become Empress of India; eight days later came the Marquess of Salisbury; and finally, in 1892, the Earl of Rosebery.§ The last Knight Queen Victoria appointed was Field Marshal Earl Roberts (within a month of her death).

---

* He died in 1700

† Presumably men such as the Earl of Athlone, and Earl Mountbatten of Burma were not deemed lineal descendents as such. At any rate they were included in the twenty-four.

§ It was then another thirty years before the next prime minister was appointed, Arthur Balfour.

A notable Knight of Victorian creation was H.R.H. the Duke of Connaught. He held the Garter longer than anyone else in the history of the Order, nearly seventy-five years, having been appointed in 1867 when he was 17, and dying in 1942, aged 91. There were few installations in Queen Victoria's reign, and equally few in the early part of this century.

KING EDWARD VII

King Edward VII's reign is notable for his revival of the habit of appointing Ladies of the Garter after a lapse of four centuries, of some magnificent Garter Missions, and of some memorable rows, concerning the Order.

The King only had the chance to create twenty-four Knights in his short reign. Of these, fifteen were royal. Two are dealt with at some length below. His first royal Knight was the Crown Prince of Prussia, who visited Osborne in 1901; then there was King Alfonso of Spain, invested in Madrid in 1902. There followed a batch of royal representatives who came to London for the coronation which was postponed due to the King's sudden illness: Grand Duke Michael of Russia (heir to the Tsar, and later murdered), Archduke Franz Ferdinand (later murdered at Sarajevo), whose insignia was delivered to him at the Castle of Konopischt; the Duke of Aosta; Luiz Filippe, Prince Royal of Portugal; the King's nephew, the Duke of Albany; Prince Arthur, Duke of Saxony (better known as Prince Arthur of Connaught – another nephew); later came the Shah of Persia (see below), King William II of Wurttemberg; the future King Gustav V of Sweden; the Emperor of Japan (see below); Friedrich, Grand Duke of Baden; the King's son-in-law, King Haakon of Norway; and King Manoel II of Portugal, who settled in England in exile in 1910 and died at his Twickenham home, Fulwell Park, in 1932.

Of Edward VII's English Knights, there were the Dukes of Bedford, Marlborough, Wellington, Sutherland, and Richmond (with whom the King stayed for the Goodwood race meeting each July). After 1906 the 9th Duke of Marlborough was allowed to attend the chapter meetings but was sent away before luncheon because he was separated from his wife, Consuelo Vanderbilt, and consequently banned from court.*

There were five others. The first was the Earl Carrington (later Marquess of Lincolnshire)†, an intimate and life-long friend of the King and one time Governor of

---

* In 1911, Winston Churchill appealed to King George V to allow the Duke to remain to luncheon, pointing out that it 'inflicted a serious humiliation upon the Duke where he is only obeying an official summons which he receives as a Knight of the Garter.' Churchill added that the ceremonies were rare and the membership of the Order small. 'On the last occasion the base press of the United States was filled with insulting references to the Duke and highly coloured accounts of his treatment at the Castle and a great deal of unkind comment was excited in London.' The King replied via Viscount Knollys, who said an invitation to luncheon would be sent, adding that the King 'is sure that the Duke of Marlborough will understand that in taking this step it must not be supposed that his Majesty proposes to abrogate the general rule, which affects him in regard to his coming to Court.' [Randolph Churchill, *Winston S. Churchill, Companion Volume II, Part 2, 1907-1911*, (Houghton Mifflin, 1969), pp.1082-1083]
† In 1914, when he was 71, the Marquess of Lincolnshire wanted to don khaki to inspect a regiment. He asked permission to wear a bit of Garter ribbon as a bar. This was refused. He then wanted to wear the actual star and riband with the khaki, again this was refused. [Rose, *George V*, pp.185-186]

King Edward VII
in Garter robes,
painted by Harold
Speed in 1905.
The King who
enjoyed some
memorable fights
over who should get
the Garter, is also
wearing the riband
of the Order of St
Patrick.

New South Wales, and later Lord Chamberlain. A keen diarist, he left an account of his investiture, which was a much simpler process than nowadays. King Edward offered him the Garter at Balmoral where he was a guest in October 1906. The investiture took place at Buckingham Palace three weeks later. The King was dressed in field marshal's uniform with Garter riband and star. Carrington recorded:

> I knelt – he put the ribbon over my shoulders, fixed the star, and handed me the
> Garter and Collar, and gave me his hand to kiss. Then, holding my hand, he said:
> 'I have the greatest pleasure in giving the Garter, the finest Order in the world, to
> you – one of my oldest and best friends, and I have selected this room as it is
> filled with reminiscences of my Indian tour when we went there in 1875.[4]

Of the other five, there was the Earl of Crewe (later Marquess of Crewe), another old and valued friend of the King and senior Liberal politician in the Lords. His Garter, unlike that of Lord Carrington, was entirely the gift of the Prime Minister, Henry Campbell-Bannerman, to replace the lately deceased 8th Duke of Devonshire. The Prime Minister made the appointment from his death-bed. 'Is it not pathetically kind with a sort of personal touch which one can never forget?' wrote Lord Crewe[5]. The other three were the Marquess of Northampton, the Earl of Durham and the Earl of Selborne (the retiring High Commissioner to South Africa)*, all safe and grand Establishment figures.

Edward VII had some memorable fights. In 1902 the then Shah of Persia, Muzzafer ed-Din, was invited on a state visit to Britain for political reasons, but was reluctant to accept. Lord Lansdowne, the Foreign Secretary, was particularly anxious that he should come as there was danger of the Shah siding with the Russians. Sir Arthur Hardinge, British Minister in Teheran, suggested to the Shah that he would be sure to receive the Garter if he came, and so the Shah came, the Garter being his sole reason for coming. King Edward warned Lord Lansdowne that he had no intention of making the Shah a Knight of the Garter as the Order was now reserved exclusively for Christians.

The King had been convalescing on his yacht after his illness and the strain of the coronation, but went to Portsmouth to greet the Shah. They lunched together on his yacht, the *Victoria and Albert*. Lansdowne prepared a memorandum indicating that the officers of the Garter would draw up some special non-Christian insignia for such people as the Shah and gave it to the King to read in the presence of the Shah himself. But the King did not look at it, merely nodding twice, before laying it aside for later study. Lansdowne interpreted the King's nods as assent being given, and assured the Shah that the King would appoint him within the next week. The Shah, aware of the scheme, said that he would be happy to receive the Garter in its Christian form, as that was how his father had received it.[†] He proceeded to decline a miniature of the King, encrusted with gold and with South African diamonds, and he instructed his staff to decline any decorations offered them.

---

* His citation read that the Garter was given in recognition of 'the strong and grateful sense on the part of H.M. present Government of his loyal and efficent co-operation during the last four years in a peculiarly difficult situation'.

† Nasr ed-Din, Shah of Persia, was created K.G. in 1873, and died in 1896.

King Edward VII, the Shah of Persia and Queen Alexandra on board the royal yacht, Victoria and Albert, *August 1902. All three are wearing Persian Orders, as the Shah had not yet succeeded in getting his Garter. King Edward also wears the Royal Victorian Chain.*

Lord Lansdowne then instructed the crown jewellers to make a non-Christian Garter star in three days, omitting the Cross of St George. And he informed the Persian Minister in London that the Order had been conferred. He wrote to the King, explaining what he had done and enclosed some coloured illustrations of the new insignia.

The King was still aboard his yacht, when the letter arrived on the morning of 24 August 1902. He exploded with rage. And he flung the Foreign Secretary's letters, with its painted enclosures, through a port-hole.* The King dictated a fierce letter to Lansdowne, which Sir Frederick Ponsonby, his Assistant Private Secretary, moderated somewhat. The letter nevertheless read: 'The Shah forced himself upon the King when he knew his visit this year was most inconvenient . . . and if the Shah leaves this country in the sulks like a spoilt child, because he cannot get what he wants, then it cannot be helped'[6].

The Shah did leave in a sulk, but when Lansdowne threatened to resign, and the opinions of the Duke of Devonshire, Lord Curzon, Lord Knollys and Mr Arthur Balfour were canvassed, the King realised he would have to give way. The Shah was nominated by special statute on 12 December, and invested in Teheran by Viscount Downe the following February.

* The designs survived and are now in the Royal Library.

The King made certain stipulations. He declared that the Garter should never again be conferred on an infidel*; that members of the Shah's suite who refused decorations should be offered no more[†] and that Sir Arthur Hardinge be reprimanded[§].

It was also decided that the King should confer the Garter only after consultation with, and on the advice of, the Prime Minister in future. The same went for all the other orders except the Order of Merit, the Royal Victorian Order and the Royal Victorian Chain.

In June 1907, there arrived in London the King of Siam, again expecting the Garter. Many officials, both British and Siamese, watched developments with anxious interest. The Foreign Office were keen to avoid any unpleasantness, while the Siamese ministers, fearing they had misled their King, believed their heads might be chopped off. Edward VII refused this time, and the King of Siam was offered the Royal Victorian Chain instead, which he declined on the advice of his Government. 'It was an awkward affair altogether', recalled Lord Hardinge of Penshurst.[7]

Then in 1909 there was a vacancy, which Asquith suggested should be filled by Sir Edward Grey, the Foreign Secretary. The King was reluctant to give the Garter to a man who was not, at least, an Earl, so appointed the Marquess of Northampton instead.[¶]

GARTER MISSIONS

Garter Missions have always been splendid affairs, greatly enhancing the prestige of the Order in the eyes of the receiving Sovereigns. There have been numerous of these since 1469 when Charles, Duke of Burgundy was invested by a group sent from England. There have been five such missions this century. Three occurred in the reign of Edward VII.

In 1902 the Duke of Connaught was sent to Madrid to invest King Alfonso XIII of Spain. There was the investiture of the Shah, mentioned above, in 1903. In 1904 the Prince of Wales, later George V, went to Stuttgart to invest King William II of Wurttemberg, in 1906 Prince Arthur of Connaught went to Japan to invest the Emperor, and in 1929, the Duke of Gloucester also went to Japan to invest Emperor Hirohito.

Lord Redesdale, grandfather of Nancy Mitford, accompanied Prince Arthur on the Garter Mission to the Mikado in 1906, and wrote a book about the trip. They were abroad for many weeks. Six men accompanied the Prince, and they sailed from Marseilles on 12 January 1906. H.M.S. *Diadem* sailed into Yokahama harbour just over a month later. The Garter party was met by the Ambassador and two distinguished Japanese war leaders, General Kuroki and Admiral Togo (the latter one of three invested with the Order of Merit). Breaking centuries of tradition, the Emperor himself greeted Prince Arthur on his arrival in Tokyo.   The day of the ceremony dawned

---

*   Emperor Mutsuhito of Japan was nominated in 1905.
†   They were.
§   .Sir Arthur was reprimanded.
¶   When George V gave Grey the Garter in 1912, there were some in grand society who disapproved.

and the group made their way to the Emperor's Palace. Here the insignia, including a Garter star, emblazoned with diamonds, and a George carved in onyx and mounted in brilliants, were laid out in readiness. Prince Arthur was in his Garter robes, a procession formed and they wound their way along the long corridors of the Palace to the Throne Room. Redesdale described the scene:

> Imagine to yourself a vast room or hall, square, or nearly so, in shape. The floor is parquetted; the walls panelled with silk brocade surmounted by a frieze of the most elaborate carving, coloured and gilt; the ceiling coffered, finely lacquered and enriched with gold decoration. Opposite the entrance is a raised dais carpeted with crimson and canopied with a baldacchino of silk and velvet of the same colour, supported by two huge gilt spears springing up from the wall at an angle of about forty-five degrees. On the dais is the throne of gold and velvet, in front of which stands the Emperor in Field Marshal's uniform, with white breeches and jack-boots . . .
>
> At His Majesty's right hand, also below the dais, are the Princes and Princesses of the Blood, and at right angles to them are the great nobles, generals, admirals, statesmen, and the ladies of the Court – all in European uniforms and dresses . . .
>
> Not a sound was heard, not a movement of a finger, not the rustle of a dress, as very slowly each one of us in turn, carrying the insignia on a red velvet cushion, advanced alone towards the throne, making the three prescribed obeisances, and drawing up on each side to make a lane for the Prince, who, of course, came in last.[8]

Prince Arthur then addressed the Emperor on behalf of his 'august master and royal uncle' and asked him to accept 'the highest mark of his friendship and esteem which it is in His Majesty's power to bestow'.[9] His speech over, the Emperor replied. Then came the investiture, and just as Prince Arthur was buckling the Garter around the Emperor's knee, the invisible band struck up 'God Save The King'. 'The effect' wrote Lord Redesdale 'was electric'. The ceremony over, Prince Arthur and his party backed out of the imperial presence. Lord Redesdale concluded:

> The central figure, the Tenshi Sama, the Son of Heaven, a monarch the origin of whose ancestors is lost in the dimness of myth and fable – himself, until a few short years ago, as great a mystery even to his own people as those very ancestors – now a Ruler whom all may see, and whom all revere, not only as the symbol of authority, but because, during the whole thirty-eight years of his reign, he has never done a deed in public or in his private life of which either he or his people can be ashamed.[10]

In 1929, Prince Henry, Duke of Gloucester went on a similar mission to bestow the Garter on Emperor Hirohito. He described the investiture as 'a very impressive ceremony, and luckily none of us made a mistake. I found it very difficult walking backwards when wearing the mantle!'[11]

George V, an ardent Christian, was not enthusiastic about conferring the Garter on a non-Christian. Wriggle as he did, though, he could not escape his Government's wish that it be conferred on Emperor Hirohito. The matter dragged on, but Sir Austen Chamberlain secured the King's agreement and then informed Emperor Hirohito of his good fortune. He duly cabled the King to thank him in advance. Thus, the Duke of Gloucester followed in Prince Arthur's footsteps. The ceremony was as splendid and impressive as before. And the Duke negotiated the difficult task of walking backwards in his mantle after the investiture. As the Duke's biographer concluded: 'This was all very grand, almost medieval stuff'.[12]

The later history of Emperor Hirohito's Garter was a less happy one. Due to Japan being at war with Britain, the Emperor's banner was quietly removed from over his stall on 20 December 1941, though the stall-plate remained. After the war, when more amicable relations were restored, Princess Alexandra visited Tokyo (in 1961) and the Emperor was allowed to wear his star. In May 1971, before his state visit to Britain that autumn, the Emperor's banner was again hung in St George's Chapel, this act and the visit itself being the subject of some hostility, the mood of which was captured by a *Private Eye* front cover, depicting the Emperor and proclaiming: 'There's a nasty Nip in the air'.

Emperor Hirohito of Japan wearing his Garter riband during his 1971 State Visit. Also in the photograph (from left to right) are the Duchess of Kent, the Queen Mother, the Prince of Wales, Prince Richard of Gloucester, Empress Nagako, Lord Snowdon, the Duke of Beaufort, Prince William of Gloucester (partly hidden), the Queen and Princess Alice, Countess of Athlone. The Prince of Wales and the Queen are wearing the Order of the Chrysanthemum of Japan.

49

LADIES OF THE GARTER

There were some Ladies of the Garter in the very early days of the Order's life, Edward III appointing his wife, Queen Philippa, and his daughters, and assigning them robes and Garters (worn on the left arm). But they had no stalls in St George's Chapel. Some sixty-four ladies received this privilege between 1358 and 1488. It was another feature of the reign of Edward VII that he revived the practice, appointing Queen Alexandra by special statute in 1901. George V then appointed Queen Mary in 1910. And George VI appointed his Queen Elizabeth in 1936, Queen Wilhelmina of the Netherlands in 1944, and Princess Elizabeth (the present Queen) in 1948. In her turn the present Queen has appointed three ladies, Queen Juliana of the Netherlands in 1958, Queen Margrethe of Denmark in 1979, and Queen Beatrix of the Netherlands in 1989.

KING GEORGE V

King George V's early Garter Knights were mainly members of his family – Queen Mary, and his son, the Prince of Wales (automatically). He held an installation ceremony at Windsor in June 1911, during which he installed his son, with a full procession down the hill to St George's Chapel. The young Prince of Wales wore the fullest possible robes of the Order, with a huge hat, over a costume of cloth of silver, with stockings and white satin slippers under his robes. Sponsored by his great-uncle, the Duke of Connaught and by Prince Arthur of Connaught, he was escorted into the Garter Throne Room. After the King had invested him, he circled the room, shaking hands with each Knight in turn.* The young Prince, who later took a great dislike to such robes, was pleased that he could use his father's and not incur additional expense. Queen Mary described him to her aunt as looking 'too sweet'.[13]

Before the war George V gave the Garter to the old Prince Regent of Bavaria, the Grand Duke of Mecklenburg-Strelitz, to his uncle, the Duke of Argyll and his brothers-in-law, the Duke of Fife (who died within the year of a chill contracted due to a shipping accident off Cape Spartel), and King Christian X of Denmark; and to Emperor Yoshihito of Japan. He also appointed the retiring Viceroy of India, the Earl of Minto; the Foreign Secretary, Sir Edward Grey (later Lord Grey of Fallodon)†; and the Lord Chamberlain, Earl Spencer. A less satisfactory appointment was that of the 7th Earl Beauchamp, the holder of many public offices, who was later drummed out of

---

* Not having been invested as Prince of Wales at this point, the young Prince wore the Garter regalia at the coronation twelve days later.

† Sir Edward Grey, oblivious of the earlier attempts to have him appointed, wrote to a friend: 'I suppose my real feeling about the Garter was that I was very pleased at being offered it, but shrank from having it. It will make life a little more conspicuous and more complicated: and it gives me a feeling of being still deeper in.' [G.M. Trevelyan, Grey of Fallodon (Longmans Green, 1937), p.164] Lord Hardinge of Penshurst noted that Grey had declined the G.C.V.O. on the grounds that he disliked orders and did not think it right for Cabinet ministers to accept them. 'Yet a few years later he accepted the Garter while still a Cabinet minister! which however, I learnt later, had been bestowed upon him in answer to attacks made upon him as Foreign Secretary by the German Government and Press.' [Lord Hardinge of Penshurst, Old Diplomacy (John Murray, 1947), p.179]

Britain by his brother-in-law, 'Bendor', Duke of Westminster, for sins unmentionable. Contrary to the belief held by many at the time (including the Duchess of Windsor), he never lost his Garter.

At the beginning of the Great War, King Albert of the Belgians was appointed, and in 1915, the Earl of Derby, a larger-than-life figure known as 'the King of Lancashire', and the 10th Earl of Chesterfield. Later that year the famous World War I general, Field Marshal Earl Kitchener of Khartoum, was appointed, but died almost exactly a year later, being drowned at sea by enemy action with his Garter star aboard and lost forever.

On 13 May 1915, with some reluctance, the King sanctioned the removal of the banners of certain stranger Knights from above their stalls, due to their countries being at war with Britain. The King was uncomfortable about the idea of removing honours that had been given in peacetime and had nothing to do with the present war. The Knights were struck from the roll of the Order but their stall-plates remain, though their banners were not re-hung in peacetime. These were the Kaiser, King William II of Wurttemberg, Crown Prince William of Germany, Ernst, Grand Duke of Hesse, Prince Henry of Prussia, the Duke of Coburg*, the Duke of Cumberland, and Emperor Franz Josef of Austria. Private files in the Royal Archives apparently indicate that 'a good deal of hostile criticism had been incurred by the fact that the Garter banners of the foreign royalties, who were engaged in war against us, had been allowed to remain hanging in St George's Chapel'[14]. And Queen Alexandra herself wrote to the King, her son: 'Although, as a rule I never interfere, I think the time has come when I must speak out. It is but right and proper for you to have down those hateful German banners in our sacred Church'[15]. The King agreed, commenting privately that otherwise 'the people would have stormed the chapel'.[16]

In 1916 the King appointed Earl (later Marquess) Curzon of Kedleston, a former Viceroy of India, who went on to be Foreign Secretary in the 1920s, and the 9th Duke of Devonshire, who served for the next five years as Governor-General of Canada. Lord Curzon was characteristically arrogant to his fellow Knight, the 9th Duke: 'You, Victor, of course, have got the Garter as the head of a Garter family. Dukes of Devonshire always get the Garter. It is no credit to you at all. But for me it is a personal honour'. The Duke protested that he had been an MP and served in the Lords, but Curzon would brook no excuses.[17]

Also in 1916 came Lord Hardinge of Penshurst, who retired as Viceroy of India, having survived a serious assassination attempt out there. And the King gave it to his second son, the Duke of York, who received it with almost undue pride, on his 21st birthday.

The appointment of the 4th Marquess of Salisbury in 1917 was in line with many Garters given to that family, and the Marquess of Bath, on the same day, represented a more lofty Establishment position held by the family before they descended into the

---

* The Duke of Coburg was a grandson of Queen Victoria and the brother of Princess Alice, Countess of Athlone. In 1936 he attended the funeral of King George V in the chapel, "a rather bent figure in obviously German uniform with what looked like a storm-trooper's helmet". [Lord Harewood, *The Tongs and the Bones* (Weidenfeld, 1981), p16]. So sinister did he look that the young Gerald Lascelles, son of the Princess Royal, burst into tears at the sight of him. He was a prisoner of war of the Americans at the end of the Second World War, and died, a severe arthritic, in Coburg in 1954.

wilder realms of the stately home business. Of George V's later Knights, the Duke of Rutland (1918), the Marquess of Londonderry (1919), the Duke of Northumberland (1925), the Duke of Abercorn (1928), the Earl of Scarbrough (1929), and the Earl of Yarborough (1935), fell into the category of Establishment figures.

George V was sparing with the Garter as far as foreign kings were concerned. In 1924 he gave it to King Ferdinand of Roumania, who had married his cousin, Princess Marie of Edinburgh (a girl he had at one time wished to marry), to Emperor Hirohito of Japan (1928), and to the young King Leopold III of the Belgians (in December 1935), whose wife, Queen Astrid had been killed a few weeks earlier. He gave it to his sons, Prince Henry, later Duke of Gloucester, and Prince George, later Duke of Kent. He also gave it to Queen Mary's brothers, the Marquess of Cambridge and the Earl of Athlone, and to his son-in-law, Viscount Lascelles, later 6th Earl of Harewood.

Kenneth Rose has examined the whole question of honours in his biography of George V. He wrote: 'Honours there had always been. Not until the reign of King George V, however, did they cease to be the almost exclusive preserve of the well-born and the well-established. The Orders of the Garter, of the Thistle, and of St Patrick were confined to the Sovereign's family, the landowning nobility, elder states-men and the occasional hero of the battlefield or the war at sea'[18]. The later choices of George V's Garter Knights in no way contradicts this.

Alfred, Viscount Milner was appointed in 1921. This former Colonial Secretary and able colleague of Lloyd George was unaware that the Garter riband was worn from left shoulder to right hip. Thus he wore it the same way as his G.C.B. and duly arrived in the ante-chamber of St James's Palace for a levee. Here he had the misfor-tune to encounter Lord Curzon, who was so shocked that he wrote him a letter say-ing that it was 'almost inconceivable that anyone who had been given this ancient Order, the highest order in the land, should not even take the trouble to ascertain how it was worn'[19]. Some months later a further levee occurred on what is known as 'a Collar Day'*. These occasions often caused problems to eminent men, who were, in the words of Sir Frederick Ponsonby 'inclined to be vague about their dress'. Lord Curzon arrived late, wearing both the Garter collar and a riband. King George V, a stickler for detail as are all monarchs, teased the Marquess gently. But a few days later a letter arrived from Lord Milner, repeating Curzon's rebuke to him almost word for word.[20]

Arthur Balfour, the Prime Minister (1922), and later H.H. Asquith, Earl of Oxford and Asquith (1925) and Sir Austen Chamberlain (1925)[†] were given the Garter as senior politicians.

Viscount Fitzalan of Derwent, former Lord Lieutenant of Ireland, was appointed in 1925.

In 1926 the Earl of Reading was bidden to Windsor on his retirement as Viceroy of India. This was a post that made a Garter a near certainty, but none came. Instead Reading was raised to a marquessate. As his son explained: 'There could, in fact, never

---

* These are certain Saints' days and days of high festival when the collar of the Order is worn and not the riband.

† Sir Austen was an example of a Knight appointed by special statute, extra to the complement of twenty-four. He became an Ordinary Knight on the death of the Marquess of Lansdowne on 3 June 1927. This situation arose occasionally during the reign of George V and indeed of George VI.

have been any question of a choice, since, as he learnt later, the Garter is an exclusively Christian Order'.* [21]

The Garter needs a few more Knights of the calibre of Hugh, 5th Earl of Lonsdale, created K.G. in 1928. The 'Yellow Earl' was a keen sportsman, rider, yachtsman and boxer, who had toured with a circus as a young man. He lived in splendour, drinking white Burgundy for breakfast, and when he arrived at Ascot it was in his famous yellow and black wagonette, drawn by perfectly matching chestnuts and grooms and postilions in yellow livery, every buckle gleaming. When given the Garter, the Earl treated himself to a Garter star set in diamonds with a ruby cross and more diamonds on the blue enamel surround, a Lesser George in a diamond frame, a garter with diamonds on blue velvet, and diamond buckle.[†] The 2nd Earl of Lytton (1933), Governor of Bengal, and a supporter (with his sister, Lady Constance Lytton) of the cause of women's suffrage, is best remembered now as the author of the book, *Antony*, a tribute to his son, Lord Knebworth, who died in a flying accident in 1933. He married Pamela Plowden, an early love of Sir Winston Churchill.

Lord Irwin, destined to be the Earl of Halifax, was appointed in 1931. He was an important Knight of the Garter, serving as Chancellor of the Order from 1943 till his death in 1959. His distinguished career included being Viceroy of India, Lord Privy Seal, Lord President of the Council, Foreign Secretary and then (somewhat in wartime exile) Ambassador to Washington. As Chancellor he played an important role in the selection of Knights of the Garter and the revival of the annual ceremony in 1948.

The last Knight appointed by George V was James, Earl Stanhope, in 1934. He lived on until 1967, and in his later years the Garter ceremony was his only public appearance. He was given the Garter having served as Civil Lord of the Admiralty, and later as Under-Secretary of State for War. (Later he was in the Cabinet as First Commissioner of Works and then Lord President of the Council). He caused a stir in April 1939 when he announced that the Fleet had been re-armed with anti-aircraft guns, at a time when Chamberlain was still believing in his Munich pact. Churchill removed him from office.

The Earl, 'a holy and humble man of heart, who tried to do his duty to God and his Sovereign'[22], left his eighteenth century mansion, Chevening, in Kent, to the nation, hoping that the Prince of Wales would live there (as he did for a while in the 1970s), or that another descendant of George VI would occupy it as 'a family home and a worthy part of our national heritage'.[23] It is now the weekend home of the Foreign Secretary,[§] and in 1993 some of the contents were sold by the Trustees for £451,000.

---

* Lord Reading was Jewish, born Rufus Isaacs. Yet non-Christians were appointed to the Order, as we have seen. Reading was a Privy Councillor, a G.C.B., G.C.I.E. and G.C.V.O. without any problems.

[†] These were variously sold over the years. Frank Partridge bought them for £3,000 in the 1947 Christie's Lonsdale sale. They were sold again in 1955 for £2,000, and again in 1959. They are now in the Royal Library.

[§] A Foreign Secretary, Geoffrey Howe and his wife lived there until he was removed from office in 1989. Amongst other reasons for shifting him, wrote Mrs Thatcher's biographer, 'he had grown too attached to his official residence at Chevening which he and his wife used intensively as a place to entertain Tory allies as well as foreign officials.' [Hugo Young, *One of Us* (Macmillan, 1991), p.560] It was after Mrs Thatcher moved him out of the house, that the Howes began to seethe, and in due course the woolly Howe seized the dagger and delivered his withering 1990 speech that precipitated the leadership contest in which Mrs Thatcher was ousted from power.

KING GEORGE VI

King Edward VIII created no Knights of the Garter in his brief reign.

It was King George VI who converted the Garter back to being an entirely personal gift of the Sovereign. He loved the Garter and took a most particular interest in it. One of his first acts as King was to bestow it on Queen Elizabeth on his birthday, and he immediately decided to hold a Garter service[24]. He redesigned the star to the Stuart style in 1946, fixed the riband's colour as 'Kingfisher blue', and but days before he died, was in the process of designing a new style of trousers, which would enable the Garter to be worn – instead of over-knee breeches.

In 1937, George VI gave the Garter to his Lord Chamberlain, the Earl of Clarendon, who had just retired as Governor-General of South Africa. Then at the time of his coronation he gave it to the Duke of Norfolk (Earl Marshal), the Marquess of Exeter, the Earl of Strathmore (his father-in-law), the Duke of Beaufort (Master of the Horse)* and a few days later, Stanley Baldwin, the retiring Prime Minister.

King George VI held an investiture and installation service that summer. The eloquent Duchess of Sermoneta left an account of this ceremony:

> On this occasion the heralds who headed the procession looked like so many Knaves
> of Hearts, and the Knights of the Garter who followed wore long blue velvet cloaks
> that trailed behind them, and round hats trimmed with a profusion of white ostrich
> feathers. The Queen [Queen Elizabeth], very sweet in her robes, walked beside the
> King, and Queen Mary, splendidly dignified, swept along by herself. Except for the
> King and the Duke of Norfolk[†], all the Knights were very old, and the procession was
> held up by a Duke[§] who could not be persuaded to remain at home and had insisted
> on taking part, though he leant on a stick and could scarcely toddle.[25]

Unfortunately one of the escort fell over during the procession, and this and the absence from the ceremony of the Duke of Windsor seemed to be of great interest to the lower echelons of the press who depicted the first and made extensive comment on the latter. Lord Wigram, Keeper of the King's Archives thought some of them 'used the occasion as propaganda for the Duke of Windsor'.[26]

The next years saw three kings appointed, King George II of Greece (on a short private visit to London, November 1938), King Carol of Roumania (on his state visit in 1938), and Prince Paul of Yugoslavia (on his London visit, July 1939).

At the beginning of the war, the King's Private Secretary, Sir Alexander Hardinge, suggested that the King of Italy's Garter banner be removed 'without delay'. This came down as did that of Emperor Hirohito of Japan. There was discussion about the banners of the King of the Belgians, the King of Roumania and Prince Paul of Yugoslavia, but these remained.[¶]

---

* These last two were by special statute, exceeding the number of Knights.
† She could have mentioned the Duke of Beaufort, then a mere 37.
§ The Duke of Portland was born in 1857, and the Duke of Bedford in 1858.
¶ King Carol of Roumania was in exile during the war, and Prince Paul was a close personal friend of Queen Elizabeth, and indeed spent most of the war in exile.

*Queen Mary
'sweeping along by
herself' in the 1937
Garter procession,
her train carried by
the young Captain
Alexander Ramsay
of Mar and the
present Earl of
Harewood.*

In 1940, shortly before he died, the King offered the Garter to his outgoing Prime Minister, Neville Chamberlain, but he felt too unwell to accept it.

There were three wartime appointments, Edward, 10th Duke of Devonshire (1941), the 2nd Marquess of Zetland (former Secretary of State for India) (1942) and the 2nd Marquess of Linlithgow (retiring Viceroy of India) in 1943. In July 1945, following his defeat in the General Election, Winston Churchill tendered his resignation to the King. Having accepted this, the King offered him the Garter but he declined, feeling that 'the times were too sad for honours or rewards'.[27] Churchill recommended that Anthony Eden should have it, but he declined too on the grounds that 'I could not possibly agree to accept such a distinction after five years service under a Chief who accepts nothing for himself.'[28]

On his 86th birthday, in 1944, the Marquess of Crewe mused on the comparative longevity of the 'comfortable classes' as opposed to 'the working population'. He cited the Garter as an example: 'I think that more than a third of the K.G.s are men over eighty, which I am sure never happened two generations ago.'[29] By the end of the war, inevitably there were many unfilled vacancies. At this point, the King managed to persuade Clement Attlee that the Garter (and the Thistle) should be entirely in the gift of the King, and so it has been ever since. In December 1946 the King rewarded the war leaders – Viscount Addison (the Lord Privy Seal and Leader of the Lords); Viscount

Cranborne (the Secretary of State for the Dominions, and Opposition Leader of the Lords and later 5th Marquess of Salisbury); Admiral (of the Fleet) Viscount Mountbatten (later Earl Mountbatten of Burma); Field Marshal Viscount Alanbrooke; Marshal of the Royal Air Force Viscount Portal of Hungerford; Field Marshal Viscount Alexander (later Earl Alexander of Tunis); and Field Marshal Viscount Montgomery of Alamein.

In December 1946 the King invested six of his seven new Knights* in the Bow Room of Buckingham Palace. All the Knights were present except the 81 year old Earl of Derby. They wore robes and collars over plain clothes or service dress, and the King made a speech explaining that it was the first such investiture since the Great War, and the first in which any of the present Knights had taken part. He said: 'During the actual Investiture you will find that the Ancient Admonitions will be said as the separate emblems of the Order are presented, signifying their Christian purport. These Admonitions have been revived after many years of disuse.'[30]

Princess Elizabeth was appointed in 1947, and Prince Philip, Duke of Edinburgh a few days later. (The King did this expressly: 'so that she will be senior to Philip'[31].) Then in 1948 the King appointed the 7th Duke of Portland, the 4th Lord Harlech (former British High Commissioner in South Africa), the 11th Earl of Scarbrough (Governor of Bombay before and during the war, and later Lord Chamberlain) and the 2nd Lord Cranworth, and on 23 April that year, he installed Princess Elizabeth, the Duke of Edinburgh and some thirteen Knight Companions one after another.[†]

The 1948 Ceremony was a high point in the history of the Garter, marking its sex-centenary and the full revival of the medieval ceremonies. Again the King addressed the Knights before the investiture. *The Times* noted that the ceremonies had not been used since the reign of King George III and that this was a festival of old England. The new Knights were particularly appropriate, 'many of them heroes of the late victory worthily continuing the succession of the knights of Crecy and Poitiers, but headed on this occasion by the heiress presumptive and her husband'.[32] A large crowd thronged the Castle to witness the procession, and Queen Mary drove down before the ceremony and joined the procession at the Great West Door. The Duke of Gloucester and the Earl of Athlone walked side by side after the Knight Companions.

His later appointments were the 7th Duke of Wellington, 5th Earl Fortescue and 2nd Viscount Allendale, all in 1951[§] These three were installed along with King Frederik IX of Denmark in May 1951, during the King's state visit to Britain. Within a year George VI was dead.

---

* Lord Alexander was in Canada as Governor-General.

† Besides the 1946 and 1948 creations mentioned above (with the exception of Mountbatten, who was in India), the King installed the Duke of Devonshire, the Marquess of Zetland, and the Marquess of Linlithgow, the earlier wartime appointments.

§ Lord Hardinge of Penshurst, the King's former Private Secretary, noted that the re-arrangement whereby the King alone selected Knights of the Garter was a great improvement, though in the choices of Lords Cranworth, Fortescue and Allendale, 'in preference to Bledisloe [former Governor-General of New Zealand], Selborne [Minister of Economic Warfare] and others' he spotted 'a preference for personal friends which, if persisted in, would do the Order no good'. [Private notes] Christopher Hibbert, writing in *The Court at Windsor*, was also disappointed in the King's later choices of Knights.

QUEEN ELIZABETH II

Happily the Order of the Garter has flourished during the present reign, the Queen having made sixty-one appointments to date. This section deals with those that no longer survive.

The Queen's first Knight was her uncle, Earl Granville, the Governor of Northern Ireland.* Appointed in December 1952, he was already a sick man. He was never invested or installed, nor did his banner hang in the chapel. He died in June 1953.

Next came the Queen's most famous appointment, Sir Winston Churchill, nominated in April 1953 so that he could wear his robes at the Coronation, and installed in June 1954. Sir Winston had been offered the Garter twice before by George VI, but turned it down. He was delighted to accept it from the young Queen. 'I refused it before but then the Prime Minister had a say in it. Now only the Queen decides,' Sir Winston told his doctor.[33] Sir Winston was the first prime minister since Disraeli to receive the Order while still in office.

Churchill wore the splendid diamond Garter star of Lord Castlereagh at the pre-coronation dinner at Ten Downing Street. Though his health was poor, Churchill managed the installation ceremony gamely in 1954. The next day he was busy looking at press cuttings and told his doctor: 'The scene in the Chapel was lovely.'[34] He went on: 'I had to climb a great many steps up to the Chapel and afterwards in the Castle; and there was a lot of standing, and I'm no good at that. . . .'[35]

King Gustav VI Adolf of Sweden sailed into Greenwich on his state visit in June 1954 and received the Garter that day. On 15 October the Queen presented the Garter to Emperor Haile Selassie of Ethiopia at the State Banquet at Buckingham Palace during his very brief state visit to London. And five days later she appointed the Foreign Secretary, Anthony Eden, who now accepted it.[†] Eden had to wait until 1956 to be installed as the 1955 ceremony was cancelled at the last minute due to the rail strike. Sir Winston Churchill, who attended a rehearsal of the ceremony at St James's Palace, commented later from his bath: 'Certainly if there is a general strike it would be ridiculous for Anthony to prance about in his Garter robes.'[36]

In 1955 the Queen gave the Garter to the Earl of Iveagh, head of the Guinness family, who was also Lord Halifax's brother-in-law.[§] Then Earl Attlee, the former Labour Prime Minister, joined the Order in April 1956, on his retirement as Leader of the Labour Party. *The Times* welcomed the appointment, noting that now all the three living prime ministers, Churchill, Eden and Attlee, were in the Garter, and that the honour transcended party politics:

> These three are the outstanding survivors of the Cabinet that conducted the Second
> World War. The service commanders were installed in the centenary celebrations of
> 1948. The statesmen were needed to complete the company. It is this which should
> preserve the Garter from becoming a conventional ornament of the highest political
> office, as (should a former Prime Minister desire it) an earldom is at present[37].

---

* He was married to Lady Rose Bowes-Lyon, sister of Queen Elizabeth the Queen Mother.
† He served as Prime Minister from 1955 to 1957.
§ Halifax first proposed him in 1949, along with his son-in-law, the Earl of Feversham, an unsuccessful candidate.

The 1956 ceremony saw the investiture of the three new Knights, Eden (sponsored by Montgomery and Churchill), Iveagh (sponsored by Stanhope and Salisbury), and Attlee (sponsored by Alexander of Tunis and Wellington)*. Sometimes Knights of the Garter are old friends. For example, the appointment of Viscount Chandos in 1970 was particularly welcomed by the Marquess of Salisbury and the Duke of Portland. All three had messed together in the Reverend Bowlby's house at Eton in the early years of the century. Thus Oliver was re-united with 'Bobbety' and 'Chopper'. On the other hand, in 1956, Sir Winston Churchill found himself joined by the Earl of Iveagh, now leaning on a heavy stick. The two had been at prep school together and loathed each other. Now, unexpectedly reunited as octogenarians, their displeasure was further incurred when they realised they had to sit next to each other in chapel. They studiously ignored one another.

The next day Churchill confessed to his doctor that he had walked in the procession: 'I had to sit down during the Service. Even when they sang 'God Save the Queen' I did not stand up. My legs felt wobbly. It wasn't the length of the walk that tired me, but the way they tottered along and dawdled.'[38]

There was a considerable royal turn out at the 1956 service (several of whom had recently accompanied the Queen to watch part of the Olympic Games in Sweden) and the young Duke of Cornwall and his sister, Princess Anne, watched the installation service for the first time from the Catherine of Aragon loft.

In 1957 General Lord Ismay, a wartime leader, who was later the extremely successful first Secretary-General of NATO, was appointed immediately on his retirement. He asked Churchill to sponsor him on what turned out to be the hottest day of a hot summer. So too the 11th Lord Middleton who was reported to 'dumbfounded'[39] when he was made a Knight of the Garter. He was a popular Yorkshireman, who advertised for clergymen for his livings in the *Horse and Hounds*. The present Prince of Wales automatically became a Knight of the Garter when the title was conferred on him in 1958, though he was not installed until ten years later.

In 1959 the Queen appointed Field Marshal Sir William (later Viscount) Slim, the outgoing Governor-General of Australia, who later became Governor of Windsor Castle, and the 10th Duke of Northumberland, a young appointment at the age of 35 (an attempt to introduce younger blood which has not been repeated)[†]. In May 1959 King Olav of Norway was given the Garter during a four-day private visit to Windsor, and invested with the same insignia as had been worn by his late father, King Haakon.

In 1960 came the 7th Earl of Radnor (Lord Warden of the Stannaries), the 11th Lord Digby (Lord Lieutenant of Dorset)[§] and Lord Wakehurst, another Governor of Northern Ireland. The 1960 ceremony was the last one attended by Sir Winston Churchill.

Sir Winston Churchill, K.G. emerging from the 1956 Garter Ceremony. His legs felt wobbly.

---

* The Duke of Wellington also presented the Wellington banner as rent for Stratfield Saye on this day, which happened also to be Waterloo Day.

† Lord Halifax first proposed him in 1956 in favour of the Earl of Derby on the grounds that 'the domestic menage I should judge to be rather more secure'. [Andrew Roberts, *The Holy Fox*, (Weidenfeld, 1991), p.300]

§ He was the father of the celebrated Pamela Digby, who married Randolph Churchill, Leland Hayward and Averill Harriman, and was appointed President Clinton's Ambassador to Paris in 1993.

In 1963, King Baudouin of the Belgians received the Garter on his state visit to Britain. He died in July 1993. And later in the year King Paul of Greece received it on his state visit, but died the following March, before his banner could be raised.

Field Marshal Sir Gerald Templer was appointed K.G. in 1963 on the day the Federation of Malaysia was announced – a 'Malaya Garter' therefore, and the next year came Earl Alexander of Hillsborough, another short lived Knight, installed in June 1964 and dead the following January. His banner was never raised. He was better known as A.V. Alexander, the son of a blacksmith, and a Labour First Lord of the Admiralty*. Appointed with him was the 10th Viscount Cobham, a keen cricketer and a former Governor-General of New Zealand.

Sir Gerald Templer, Lord Alexander of Hillsborough and Lord Cobham were all installed on the same day in 1964. The rehearsal that day had been a bit of a fiasco as the Garter King of Arms apparently got the Knights muddled. And after a long day, when the ceremony was over and they were back at the Castle, the Field Marshal turned to Lord Cobham and said: 'At last we can smoke; there are no Royals now!' Then he spotted the Princess Royal, who fortunately laughed[†40].

If the Queen had had her way, Harold Macmillan would have been one of the Knights installed that day. She offered him the Garter in March 1964, but he declined it, saying that it should only be awarded for service in times of national emergency. To Lady Waverley he wrote that it would have given him 'the substance without the shadow'.[41]

The following January, Sir Winston Churchill died after a ten day illness at the age of 90. When his coffin lay in state in Westminster Hall, it was covered with the Union Flag, and a dark blue velvet cushion, bearing the star, Garter, and collar of the Order, probably the most prominent time when the Garter insignia impinged itself on the public conscience. A long crowd passed through Westminster Hall, queuing through the cold January days and nights, and then on Saturday 30 January, the coffin, similarly adorned, was borne to St Paul's Cathedral for the state funeral.

In April 1965 came Viscount Brookeborough, former Prime Minister of Northern Ireland, and Lord Bridges, former War Cabinet secretary. No Knights were appointed until 1968, when the Queen appointed Viscount Amory, the former Conservative Chancellor of the Exchequer and Viscount De L'Isle, a rare holder of the Victoria Cross and Garter,[§] and the last English Governor-General of Australia. The Queen's fondness for the Commonwealth was reflected in her choice of another Governor-General of Australia, this time an Australian by birth, Lord Casey. He was installed in 1969 with 6th Lord Ashburton, who attended Garter services until 1988, when he was 90.

In 1970 there were four Knights, of whom Sir Cennydd Traherne survives and is the senior Knight of the Order. The others were Viscount Chandos, Lord Cobbold

---

* He did not walk in the procession.
† Occasionally other members of the Royal Family attend Garter ceremonies. The Princess Royal died the following March. In 1968, the Duke and Duchess of Kent attended Prince Charles's installation with Princess Marina. She died that August. Canon Bentley, who had to look after those princesses on each occasion, can be forgiven for thinking it a bad omen.
§ Field Marshal Lord Roberts was a V.C.

The Prince of
Wales and his
cousin, the Duke of
Kent, in the Garter
procession.

(former Governor of the Bank of England, and Lord Chamberlain), and Sir Edmund Bacon, Lord Lieutenant of Norfolk. Sir Edmund was asked how he felt after his installation service in 1970, and said: 'It felt like a mixture between being elected to 'Pop' and Holy Communion.'[42]

The present Knights are treated separately below, but eleven of those appointed since 1971 have died: Lord Butler of Saffron Walden (1971), dubbed the best Prime Minister we never had; Lord Rhodes (1972), the most humbly born ever appointed, who began life as a mill hand and travelled via politics to be Lord Lieutenant of Lancashire*; Lord Howick of Glendale (1972), a former Governor of Kenya†; the 11th Earl of Drogheda (1972), who combined being Chairman of the *Financial Times* with being Chairman of the Royal Opera House; Lord Trevelyan (1974), former Ambassador to the Soviet Union and last British Governor of South Yemen; the 3rd Earl of Cromer (1977), former Governor of the Bank of England; Marshal of the RAF Lord Elworthy (1977), a New Zealander, who was a popular Governor of Windsor Castle; Sir Paul Hasluck (1979), another Australian Governor-General; Sir Keith Holyoake (1980), Maori born Prime Minister and later Governor-General of New Zealand§; Field Marshal Sir Richard Hull (1980); and the Marquess of Normanby (1985).

Garter insignia is not normally allowed to be sold. In 1938, the step-daughter of the murdered Grand Duke Michael of Russia attempted to auction his Garter insignia, but it was claimed by the Crown the day before the sale. But the present Duke of Beaufort sold some Garter insignia at Christie's in the late 1980s.

THE ANNUAL GARTER CEREMONY

The Garter Ceremony has been an almost annual event since 1948, and during this reign has most usually been held on the Monday before Royal Ascot in June.¶ It is the occasion when the Sovereign and her Knights of the Garter gather at Windsor for a chapter meeting, a luncheon, a procession and a service at St George's Chapel. The occasion has been jokingly described as 'The Ascot Vigil', when the Knights kneel to pray for a winner later in the week, and also as 'the March of the Lame Dukes'.

Each year the Knights (with one Lady Companion) have come to Windsor to take part in this, the most colourful of all the annual pageants.

New Knights are announced on St George's Day, 23 April. Many appointees are sufficiently modest to suspect a friend playing a practical joke. Lord Drogheda, for example, was convinced it was 'some kind of leg-pull'.[43] Lord Trevelyan had to telephone his acceptance from a public call box in Italy.

---

* In 1918 he was shot down when serving in the Royal Flying Corps, hospitalized for three years, and one wound needed dressing every day of his life. He continued to attend Garter ceremonies until his death at the age of 92 in 1987, though latterly arrived at the chapel by car.
† His banner never hung in the chapel.
§ He came to be installed at Windsor, but was not well enough to walk in the procession.
¶ There were no Garter ceremonies in 1949, 1952, (following the King's death), 1953 (following the coronation), 1955 (because of the rail strike), 1959 (the Queen was in Canada), and 1984 (the Queen chose to visit the Royal Highlands Show in Ingliston, Scotland to mark its bicentenary).

If there are new Knights, they are invested privately in the Garter Throne Room (one of the rooms happily untouched by the dreadful fire of November 1992). Only the Knights and officers of the Order are present, with their wives and a few courtiers. The Queen is Sovereign of the Order. She was appointed to the Order in 1947 and automatically became Sovereign on her father's death in February 1952. The Duke of Edinburgh was appointed a few days after the Queen, also in 1947. One of the first things that George VI did was to appoint Queen Elizabeth (now the Queen Mother) a Lady of the Order on 14 December 1936, choosing his birthday as an appropriate day. She has thus held the Garter for fifty-seven years. The Prince of Wales is automatically a Knight as Prince of Wales. He became so in 1958, and was installed ten years later just prior to his investiture. (In his early days he looked rather bashful and consequently red of cheek as he walked with his grandmother in the procession). The other Royal Knight is the Duke of Kent, appointed on his fiftieth birthday. (The Duke of Gloucester, a senior Duke in line to the throne, is not a Knight, but may well become so on his fiftieth birthday in August 1994).

The other Knights have been personally selected by the Sovereign. The Senior Knight is Sir Cennydd Traherne, a spry 83 year old and one of the so-called 'regional' Knights. He was Lord Lieutenant of Glamorgan in Wales and was prominent during the year of the Prince of Wales's investiture. He enjoys his association with the Order and is often present at ceremonies such as the laying up of banners.

The Earl of Longford, made a K.G. in 1971.

There are several dukes: the Duke of Grafton, an old friend of the Queen (and some say a candidate for her hand in marriage before his promotion – on the inspiration of Lord Louis Mountbatten – to serve as A.D.C. to the Viceroy of India, Lord Wavell in 1943), whose wife is her Mistress of the Robes. There is the Duke of Norfolk, the Earl Marshal and Premier Duke – (10 of the 17 Dukes and various other predecessors have been holders), and there is the Duke of Wellington, whose father was a Knight till his death in 1972, a Lord Lieutenant and friend of the Royal Family. In a sense the presence of a few dukes gives the Order a certain old-world prestige.*

Politics is represented by several distinguished socialists: the Earl of Longford, politician, prison visitor and anti-pornography campaigner; Lord Shackleton; and two Labour Prime Ministers, Lord Wilson of Rievaulx, Prime Minister from 1966 to 1970, and from 1974 to 1976, and his successor, Lord Callaghan of Cardiff, who served from 1976 to 1979. There are some high Tories as well, Lord Carrington, holder of many Government offices, Lord Hailsham of St Marylebone, former Lord Chancellor, and Sir Edward Heath, Wilson's rival for many years and currently Father of the House of Commons, whose delight at receiving the Garter was demonstrated by his grand piano smile, which beamed all the way down the hill the day of his installation.

---

* Dukes sometimes express their membership of the Order in what is perhaps best described as a perdictably ducal way. The late Duke of Portland, invested in 1948, turned to the Knight next to him and in a voice, unfortunately overheard by the King, intoned: 'Rather like taking part in amateur theatricals, what?'

The late Duke of Wellington, appointed in 1951, opined that Garter Knights were not what they used to be: 'It's full of Field Marshals and people who do their own washing up,' he said. He was, however, generous to lend Sir Winston Churchill the splendid large and bejewelled 'George' that came to him via Queen Anne, the great Duke of Marlborough, the Prince Regent and his ancestor, the 1st Duke of Wellington. As a Knight of the Garter, he could have worn it himself. (This 'George' was sadly stolen from Apsley House in 1965.)

The services are less well represented these days than in the post-war years when the Order contained great war victors such as Alanbrooke, Montgomery, Mountbatten, Alexander of Tunis, Portal of Hungerford, Slim and Sir Gerald Templer. But the senior rank of each service is usually there: Admiral of the Fleet Lord Lewin, a Falklands Garter, and Field Marshal Lord Bramall (also Lord Lieutenant for Greater London). Since the death of Marshal of the RAF Lord Elworthy in 1993, there is no Air Force man.

Of the other Knights, the Marquess of Abergavenny was a Lord Lieutenant and Her Majesty's Representative at Ascot. Lord Hunt climbed Everest, and Lord Richardson of Duntisbourne was Governor of the Bank of England. Viscount Leverhulme was a benefactor of St George's House as well as a keen figure on the Turf. Viscount Ridley is a Lord Lieutenant (Northumberland) and also Lord Steward of the Household, and Lord Sainsbury of Preston Candover represents considerable benefaction of the arts. (On the day of his appointment the audience at the Royal Opera House, Covent Garden, were invited to applaud him in his seat.)

There is another interesting choice, that of Lavinia, Duchess of Norfolk, to date the only Lady Companion. When the Queen announced in 1987 that ladies would now be eligible, she waited a year or two and then appointed the Duchess, a highly suitable choice, since she was the widow of a former Senior Knight, and had been the first lady Lord Lieutenant (of East Sussex), and was therefore a safe Establishment forerunner so that if the Queen appoints Baroness Thatcher in the fullness of time, she will be following an already established pattern, not breaking new ground.[3]

At present (February 1994) there are three vacancies in the Order.

At the investiture, the Knights are assembled in facing rows, with the Queen at the end and the Gartered members of the Royal Family near her. The new Knight is summoned and enters the Garter Throne Room, escorted by two supporting Knights whom he chooses himself. The Queen hands her page the Garter, and it is he who kneels down and attaches it around the trousered leg of the new Knight. The Queen then puts the Garter riband over the Knight, from his left shoulder to right hip, and she attaches the star to a hook on his left breast. The supporter Knights help robe him in the mantle, but the Queen herself, robed and be-spectacled, pulls the cord through the robe and ties him into it. She also places the great collar over him and each supporting Knight ties it in place on right and left shoulder. The new Knight then shakes his Sovereign's hand.[†]

After the investiture a mighty luncheon is served in the Waterloo Chamber (again undamaged by the fire, though the smell of damp embers still permeated there well into 1993).[§] The Knights are joined by their wives, members of the Royal Household and a few other guests.

The Queen circulates before luncheon, meeting the Knights and their wives. In 1981 she singled out Lord Trevelyan for 'special kindness' as he was in a wheelchair. Afterwards his former prep-school colleague, Lord Longford, said to him: 'Next year I'll get into a wheelchair! You can't have the Queen all to yourself.'[44]

[*]   The Duchess fell badly at the 1992 ceremony, suffering a well-publicised nosebleed. There is always a doctor on hand to cope with such emergencies. The Duchess was not well enough to appear in 1993.
[†]   A television film, *Days of Majesty*, was allowed to film Sir Edward Heath going through this process in June 1992, supported by Lords Carrington and Callaghan.
[§]   In 1993 the luncheon was prepared by the chef at Buckingham Palace and served cold at Windsor, due to the fire.

In the days of the Great War leaders and people like Lord Avon, these were always times of great reunion. Nowadays fewer of the Knights are such intimate friends, though there are still groups. But these reunions did not always run smoothly. One year Lord Mountbatten had been quoted on Suez in one of the Sunday papers. Field Marshal Sir Gerald Templer (no fan of Mountbatten's) took the opportunity to reprimand him, displaying all the ferocity with which he terrified the natives in Malaya and elsewhere. (It will be recalled that Sir Gerald once told Mountbatten: 'Dickie, you're so crooked that if you swallowed a nail you'd shit a corkscrew.'[45])

In 1976, there was a meeting between Lord Avon and Mountbatten the evening before the Garter ceremony, during which the former Prime Minister reprimanded the sea-dog for revealing (to Robert Lacey) that the Queen had disapproved of the combined operation against the Egyptians in 1956 but had no constitutional means to stop it. Lord Avon informed his fellow Knight that if this information appeared in Lacey's book, he 'would have to take official action on this'[46]. The next day Sir Harold Wilson was installed K.G., with Mountbatten commenting: 'I do think that Lilibet had been wise to get Harold Wilson to become a Knight of the Garter because to have a Labour Prime Minister, like her father had Attlee, is an excellent idea to keep a balance between parties and classes.'* [47]

Another year the wife of one of the Knights advanced the theory that the Garter was based on 'the old religion' and that the composition of the Order was a witches' coven times two. The late Duke of Wellington was enraged by this suggestion.

Outside, the Military Knights walk up the hill from their houses in the walls of the castle. The Officers of Arms (or heralds) come from their picnic at Runnymede in time to see the Knights emerge from the Waterloo Chamber 'in a haze of cigar smoke and general euphoria'.[48] The Knights are then robed in preparation for the procession down the hill to St George's Chapel. The late Earl of Drogheda recalled that as they were robing up for the 1972 procession, the late Lord Rhodes turned to him and enquired in his Yorkshire accent: 'Do you think we'll be the last?'[49] Another Knight of advanced years looked round anxiously one year and said: 'Can we go home now?'[50]

The old or infirm Knights drive to the Chapel by car. The late Viscount Amory, who was very lame, complained in the 1977 procession: 'Why do they go so damn fast?' and elected to travel by car in future and watch the procession from the Galilee Porch. Sir Gerald Templer was furious when he was forced to travel by car. Members of the Royal Family who are not in the Order, stand and watch at the Galilee Porch, as do the wives of the Knights. The crowd are notoriously hopeless at recognising the Knights. Old Earl Stanhope had lost his leg below the knee, and used to arrive by car to a great cheer and a ripple through the crowd mis-identifying him as 'Attlee, Attlee, Attlee'.

There is something magnificently medieval about the Garter procession as it winds its way through the crowds in the different wards of the castle.§ It manages to be both grand and intimate at the same time. The bands play outside, and with luck the sun

---

* In fact it was the present Queen who appointed Attlee a K.G. in 1956.
§ Occasionally rain has forced the cancellation of the procession, in which case everyone travels to the service by car. This happened in 1961 and 1971. Often Garter Day is one of broiling heat and the press the following day delights in printing pictures of fallen Life Guards, whose collapse is the more noisome due to their breast-plates, or of tourists borne away on stretchers by ever-vigilant nurses from St John's Ambulance Brigade.

beats down. The procession itself is led by the Governor of the Castle, currently General Sir Patrick Palmer. He is a sprightly, tall and healthy 60 year old, a great contrast to the days of General Lord Freyberg, V.C., frail in his scarlet uniform and plumed hat, strapped up underneath due to his many wounds. Next come the Military Knights, then the heralds, then the Knights (two by two). The Queen Mother (at 93 the oldest but by no means the frailest participant) walked in the procession every year until 1992, usually with the Prince of Wales,* behind the Duke of Kent.† Then come the officers of the Order – the Secretary (who arranges the ceremonial), Black Rod, who can demote a Knight by touching him on the shoulder with the Black Rod of his office,§ the Register (who is the Dean of Windsor), Garter King of Arms, the Chancellor (the Marquess of Abergavenny, K.G.) and the Prelate (the Bishop of Winchester).

At the end of the procession come the Queen and the Duke of Edinburgh, followed by the Yeomen of the Guards and their various officers. Amongst these are Silver Stick-in-Waiting, a position occupied for some years by Brigadier Andrew Parker-Bowles, who could sometimes be observed discussing the progress of the procession with the Queen as they walked along.

Major-General Sir Edmund Hakewill-Smith (centre) and the Military Knights of Windsor in 1966. Major H.K. Clough (front left) was then 90.

---

*   From 1937 to 1952, she walked with the King, then until 1965 with the Duke of Gloucester. Occasionally she has been escorted by a visiting monarch from overseas.

†   In 1993, the Queen Mother, who had lately undergone a general anaesthetic in Scotland, attended the Garter luncheon, but was advised by the Queen not to come to the service at the last minute. The Queen Mother said: 'But I must go, because of Arthur [her page, Lord Mornington, grandson of the Duke of Wellington].' The Queen said: 'I'll take Arthur,' and thus had three pages that year, all much needed as it was a wet day, and the train became as heavy as a marquee in the rain.

§   Black Rod has to be 'a gentleman of Blood and Arms born within the Sovereign's Dominions'. These days he is, by rotation, a sailor, soldier, and then airman. He used to be paid £5 for performing the business of demoting a miscreant K.G.

Occasionally there is extra glamour when one of the Extra Knights attends. There are presently six of these and all have attended and been installed except the oldest, Princess Juliana of the Netherlands, appointed in 1958.* The Extra Knights or Ladies have usually come within a year of their appointment: the Grand Duke of Luxembourg (appointed in 1972, but installed in 1980), Queen Margrethe of Denmark (1979), who looked like a medieval monarch in her robes, worn over a white dress with white ruff collar, King Carl Gustav of Sweden (1983), King Juan Carlos of Spain (1988) and Queen Beatrix of the Netherlands (1989).

The ill-fated Emperor Haile Selassie of Ethiopia was present in 1972, walking with the Queen Mother. Unlike the other Knights he did not take his hat off when he arrived at the Great West Door. (Two years later he was imprisoned in his country, and died in 1975. Numerous Rastifarians attended his banner presentation).

Cheering is very much a feature of Garter Day. Indeed the crowd appear to cheer almost anything that moves. When Sir Harold Wilson was installed, he wore a slightly sheepish look as if to plead: 'I'm still one of you, lads. They made me do it!' Meanwhile Bernard Levin, the redoubtable columnist of *The Times*, explained his presence at the ceremony by saying: 'I couldn't miss the chance of seeing Harold in a floppy hat!'[51] Evidently Wilson had contemplated asking for a G.C.V.O. as this was in the personal gift of the Sovereign. He even considered the Order of Merit, so was hurriedly offered the Garter, as the O.M. did not seem quite suitable. In 1992 a soldier was delegated to walk beside Lord Wilson, who has succumbed to the vagueness of the years and was inclined to drift out of line. In 1993 he travelled by car.

One year the late Lord Mountbatten promoted himself to escort the Queen Mother to the annoyance of the other Knights. But he did not try that again, perhaps because he was unable to gauge exactly how much he was being cheered on his own merit. On another occasion the Bishop of Winchester's velvet hat blew off in the wind and was rescued by a smiling Prince Philip.

All in all it is a magnificent sight, the blue velvet gowns shimmering in the June sunlight, the hats of ostrich plumes bobbing up and down as the procession winds its way down between the lines of Life Guards and the crowds of camera-happy tourists. Outside, the band plays, while inside the chapel the atmosphere is solemn and ecclesiastical. The procession is met and preceded by the choristers and Canons and all enter the Quire. On the arrival of the Queen at the West Door a fanfare sounds. In the Quire itself the new Knights are installed. From then until the day they die their banner will hang over their stall and they will be able to wear the star and blue riband of the order on all full-dress occasions.

The Knights join a select group. They will be invited to events such as the Prince of Wales's wedding, even if they are not close friends of the Royal Family. If there is a coronation, four of them will hold the canopy over their sovereign during the anointing. When they die, the Queen will send another Knight to represent her at their memorial service. And in St George's Chapel, there will be a short and moving ceremony during which the Military Knights fetch the banner of the deceased Knight and

* King Baudouin of the Belgians, appointed in 1963, was installed as recently as 1991. He died in July 1993.

march it to the Quire, the sound of their heavy boots on the Chapel floor, heralding their approach. The Dean then lays the banner on the altar.*

By a strange coincidence two Knights have died on the very morning of the service – Viscount Alanbrooke, whose cup of tea slipped from his hands at home in bed in 1963 and Earl Alexander of Tunis who suffered a perforated aorta and died at Wexham Park Hospital, Slough, in 1969.†

After the prayers and blessing, the procession re-forms and returns to the Nave. In 1978 the retiring Governor of the Military Knights, Sir Edmund Hakewill Smith, was asked by the Governor of the Castle, then Lord Elworthy, to come onto parade for the last time. Aged 82, he marched valiantly but shakily and without a stick. At the West Door, his stick was handed to him so that he could support himself down the steps outside. One old Military Knight, Brigadier Crook, a splendid man, marched down the aisle with another Military Knight. As he reached the West Door, he said in what he thought was a stage whisper: 'Well done, Old Boy!' but his voice boomed out over the organ voluntary. As ordained, he then dropped out of the procession. Having gained considerable momentum during the walk from the Quire and intent on regaining the sanctuary of a seat behind the West Door, he stormed the ranks of some Household Cavalry trumpeters who promptly parted to let him through.

Thereafter the Knights spill out onto the steps and form up either side so that the Queen and Prince Philip may walk between them to a waiting carriage. The Knights then return by car to the State Apartments, leaving in order of seniority. Lavinia, Duchess of Norfolk would have been in car 'one' from 1968 to 1974 as wife of Duke Bernard. But as a new recruit to the Order in 1990, she was in car 'twenty-four', one of the penalties of joining a club.

One year Viscount Montgomery's car, driven by the famous and faithful Sergeant Parker, met a detachment of Guards advancing toward them. Hastily reversing, the Field Marshal heard a member of the crowd call out: 'Look, there's Monty retreating at last!'[52]

In the privacy of the State Apartments the ceremonies come to an end, the Knights disrobe and tea is served. In 1972, Sir Gerald Templer turned to the newly installed Lord Drogheda and said: 'I suppose you feel very virtuous now! You'll find it wears off'[53].

Sooner or later, in a variety of vehicles from Rolls Royces to small cars, they go their separate ways.

Anyone who takes a stroll down the Long Walk is likely to see Prince Charles, converted from medieval Knight to twentieth-century sportsman, driving in an open car to Smith's Lawn for a little polo practice. As we head into the twenty-first century the contrast between a ceremony such as that of the Garter and modern life becomes the more acute, and for such reasons the day retains a unique quality.

---

* Sir Winston Churchill's banner was displayed before the Nave altar for some weeks before its presentation. After the laying-up ceremony, which was witnessed by the Queen from the Catherine of Aragon loft, it was given to his son Randolph. He rolled it up and flung it into the boot of his car under the disapproving eye of the Dean's Virger, who had treated it with great reverence until that moment.

Many garter banners can be seen in churches. The Earl of Radnor's is in Salisbury Cathedral, Viscount Portal's is at St Clement Dane's, and the Duke of Wellington's hangs in the hall at Stratfield Saye.

† Field Marshals who are Knights of the Garter often have their funeral services at St George's Chapel, complete with gun carriages - Alanbrooke, Alexander of Tunis, Slim, Montgomery, Templer, and Hull for example..

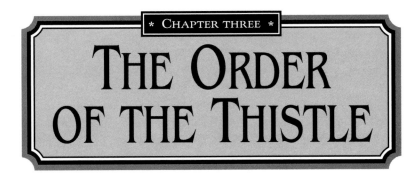

* CHAPTER THREE *

THE ORDER OF THE THISTLE

HE MOST ANCIENT and Most Noble Order of the Thistle is the Scottish equivalent of the Order of the Garter. In 1687 the present Order was put on a regular foundation, confirming the existence of an Order of some antiquity. And it was re-established by Queen Anne on 31 December 1703. The origins of the Thistle are lost in the Scottish mists. Some say that it was founded in 809 as the Order of St Andrew. At that time King Achaius of the Scots entered into an alliance with the Emperor Charlemagne. There is also a story that Hungus, King of the Picts, was being attacked by Athelstan, King of the West Saxons, and asked Achaius to support him. This he did with some 10,000 men. During the night before the battle, King Hungus had a vision in which the Cross of St Andrew appeared to him in the heavens. He took this as an omen for victory. The enemy was duly routed at Athelstan's Ford in East Lothian. Thereafter, Hungus evidently used the Cross of St Andrew as his symbol and built a temple in his honour.

Whatever the exact origins of the Order, the Knights of the Thistle have taken the view that their Order is of more ancient foundation than the Garter, and that in Scotland it should take precedence over the Garter. The present Queen certainly makes the point of wearing the Thistle when in Scotland, and in the days when she wore uniform at the Queen's Birthday Parade, she always wore the riband of the Thistle when the colour of the Scots Guards was being trooped.

St Andrew (said to have been crucified in AD 69) was accepted as the titular saint for Scotland from early times, but the thistle became an emblem of Scotland at some later time. It appeared on Scottish coins in the fifteenth century, but was only formally adopted as the Badge of Scotland by King James III as 'a native Scottish plant of which the self-protective qualities illustrated most aptly the Royal motto *In Defence*'[1].

In 1535 King James V of Scotland conferred the 'Order of the Burr or Thissil' on King Francis I of France, whose daughter he was marrying. There are further references in the middle ages to the Order of St Andrew and to the bestowal of Thistles, but the Order did not become a regulated thing until May 1687. In the new statutes,

ABOVE: *The star of the Order of the Thistle.*

OPPOSITE: *The Queen receiving the Honours of Scotland in 1953. The Queen upset the more traditionally-minded by wearing day-dress but Prince Philip wore the uniform of Field Marshal with the collar of the Order of the Thistle.*

69

King James II made it clear that he was reviving an Order originally founded by King Achaius, and that this was to consist of the Sovereign and twelve Knights, like 'the Blessed Saviour and his Twelve Apostles'[2].

The Order fell into abeyance after the abdication of James II the following year, and was then revived by Queen Anne. Certain modifications were made to the robes and insignia in the ensuing 120 years, and now the riband is green and there has been a star since 1714. The robes are a green velvet mantle, with a purple hood worn on the left shoulder. The Thistle badge is embroidered on the left shoulder, and there is a collar of golden thistles, and a black velvet bonnet with plumes similar to that of the Garter. In 1827 the number of Knights was increased to sixteen and in Queen Victoria's reign additional statutes allowed for the creation of Extra Knights (members of her family).

The star and collar of the Thistle, with the badge appended.

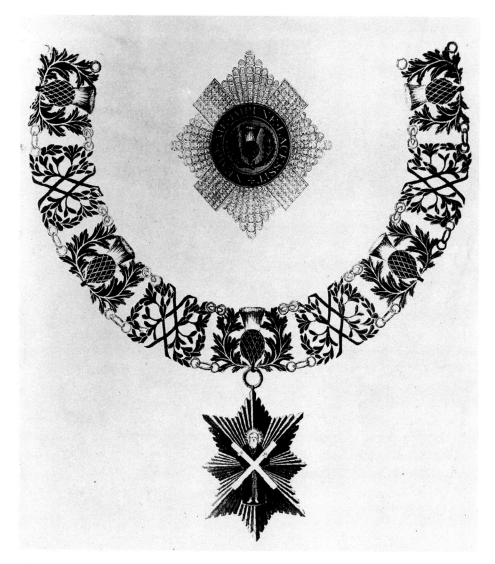

70

Since 1973, the Queen has traditionally appointed new Knights of the Thistle on St Andrew's Day, 30 November. Ladies have been eligible since 1988 but none have been appointed. The chapel of the Order is part of St Giles's Cathedral, Edinburgh, not as impressive as the Garter chapel at Windsor, or the Henry VII Chapel at Westminster Abbey, chapel of the Order of the Bath. It was built by the 12th Earl of Leven and his brothers in deference to their father's wish that a new Thistle chapel should exist. It was designed by Sir Robert Lorimer and is considered the most ornate building erected in Scotland since the Middle Ages. With the stalls of the Knights of the Thistle on each side, and the Sovereign's stall at the west end, the chapel was inaugurated by George V in July 1911*. Here the occasional installation services take place.

On these occasions, the Royal Company of Archers and divisions of certain Scottish regiments are on duty at the Cathedral. Her Majesty's Household Trumpeters in Scotland sound a fanfare on the Sovereign's arrival at the Cathedral.

On the morning of the Ceremony, the Sword of State is fetched from Edinburgh Castle and brought to the Signet Library 'with due Honours' by Lord Lyon King of Arms. The Thistle procession is lined up by the heralds and joined by members of the Royal Family just before the ceremony. In 1979 it proceeded into the Cathedral in the following order:

The Pursuivants and Heralds (one by one)
The Usher of the Green Rod
The Secretary (Lord Lyon)
The Dean of the Thistle

The Knights of the Thistle (junior first, senior last)

The Chancellor of the Thistle
(Lord Home of the Hirsel)

H.R.H. the Duke of Rothesay
(H.R.H. the Prince of Wales)

The Earl of Wemyss and March, K.T.
(bearing the Sword of State)†

H.R.H. the Duke of Edinburgh   H.M. the QUEEN
                                                    page
                    Two Archers

*   There was briefly a Thistle chapel in the Abbey Church, near Holyroodhouse in 1668, but it was very soon destroyed by the mob.
†   By custom the senior Earl being also a Knight of the Thistle carries the Sword of State at these ceremonies. Since his appointment in 1981, this privilege is granted to the Earl of Elgin and Kincardine.

*Members of the
Royal Company of
Archers at the
Thistle ceremony in
Edinburgh.*

The procession enters the Cathedral and the service begins with a fanfare and anthem.
There is a hymn, the Confession, Kyrie Eleison, Declaration of Pardon, Gloria and
prayers and a psalm. The procession re-forms as before during the psalm, except that
the Knights of the Thistle follow the Queen and Duke, this time the senior man first.
They enter the Thistle Chapel. The installation then takes place. The Dean says some
prayers and then the Queen says (for example in 1979):

> It is Our pleasure that Sir John Cameron (commonly called the Honourable
> Lord Cameron) be installed a Knight of the Most Ancient and Most Noble
> Order of the Thistle.

The new Knight is escorted to a vacant stall by Green Rod and Lord Lyon. The Dean
then administers the oath in which the new Knight promises to fortify and defend the
Christian religion, to be loyal and true to the Sovereign, to maintain the honour and

dignity of the Order of the Thistle, and never to bear treason against the Queen. The
Dean delivers the admonition and blessing and then Lord Lyon recites the titles of the
new Knight:

> Sir John Cameron (commonly called The Honourable Lord Cameron), Knight
> of the Most Ancient and Most Noble Order of the Thistle, Holder of the
> Distinguished Service Cross, one of Her Majesty's Counsel learned in the Law,
> a Senator of Her Majesty's College of Justice.

The process is repeated until all the new Knights are installed. There follows a lesson
and the prayers, which include the special prayer for the Order: 'God Save Our
Gracious Sovereign and all the Knights of the Most Ancient and Most Noble Order
of the Thistle.'

During the singing of the Magnificat, the procession re-assembles and returns to the
royal pew in the main body of the Cathedral. After a further hymn, the National
Anthem and the Benediction, the procession of Knights leaves the Cathedral.

Unfortunately there are not many services of the Order. They occur about once
every three years, the last being the installation of Lord Whitelaw in July 1991, which
was filmed for the documentary *Elizabeth R*, but ended on the cutting room floor.

The composition of the Order is generally less interesting than the Order of the
Garter, but there have been some notable exceptions especially in recent years.

By the end of Queen Victoria's reign, there were four royal Knights: H.R.H. the
Prince of Wales (later Edward VII), H.R.H. the Duke of Connaught (1869)*, H.R.H.
the Duke of York (later George V), and H.R.H. the Duke of Cambridge (1881)[†], who
died in 1904. She also gave the Thistle to the Duke of Argyll (1871)[§], at the time of his
marriage to her daughter, Princess Louise, and to the Duke of Fife (1881), who later
married her grand-daughter, Princess Louise of Wales.

The other Knights at the close of her reign were all dukes and earls, who served as
worthy lords lieutenant of Scottish counties. Men of particular note were the 5th Earl
of Rosebery (1895), Prime Minister 1894-1895, the 1st Marquess of Zetland (1900),
Lord Lieutenant of Ireland, and the 7th Earl of Hopetoun, later 1st Marquess of
Linlithgow (1900), who was Governor of Victoria and the 1st Governor-General of
Australia.[¶]

Four of Queen Victoria's Knights living in 1901 were also Knights of the Garter:
the Duke of Argyll, the Duke of Buccleuch, the Duke of Fife and the Earl of Rosebery.

It was to be expected that the Thistle would be held by a succession of Scottish
dukes. Indeed it has always been an even more exclusive order than the Garter. Firstly,
there are fewer Knights (sixteen instead of twenty-four), and then it has never been
given to anyone who had did not possess a considerable degree of Scottish blood.

---

*   Queen Victoria appointed all her sons Knights of the Thistle.
[†]   The Duke of Cambridge was a grandson of George III and held all the senior British orders, including the
Grand Cross of the Order of Hanover.
[§]   He later served as Governor-General of Canada.
[¶]   Lord Linlithgow was appointed at the age of 40 and died in 1908, aged 47.

Almost all the Knights of the Thistle have lived most of their lives in Scotland, and certain families, such as the Buccleuchs, the Montroses, the Earls of Home, Crawford and Elgin, have produced generation after generation of Knights. Looking down the list this century, many of them have been Lords Lieutenant of their counties (again in succession for generations). An almost automatic way of being appointed to the Thistle is to serve as Lord High Commissioner to the General Assembly of the Church of Scotland.* Some Knights have been Secretary of State for Scotland, and others have been involved in Scotland's heritage as Chairmen of the National Trust of Scotland and other cultural organisations. By and large the Knights of the Thistle are not household names in London, nor even really in Edinburgh. Only the exceptional choices will be given prominence in this study.

King Edward VII's Knights were of the traditional mould, but noteworthy is the 1st Marquis of Aberdeen (1906) who served as Lord Lieutenant of Ireland and Governor-General of Canada.

KING GEORGE V

King George V's royal Knights were H.R.H. Prince Arthur of Connaught (1913), a rare occasion when a grandson of Queen Victoria was appointed, and then his own sons, H.R.H. the Prince of Wales (1922), H.R.H. the Duke of York (1923), H.R.H. the Duke of Gloucester (1933) and H.R.H. the Duke of Kent (1935). The fathers-in-law of two of these also held the Thistle: the Duke of Buccleuch (1917) (father of H.R.H. Princess Alice, Duchess of Gloucester), and the Earl of Strathmore (1928)[†] (father of H.M. Queen Elizabeth the Queen Mother).

King George V appointed his fair share of Scottish grandees, but some of his Knights were men of great distinction. Lord Reay (1911) was Governor of Bombay, Under Secretary of State for India, and the first President of the British Academy. Viscount Haldane (1913) was Liberal Lord Chancellor (1912-15) and the first Labour Lord Chancellor for nine months in 1924. Lord Lovat (1915) raised the Lovat Scouts, a corps of Highlanders whose fieldcraft defeated the seemingly invincible Boers in the South African War. Field Marshal Earl Haig (1917), was the famous First World War general who shattered the Hindenburg Line and made 8 August 1918 'the black day of the German Army', and the only Field Marshal (other than the Royals) to hold the Thistle.[§] Appointed on one of the King's visits to the Front, Haig was the prouder when the King told him that the Duke of Buccleuch had refused to become a Knight of the Thistle until it was bestowed on the 'greatest living Scotsman'[3].

* The sovereign has been represented at the annual General Assembly of the Church of Scotland by the Lord High Commissioner since 1690. During his two-year time of office, he takes precedence after H.R.H. the Duke of Edinburgh in Scotland, and while the General Assembly is in session, he resides at Holyroodhouse, where he entertains a great number of guests. He is addressed as 'Your Grace'.

[†] Lord Strathmore was also made a Knight of the Garter, and was thus a member of both Orders with his daughter. Interestingly another of his sons-in-law was already a Knight of the Thistle, Lord Elphinstone, appointed in 1927.

[§] Lord Haig's Thistle star and collar were particularly splendid, adorned with many jewels, and given to him by Sir Philip Sassoon, the rich connoisseur and politician. Sassoon served Haig as his Private Secretary from 1915-1919.

Of the other Knights, the 27th Earl of Crawford (1921) served as Lord Privy Seal and Minister of Transport; the 9th Earl of Kintore (1923) was Governor of South Australia and a Lord-in-Waiting; the 1st Viscount Novar (formerly Sir Ronald Munro-Ferguson) (1926) was Governor-General of Australia in the First World War and responsible for the training of the Australian Expeditionary Force; the 2nd Marquess of Linlithgow* (1928) was Civil Lord of the Admiralty and went on to be Viceroy of India; and the 5th Duke of Sutherland† (1929) served as Paymaster-General and Lord Steward of the Household. Sir John Stirling-Maxwell was appointed in 1929, the year that young Lord Dunglass (Alec Douglas-Home) entered politics. He advised him that if a heckler asked an aggressive question likely to be tricky, the thing to do was to ask him to repeat it. 'Almost always the questioner, having made his effort, will not be able to repeat the question, or if he tries will fumble it,' reported Home many years later.[4]

There was another delightful character in the Order, the 13th Earl of Home (1930), Alec's father. When his son William, the playwright, was imprisoned during the war, Lord Home often visited him in prison. On one such visit, Lady Home saw him going off on his own, and asked him where he was off to. 'I'm just going along to thank the dear little Governor for having William here,' he said.[5]

In May 1935, George V offered the Thistle to Ramsay Macdonald, his outgoing Prime Minister, who hailed from Lossiemouth. But Macdonald's Labour principles would not allow him to become a Knight. Had he accepted, he would have been one of those rare inspired choices. The son of a girl working on a farm, who was impregnated by a ploughman, he was born illegitimate. But, it was not to be.

KING GEORGE VI

King Edward VIII appointed no Thistles, but King George VI appointed Queen Elizabeth a Lady of the Order in the Coronation Honours List of May 1937, reflecting her Scottish ancestry.§ He made ten other appointments during his reign. The most interesting of these were Sir Archibald Sinclair (1941) (later Viscount Thurso), who was Leader of the Liberal Party during the war and Secretary of State for War. After the war the King gave the Thistle to Admiral of the Fleet Lord (later Viscount) Cunningham of Hyndhope (1945), described by Field Marshal Lord Alexander of Tunis as 'one of the great sea commanders of our island race', for holding the Mediterranean with but a handful of British ships. He was installed by the King during his 1945 visit to Edinburgh. Cunningham prized his Thistle more than any other honour.[¶]

The King's other Knights were grandees: Sir Iain Colquhoun (1937), Chairman of the National Trust of Scotland; the Earl of Stair (1937), Lord Lieutenant; the Earl of

---

*   He was later appointed a Knight of the Garter.
†   The Duke was invested quietly at Buckingham Palace, soon after George V recovered from his serious illness.
§   Queen Alexandra and Queen Mary were not made Ladies of the Thistle in their day.
¶   Lord Cunningham died in a taxi in London. One friend said: 'So like him. He just hailed a taxi and went straight to Heaven.'

Airlie (1942), Lord Chamberlain to Queen Elizabeth 1937-65; the Duke of Montrose (1947), Chairman of the Scottish National Party; the Earl of Rosebery (1947), famous man of the turf and Secretary of State for Scotland; the Duke of Buccleuch (1949)*; the Duke of Hamilton (1951); Lord Steward of the Household 1940-64 and the man visited by Rudolf Hess in the war; and the Earl of Haddington (1951), a long serving Representative Peer for Scotland and Lord Lieutenant.

QUEEN ELIZABETH II

The Queen came to the throne without having been appointed a Lady of the Thistle, but she became Sovereign automatically. Her first appointment in 1952 was H.R.H. the Duke of Edinburgh. The Duke wore his Thistle collar at the strange ceremony called the National Service at St Giles' Cathedral, when the Queen in day dress and hat received the honours of Scotland, 24 June 1953. As part of the Queen's coronation visit to Scotland, on 28 June she held an installation service of the Order of the Thistle and installed the Duke of Edinburgh at the Cathedral. 'I shall never bear treason about in my heart against our Sovereign lady the Queen, but shall discover the same to her,' promised the Duke during the ceremony.[6]

During her reign the Queen has made two other royal appointments: H.R.H. the Duke of Rothesay (as the Prince of Wales is known in Scotland) was appointed in Silver Jubilee Year (1977)[†], and the Queen also gave the Thistle to King Olav V of Norway. The occasion was the King's state visit to Edinburgh in October 1962. The King was appointed an Extra Knight of the Thistle the day before he arrived, and on 18 October both he and the Earl of Home (now Lord Home of the Hirsel) were installed as Knights in St Giles' Cathedral. The granting of this honour to King Olav was partly to mark his close relationship to the British Royal Family as a grandson of King Edward VII.[§]

Let us now examine the Queen's appointments who have died, before turning to the present Knights. The Queen has only appointed thirty-one Knights since her accession, and sometimes as long as five years has passed without a new appointment. This is in part a tribute to the longevity of some of the Knights, many of whom have reached the age of 90 despite (or perhaps because of) the rigour of Scottish life and the icy winters.[¶]

---

* The Duke's appointment shows the particular esteem in which the King held him. He was appointed Lord Steward of the Household at the beginning of the reign. His sympathy for the Fascist regime was well known before the war and in April 1939 he had attended the big rally in Berlin on the invitation of Hitler. When in Berlin he telephoned the King asking for a cordial message that he could give Hitler and hoping to prolong his stay. Neither permission was given. Back in Britain he expressed pro-Hitler views privately and in the New Club, Edinburgh. It proved necessary to rebuke him and to remind him that as as senior member of the King's Household, the expression of such views would reflect badly on the King. When the Coalition Government was formed in 1940, he was quietly removed from the office of Lord Steward.

† In earlier times the Queen's two younger sons would have been given the Thistle by now, but the Queen has not felt the need to give them either the Garter or the Thistle.

§ The Queen did not give the Thistle to King Carl Gustav of Sweden on his state visit to Scotland in 1975. He received the Royal Victorian Chain. On King Olav's second state visit, this time to Windsor in 1988, the Queen promoted him Admiral of the Fleet. He was already K.G. (1959), G.C.B. (1946), G.C.V.O. (1923) and held the Royal Victorian Chain since 1955.

¶ Nonagenarians or near nonagenarians include Sir John Stirling-Maxwell of Pollock (1866-1956), Sir Herbert Maxwell (1845-1933), 6th Earl of Roseberry (1882-1974), 12th Earl of Haddington (1894-1986), Lord Bilsland (1892-1970), 12th Lord Kinnaird (1880-1972), General Sir Richard O'Connor (1889-1981), Lord Home of the Hirsel (b.1903), and the Hon Lord Cameron (b. 1900).

The Queen in her
robes as Sovereign
of the Order of the
Thistle.

77

The Earl of Crawford (1955) was Chairman of the National Gallery, and the 1st Lord Bilsland (1955) was Chairman of the Scottish National Trust. Lord Mathers (1956) started life as a clerk with Northern British Railways and was a Labour Trade Unionist. Later he became an MP and Scottish Labour Whip. He also served as Treasurer to the Royal Household. He was probably the most imaginative choice to date.

Sir John Stirling of Fairburn (1956) was a Forestry Commissioner, and Lord Kinnaird (1957) was a Lord Lieutenant who lived to be 92; Lord Rowallan (1957) was Chief Scout and later Governor of Tasmania. The Thistle was again often worn in the Antipodes after the Queen gave it to Sir Robert Menzies in 1963. She conferred it on him during her visit to Australia in connection with ceremonies marking the jubilee of Canberra's foundation.

Sir Robert Menzies, a keen anglophile, was a particularly popular choice, and he chose the Thistle as opposed to the Garter, which the Queen offered him as an alternative.* He served as Prime Minister of Australia from 1939-41 and from 1949-66. So closely involved with Britain was he that he was a pall bearer at the state funeral of Sir Winston Churchill in 1965, and succeeded him as Lord Warden of the Cinque Ports. He relished his Thistle, a tribute to his descent from a long line of Scottish farming folk. Not for nothing were his memoirs bound in dark Thistle green. He is the best example of the Queen's gift of the Thistle to someone, particularly prominent in public life, who had the right balance of Scottish blood. He earned his Thistle as far from Scotland as it was possible to be. There are other later examples of the Queen giving the Thistle in lieu of the Garter to those of Scottish origin.

Sir James Robertson (1965) was another well-travelled Thistle, having served as Governor-General of Nigeria. He was later Chairman of the Commonwealth Institute, and one of the few Knights to live out of Scotland. He resided partly in Berkshire and partly in Perthshire. Lord Reith (1969) held the Thistle for two years at the end of his life. Again he was a particularly inspired choice, creator and first director of the BBC and a wartime Cabinet minister. His father was a Glasgow minister of the Free Church, and Reith began work as an apprentice of the North British Locomotive Company in Glasgow. In old age he used to sit by the telephone for hours waiting to be called to some important office. He was summoned to be Lord High Commissioner to the General Assembly of the Church of Scotland 1967-68, a path which led to his Thistle.

Sir Charles Maclean of Duart (1969), later Lord Maclean, was Chief Scout, and later Lord Chamberlain. General Sir Richard O'Connor (1971) was G.O.C. of Eastern Command and later of North Western Army in India in the war. Viscount Muirshiel (1973) was Secretary of State for Scotland, and the Hon. Lord Birsay (1973) was a Lord of Session and Chairman of the Scottish Land Court.

Another soldier, Brigadier Sir Bernard Fergusson (Lord Ballantrae) (1974) was Governor-General of New Zealand and well known as an author. And Marshal of the

Sir Robert Menzies, in his uniform as Lord Warden of the Cinque Ports in 1966. He wore the riband and star of the Thistle. Sir Robert's belt was working hard.

---

* 'Both were in our disposal at the time', recalled the Queen's former Private Secretary, Lord Charteris of Amisfield.

Royal Air Force Lord Cameron of Balhousie (1983) was the first Air Force man, a former Chief of the Defence Staff, born in Perth, but who died in 1985, aged 64.

Of the surviving Knights, the most famous is Lord Home of the Hirsel, Chancellor of the Order and Senior Knight, having been appointed in 1962, and before he became Prime Minister. He is in poor health now, having suffered a stroke, but passed his ninetieth birthday quietly in July 1993. He remains Chancellor despite his indifferent health, though in the past others have resigned the post.

It would appear that there was no Chancellor of the Order until 1913 when the 7th Duke of Atholl, the senior Knight, was appointed. On his death in 1917, the 5th Duke of Montrose was appointed. Because it has generally been given to a senior Knight, there have been quite a lot of them this century. Montrose died in 1925 and was succeeded in 1926 by the Duke of Roxburghe. On his death in 1932, the Earl of Mar and Kellie took over (The Marquis of Aberdeen being too decrepid at the age of 85). He relinquished the post in 1949 when it went to Lord Elphinstone, who died in 1955. He was succeeded by the Earl of Airlie, who relinquished the position to the Duke of Buccleuch in 1966. Lord Home of the Hirsel succeeded him on his death in 1973.

Of the other living Knights of the Thistle, the next most celebrated is the junior Knight, Viscount Whitelaw, who donned the green velvet robes in 1990. He was a leading Conservative minister, serving as Home Secretary, Lord President of the Council and Leader of the House of Lords.*

Dividing the others up, the Earl of Dalhousie (1971) was Governor-General of Rhodesia and Nyasaland 1957-63, and the Queen Mother's Lord Chamberlain for many years. The Earl of Airlie (1985) serves the Queen in that capacity, and viewers of the brilliant documentary *Elizabeth R* will recall him making jokes before the diplomatic banquet about the colours of the ladies' dresses being either Garter blue or Thistle green.

The Earl of Selkirk (1976) was prominent in British public life as First Lord of the Admiralty, and served as U.K. Commissioner for Singapore and as Commissioner-General for South-East Asia. The other Knights are more Scottish in orientation. Of these, the Duke of Buccleuch and Queensberry (1978) is the owner of many splendid Scottish castles, but also lives part of the year at Boughton, virtually a palace in Northamptonshire. He was appointed to the Order after the terrible hunting accident of 1971, which left him permanently in a wheelchair, but he takes part in the ceremonies of the Order like any other Knight. Like the Duke of Buccleuch, the Earl of Elgin and Kincardine (1981), comes from a long line of Thistle Knights.

The Hon. Lord Cameron (1976) is the oldest, having turned 94 in February 1994. As cited above, he was a distinguished Lord of Session.

The Earl of Wemyss and March (1966) was President of the National Trust of Scotland and a Lord Lieutenant, Lord Clydesmuir (1972) was a Lord Lieutenant, likewise Sir Donald Cameron of Lochiel (1973), and Captain Sir Iain Tennant (1986).

Lord McFadzean (1976) is another English resident with Scottish origins, a businessman, who was Director of the Midland Bank, and Chairman of B.I.C.C. amongst many other appointments. Lord Thomson of Monifieth (1981) was Chairman of the

---

* He and Lord Home of the Hirsel would have been prime candidates for the Garter but for their Scottish blood.

Independent Broadcasting Authority, and is better known as George Thomson, the Labour Commonwealth Secretary and Chancellor of the Duchy of Lancaster. Lord MacLehose of Beoch (1983) was Governor of Hong Kong from 1971 to 1982.

In 1993, Sir Fitzroy Maclean Bt., famous for his wartime exploits in Yugoslavia, was appointed a Knight and invested by the Queen.

The composition of present Knights shows that the Thistle is gradually evolving from its primarily aristocratic flavour to include men of more personal achievement.

KNIGHTS OF THE THISTLE

FROM 1922 to the Present Day

King George V

H.R.H. the Prince of Wales (1922)	d. 1972
The 4th Marquess of Bute (1922)	d. 1947
H.R.H. the Duke of York (1923)	d. 1952
The 9th Earl of Kintore (1923)	d. 1930
The 1st Viscount Novar (1926)	d. 1934
The 16th Baron Elphinstone (1927) (Chancellor 1949)	d. 1955
The 2nd Marquess of Linlithgow, K.G. (1928)	d. 1952
The 14th Earl of Strathmore and Kinghorne, K.G. (1928)	d. 1944
The 5th Duke of Sutherland (1929)	d. 1963
Sir John Stirling-Maxwell, of Pollok, Bt (1929)	d. 1956
The 13th Earl of Home (1930)	d. 1951
H.R.H. the Duke of Gloucester (1933)	d. 1974
Rt Hon. Sir Herbert Eustace Maxwell, Bt (1933)	d. 1937
The 10th Earl of Elgin and Kincardine (1933)	d. 1968
The 13th Earl of Leven and Melville (1934)	d. 1947
Sir Donald Cameron of Lochiel (1934)	d. 1951
H.R.H. the Duke of Kent (1935)	d. 1942

King George VI

Her Majesty Queen Elizabeth (1937)	
Sir Iain Colquhoun, 7th Bt (1937)	d. 1948
The 12th Earl of Stair (1937)	d. 1961
Sir Archibald Sinclair, 4th Bt. (1st Viscount Thurso) (1941)	d. 1970
The 12th Earl of Airlie (1942) (Chancellor 1956-66)	d. 1968
Admiral of the Fleet Lord Cunningham of Hyndhope (1945) (later Viscount)	d. 1963
The 6th Duke of Montrose (1947)	d. 1954
The 6th Earl of Rosebery (1947)	d. 1974
The 8th Duke of Buccleuch (1949) (Chancellor 1966-73)	d. 1973
The 14th Duke of Hamilton and Brandon (1951)	d. 1973
The 12th Earl of Haddington (1951)	d. 1986

Queen Elizabeth II

Her Majesty the Queen (1952)

H.R.H. the Duke of Edinburgh (1952)

The 28th Earl of Crawford and Balcarres (1955)   d. 1975

The 1st Baron Bilsland (1955)   d. 1970

The 1st Baron Mathers (1956)   d. 1965

Sir John Stirling of Fairburn(1956)   d. 1975

The 12th Baron Kinnaird (1957)   d. 1972

The 2nd Baron Rowallan (1957)   d. 1977

H.M. King Olav of Norway (1962)   d. 1991

The 14th Earl of Home (1962) (Chancellor from 1973.)

Rt Hon Sir Robert Menzies (1963)   d. 1978

Sir James Robertson (1965)   d. 1983

The 12th Earl of Wemyss and March (1966)

The 1st Baron Reith (1969)   d. 1971

Sir Charles Maclean (Lord Maclean) (1969)   d. 1990

The 16th Earl of Dalhousie (1971)

General Sir Richard O'Connor (1971)   d. 1981

The 2nd Baron Clydesmuir (1972)

The 1st Viscount Muirshiel (1973)   d. 1992

The Hon. Lord Birsay (1973)   d. 1982

Col. Sir Donald Cameron of Lochiel (1973)

The Baron Ballantrae (1974)   d. 1980

The 10th Earl of Selkirk (1976)

The Baron McFadzean (1976)

H.R.H. the Prince of Wales (1977)

The Hon. Lord Cameron (1978)

The 9th Duke of Buccleuch and Queensberry (1978)

The 11th Earl of Elgin and Kincardine (1981)

The Baron Thomson of Monifieth (1981)

The Baron MacLehose of Beoch (1983)

Marshal of the RAF the Baron Cameron of Balhousie (1983)   d. 1985

The 13th Earl of Airlie (1985)

Captain Sir Iain Tennant (1986)

The 1st Viscount Whitelaw (1990)

Sir Fitzroy Maclean, Bt (1993)

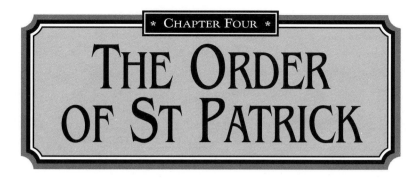

CHAPTER FOUR

THE ORDER OF ST PATRICK

T HE ORDER OF St Patrick was the third of the three great Orders of Knighthood, after the Garter and the Thistle. It was established on 5 February 1783 and the last Knight died on 10 June 1974. Since then this splendid Irish Order has been defunct.

Insignia of the Order of St Patrick.

Everything to do with the Order's foundation, its statutes, its history and decline was essentially Irish. There were haphazard plans, a great deal of money changed hands, sometimes unnecessarily, the Knights were chosen more for who they were or how useful they might be than for merit; there were tales of theft, and at times the records were badly kept. What is the Irish mentality? It is best explained by a contemporary example. The Hon. Desmond Guinness, Founder of the Irish Georgian Society, once pointed out that dry rot was not always the problem it seemed. Very few people, if indeed anyone, had died by falling through the floor due to dry rot. On the other hand a great number of people had died because they were unable to pay the bill to have the dry rot put right.

The life of the Order of St Patrick was of relatively short duration. It was founded by King George III on 5 February 1783, in the words of Brigadier Ivan de la Bere, 'as a gesture of good-will towards Ireland and in the intention of giving pleasure to a number of Irish peers who had rendered distinguished service and for whom there were no vacancies in the Order of the Garter'[1]. Ostensibly it marked the peace and harmony that reigned in Ireland and the cordiality that existed between Ireland and Great Britain. But, as the Rev. Peter Galloway, the admirable historian of the Order, has pointed out: 'Nothing could be farther from the truth. Ireland in the late 18th century was a restless, turbulent country, chafing with increasing unrest against the political and economic control exercised over her by the British government in London'[2].

In those days Ireland was ruled by the Lord Lieutenant, acting as the King's representative, and the Chief Secretary, who was the equivalent of the Prime Minister. Both were English and there was an Irish House of Lords and House of Commons. In practice the Lord Lieutenant was only in Ireland for about six months of his two years of appointment, and thus the real power was wielded by a group of Irish peers. It was partly to frustrate them and to regain a measure of control that Lord Townshend introduced the idea of an Irish Order to match the Thistle in Scotland. But it was not until Earl Temple became Lord Lieutenant in 1782, that the question of a new Order became a serious possibility.

The Order was named after the patron saint of Ireland, and ranked in precedence before the Order of the Bath. The King was its Sovereign and the Lord Lieutenant was Grand Master. There were originally fifteen Knights, but at the coronation of George IV six 'Extra Knights ' were appointed, and another four at the coronation of William IV. Thereafter the number was fixed at twenty-two. The motto was 'Quis Separabit' ('Who shall separate?') to symbolise the harmony that was sought between England and Ireland.

Dublin Castle was the base for the Order, and until the disestablishment of the Irish Church in 1871, the installations were held in great splendour in St Patrick's Cathedral. After that all the investitures were held in Dublin Castle or at Windsor.

Back in 1782, Lord Temple took soundings. He consulted the arrogant 33-year-old Duke of Leinster, 'whose power and influence were' in Galloway's words 'out of all proportion to his age and abilities'.[3] When the Order was created, the young Duke, a figure reminiscent of Max Beerbohm's creation, the Duke of Dorset in *Zuleika Dobson*, was reluctant to take the Patrick as he had his eye on the Garter.* As it turned out, matters raced ahead. The first names were submitted in January 1783, the statutes (lifted almost word for word from the Garter statutes and filled with consequent anomalies) were declared on 5 February, and the first investiture took place on 11 March.

Interestingly the first Knight was not the King's heir, the Prince of Wales, who only joined the Order as Sovereign, but the young Prince Edward,[†] later Duke of Kent, then aged a mere 15. He was invested by his father at St James's Palace, in London. The next royal Knight was Prince Ernest Augustus, Duke of Cumberland[§] in 1821; then the Prince Consort (1842); George, 2nd Duke of Cambridge (1851); the Prince of Wales (later Edward VII) (1868); then his two brothers, the Duke of Connaught (1869), and the Duke of Edinburgh (1880); and Edward VII's son, the Duke of Clarence (1887). Other Knights were Prince Edward of Saxe-Weimar (1890)[¶], the Duke of York (later George V) (1897), and then in this century three sons of George V — the Prince of Wales (1927), the Duke of Gloucester (1934) and the Duke of York (1936).

The non-royal founder Knights were Irish peers, who held influence and were supporters of the government. Lord Charlemont, the Opposition leader, was a man not to be ignored and they were pleased when he accepted the Order. The foundation was

Star, collar and badge of the Order of St Patrick.

---

* William, 2nd Duke of Leinster (1749-1804), founder K.P. (1783). He never received the Garter.
† H.R.H. Prince Edward, Duke of Kent (1767-1820), father of Queen Victoria.
§ H.R.H. Prince Ernest Augustus, Duke of Cumberland (1771-1851), 5th son of King George III, succeeded King William IV as King of Hanover in lieu of Queen Victoria, 1837.
¶ Field Marshal H.S.H. Prince Edward of Saxe-Weimar, K.P., P.C., G.C.B, G.C.V.O. (1823-1902). He was a nephew of Queen Adelaide, a childhood playfellow of Queen Victoria, and a great friend of the Duke of Cambridge. He married Lady Augusta Gordon-Lennox, daughter of 5th Duke of Richmond, K.G. He was Colonel of 1st Life Guards.

hailed enthusiastically in Dublin, the *Dublin Evening Post* pointing out that it was a boost to the economy as twenty looms were set to work to make the sky blue silk mantles of the Knights, not to mention the robes and uniforms of the various other attendants.

The Order also had a Grand Master in the form of the Lord Lieutenant, but though forty men held this post, they lost their connection with the Order when they resigned from office. Only two were ever made K.P.s.* There were a great number of other Officers attached to the Order and new Knights of St Patrick had to pay them each a fee on appointment. Thus in the late eighteenth century the cost of accepting the Order was £250, a considerable sum of money, which did not include the additional expenses of robes etc.

The first investiture took place in the ballroom of Dublin Castle, renamed St Patrick's Hall. Twelve of the fifteen Knights were present. It was followed a few days later by the magnificent installation ceremony, one of only six ever held in St Patrick's Cathedral, at vast cost, and with a carriage procession between lines of troops. At that ceremony each Knight was invested in the Choir, his banner was unfurled and his titles proclaimed. The day ended with a banquet in St Patrick's Hall. In 1800 the Irish Parliament voted itself out of existence. Thereafter the Order of St Patrick lost its essentially political bias, and knights were recommended for other qualities, such as being good landlords. There were installation ceremonies in 1821 (to coincide with the visit of George IV) and in 1868 (the sixth and last such occasion). George IV's visit was the occasion for the King to adorn himself in a 'richly trimmed silver tissue coat'[4] and much other finery.

In 1833 the number of Knights was increased to twenty-two. But besides that, little happened in the history of the Order for some years. The next great event was the 1868 installation ceremony in which the Prince of Wales (later King Edward VII) was installed in St Patrick's Cathedral. Not long after this the Order was secularised, though the banners hanging in the Cathedral in 1871 hang there to this day. Later there were investitures in Dublin Castle, followed by great banquets.

The robes of the Order were of sky blue silk, with a collar of gold composed of roses and harps, the central badge being a harp of gold surmounted by an imperial crown. The riband was sky blue and the star was a cross of St Patrick on white, surmounted by a green trefoil charged with three imperial crowns, and surrounded by the motto.

King Edward VII in the riband and star of the Order of St Patrick. He also wears the star of the Bath, and the Royal Victorian Chain.

EDWARD VII

During the reign of King Edward VII the statutes were revised. The King created only eight Knights in his short reign, the most interesting of whom was the 1st Viscount Pirrie, K.P. (1909), because he was so heartily disliked by the other Knights. He also chose the 8th Earl of Granard, K.P. (1909), who fought hard, but ultimately in vain, for the revival of the Order in later years.

---

*   Lord Talbot was created K.P. in 1821, and Lord French in 1917.

GEORGE V

In 1911 King George V and Queen Mary visited Ireland to hold an investiture of the Order. The visit was an enormous success and the investiture on 10 July a splendid occasion. All the Knights of St Patrick foregathered with the exception of the two oldest Knights, Viscount Wolseley and the Earl of Lucan, and the King invested Field Marshal Lord Kitchener, and the Queen's Lord Chamberlain, the Earl of Shaftesbury. It was the last time that a British Sovereign received a state welcome in Ireland.

King George V in the robes of the Order of St Patick.

After that, investitures usually took place at the Vice-Regal Lodge, though George V invested Field Marshal French and the Duke of Abercorn at Buckingham Palace.

Earl Kitchener of Khartoum, K.P. (1911) was George V's first Knight. Thereafter all his appointments were grand Irish peers until 1916, when he gave it to Field Marshal 10th Earl of Cavan, a rare honour for him as it was not normally given to Field Marshals, and then the next year to Field Marshal 1st Viscount French, later Earl of Ypres. His remaining three non-royal Knights were 3rd Lord Oranmore and Browne, K.P. (1918), 5th Earl of Desart, K.P. (1919), and the 2nd Duke of Abercorn, K.P. (1922).

In 1920 Northern Ireland became a partly self-governing province of the United Kingdom. In 1921 King George V and Queen Mary drove in state to City Hall in Belfast for the first opening of the Northern Ireland Parliament on 22 June. The King wore the riband and star of the St Patrick over his uniform as Admiral of the Fleet. Though the royal party were given a huge welcome, a train carrying part of the King's escort was blown up with the deaths of three soldiers and a guard. In his speech the King said that he prayed that 'my coming to Ireland today may be the first step towards an end of strife among her people, whatever their race or creed'.[5]

After 1922 there were no new appointments, other than the three royal ones, and the St Patrick gradually declined. George V did wear the St Patrick star at the wedding of the Duke of York in 1923.

And so the Knights began slowly to die off, and despite the efforts of Lord Granard, there were no new Knights chosen. Every now and again someone tried to revived the Order, but to no avail. Basically the separation of Northern and Southern Ireland put an end to the Order, and the strong opposition of the Government of Southern Ireland meant that any revival was out of the question.

However, the Prince of Wales (later Duke of Windsor) was appointed in 1927*, the Duke of Gloucester in 1934, and on St Patrick's Day 1936 Edward VIII made the last appointment, bestowing it on his brother, H.R.H. the Duke of York.

At the beginning of the present reign, only three Knights survived, the Duke of Abercorn, who died in September 1953, aged 83, the Earl of Arran, who died in December 1958, aged 90, and the Earl of Shaftesbury (formerly Lord Chamberlain to Queen Mary), who died in March 1961, aged 91. It is therefore possible that the collar of the St Patrick was worn at the Queen's Coronation in 1953, if either Lord Arran or Lord Shaftesbury attended.

Thereafter only the Dukes of Windsor and Gloucester survived. The insignia was borne at both their funerals and there were certainly a few occasions in the early 1960s when the Duke of Gloucester wore the riband and star. He did so in Kenya in 1962, and again in Enniskillen, for events in connection with the Royal Inniskilling Fusiliers. Interestingly, as late as 19 July 1927, King George V altered the wearing of the riband from right shoulder to left hip, to the same as Garter and Thistle. But the photograph of the Duke of Gloucester, adorned with the Patrick in 1962, shows him wearing the Order from the right shoulder despite his late father's edict.

*The Prince wore the star of St Patrick when he opened the Northern Ireland Parliment Buildings on 16 November 1932.

The Duke of Gloucester wearing the riband of the Order of St Patrick. He was the last Knight.

W. STRANG
1910

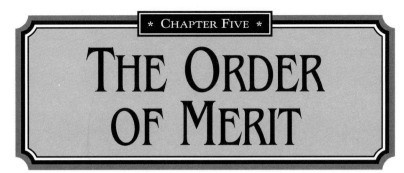

CHAPTER FIVE

THE ORDER OF MERIT

T HE ORDER OF MERIT was founded by King Edward VII on 23 June 1902, just before his coronation. The King was, in the words of his biographer, 'intensely and rightly interested in titles and decorations'[1]. Originally he had wanted sixty members, but the Secretary for War, St John Brodrick, managed to get it reduced to twenty-four. The Minister described the new order to a friend: 'It is for savants and sailors. Its chief objects are that it is worn round the neck, and puts Edward VII on a par with Frederick the Great, who invented a similar one!'[2] In founding his new order the King admitted that he had always been impressed by Frederick the Great's Order, Pour La Merite, adding: 'I should wish it to be a decoration entirely vested in the Sovereign's hands, who would naturally consult the Prime Minister and the Ministers at the head of certain Departments.'[3]

In 1873 Lord Stanhope, who founded the National Portrait Gallery, had suggested the foundation of such an order, moving an address to the Crown in the House of Lords. The motion was supported by Lord Houghton but opposed by Lord Granville. Stanhope wanted an order 'for men who deserve well of their country, and who have attained eminence in other walks of life than civil or military service'.[4]

The Order of Merit consists of the Sovereign and twenty-four members and confers no precedence on its recipients. There is a military division and a civil division, though there have been no military members since the murder of Lord Mountbatten in 1979.* The Order was instituted to include 'such persons, being subjects of our Crown, as may have rendered exceptionally meritorious service in Our Navy and Our Army, or who may have rendered exceptionally meritorious service towards the advancement of Art, Literature and Science'.[5] The appointment of certain honorary members was also allowed above the allocation of twenty-four.

The badge of the Order is worn from a two-inch riband (of Garter blue and crimson) round the neck on or a bow (for ladies). The badge is a cross of red and blue enamel of eight points, containing within a laurel wreath on a centre of blue enamel

Thomas Hardy, O.M. by William Strang, 1910. One of the series of portraits of members of the Order specially commissioned.

---

*   H.R.H. the Duke of Edinburgh is a civil member, despite holding the highest ranks in all the services.

the words 'For Merit'. On the reverse there is the royal cypher in gold. Military members have two crossed swords between the angles of the cross. The entire badge is surmounted with the Imperial Crown. The Queen does not have a badge, despite Lord Mountbatten's efforts to create one for her.

Since then the Order has become one of the most coveted of all British distinctions. There have been thirty Military Members, and 132 Civilian members. These divide into five groups: scientists, artists, musicians, writers and people active in public life. Interestingly politicians were never meant to be included in the Order as such, but six British prime ministers have been so honoured.

Between 1908 and 1914 William Strang was commissioned to make portrait drawings of fourteen of the early members, which were then signed by both artist and sitter and are now in the Royal Collection. In 1987 the Queen revived the practice and the members of the Order of Merit are now drawn in turn, always by a different artist: the Queen herself by John Merton, Lord Olivier by Derek Hill, Lady Thatcher by John Edwards*. The Queen has also made it a practice to invite all the holders of the Order of Merit to luncheon at Buckingham Palace once every five years, with a service every ten.

The first luncheon was held on 17 November 1977 to celebrate the 75th anniversary of the founding of the Order. It was preceded by a service of thanksgiving at the Chapel Royal, St James's, at which the holders gathered despite their different creeds. The service was entirely devised of words and music written by previous holders of the Order of Merit, such as Elgar, Vaughan Williams, Bridges and Walton, and the recent service included an address by the Rev. Owen Chadwick. In 1977 the Queen resisted Lord Mountbatten's plan that there should be a speech at the luncheon, but the old mariner was not deterred, and was presently tapping his wine-glass and rising to his feet. Despite this, the occasion was deemed such a success that it has become a regular feature, and a photograph is taken of the holders of the Order of Merit with their Queen.

In June 1905, King Edward VII established the ground rules for the way he intended to act as 'fountain of honour', re-emphasizing his stipulation that he should bestow the Order of Merit 'on his personal initiative and responsibility'.[6] An example of King Edward exercising his initiative occurred that very summer, when he took advantage of the prolonged absence of his Foreign Secretary, Lord Lansdowne, on his Irish estates, to confer the Order of Merit on three Japanese war victors, Field Marshal Prince Yamagata, Field Marshal Prince Oyama and Admiral Togo, who had despatched the Russian Baltic Fleet to the bottom of the Sea of Japan at the Battle of Tsushima in May that year.[†]

In the same year Edward VII gave the Order of Merit to Admiral Lord Fisher, then engaged in reorganising the British Navy, and to General Sir George White, despite warnings that the General was a man lacking any great abilities, military or otherwise, and unexceptional from the point of view of courage or character. These appointments were made without the King consulting any ministers.

---

*   An exhibition of these drawings was held at the National Portrait Gallery July to September 1992.
†   These appointments were gazetted on 21 February 1906.

Though the Order was open to women, Florence Nightingale was the only woman appointed in the early years of the Order, and Kenneth Rose wrote that this happened when she was 88 and 'even then with considerable reluctance on the part of King Edward'.[7] Indeed it was not until 1965 that another woman received the honour, Dorothy Hodgkin. Florence Nightingale received her honour when 'she had passed beyond the power of the world to please or pain' as her biographer, Cecil Woodham-Smith put it.[8] Lord Knollys called at her home in South Street on the King's behalf. Her biographer continued: 'It was not even certain that she understood the honour she had received. An explanation was attempted, but she hardly seemed to grasp it. 'Too kind, too kind,' she murmured.'[9]

The first members of the Order of Merit, appointed in 1902, numbered twelve. The military ones were Field Marshals Lord Roberts, Lord Wolseley* and Lord Kitchener, and Admirals of the Fleet Sir Harry Keppel[†] and Sir Edward Seymour. The civil ones were Viscount Morley, the English author and statesman who carried the spirit of philosophical liberalism into his public life, the physicists, Lord Rayleigh and Lord Kelvin, Lord Lister, the Surgical revolutionary, the astronomer Sir William Huggins, the writer W.E.H. Lecky, and the artist, G.F. Watts.

Edward VII's other O.M.s were George Meredith, the author, Sir Richard Jebb, the classical scholar, Sir Lawrence Alma-Tadema and William Holman Hunt, the artists, the Earl of Cromer, a Minister Plenipotentiary from 1883 to 1907 much involved with Egypt,[§] Lord Bryce, a jurist, historian and politician who served as British Ambassador to Washington, Sir Joseph Hooker (Director of Kew), Professor Henry Jackson, Regius Professor of Greek at Cambridge and a convivial man who would entertain into the small hours, then work till 6am and be lecturing brightly at 10am, and Alfred Wallace, the British scientist, who discovered the theory of evolution along with Darwin.[¶]

In 1910 King George V appointed Sir William Crookes, another scientist much pre-occupied with the property of various gases, and Thomas Hardy, author of *Far From the Madding Crowd* and other such classic novels. George V wanted to reserve the Order of Merit for people who were not politicians. Yet, as Kenneth Rose has pointed out, Lord Haldane was appointed in 1915 'not in recognition of his Hegelian studies but to solace an ill-used Chancellor'.[10] When Arthur Balfour received it in 1916 for what the King described as 'for services to philosophy and literature', Balfour almost complained, telling Lord Stamfordham, the King's Private Secretary, that the Order of Merit should not be 'another open to Party Statesmen who combine literary or other interests with

* Lord Wolseley defeated Arabi Pasha at Tel-el-Kebir and relieved General Gordon.
[†] Sir Harry was born in 1809, and was thus already 93 when appointed. A great favourite of King Edward, he had enjoyed a full naval career. He skipped arrest in Barbados to attend a ball as a young man, he appeared before a court martial and was acquitted when his ship was sunk on an unchartered pinnacle rock on its way to Hong Kong. In 1841 he stamped out piracy in the waters near Borneo, and in 1857 he defeated the Chinese at Fatshan Bay.
[§] The Under Secretary of State, Lord Hardinge of Penshurst, knew that the King disliked Lord Cromer but urged the King to appoint him in order to show support for him against the Khedive who wanted him removed. The King pointed out that the Order fo Merit was for soldiers, sailors and men of literary and artistic merit. Hardinge said that the Diplomatic Service should not be excluded. The King agreed and Lord Cromer got his O.M. Lord Cromer had once spoken disparaginly about Orders, telling Hardinge that 'it was immaterial to him whether he had a red or blue riband on his tummy!' [Lord Hardinge of Penshurst, *Old Diplomacy*, p.125]
[¶] Other candidates proposed and rejected were Swinburne, Rudyard Kipling, Bernard Shaw, and Thomas Hardy (who did receive it in 1910 from Edward VII's successor).

their political work'.[11]   Balfour noted that of thirteen recipients chosen for their emi-nence in the worlds of science, art and literature, five were Privy Councillors and for-mer Cabinet Ministers. Soon after this, David Lloyd George, the Prime Minister, was given the O.M. following strong pleading to the King by Bonar Law.

Lloyd George did not leave King George V in sole control of the Order of Merit. Kenneth Rose wrote that the King wanted to give it to Professor Gilbert Murray in 1921, but that Lloyd George objected on the grounds that he was a pacifist and 'almost pro-German'.[12]   The King, anxious to avoid a constitutional debacle with his Prime Minister, gave in over Professor Murray, who was finally given his O.M. in 1941.

King George V took great care in selecting members of the O.M. He was proud to have given it to an author such as Thomas Hardy and to the poet Robert Bridges. He offered it to Rudyard Kipling, Bernard Shaw and A.E. Housman, but they declined. In 1928 Lord Stamfordham, the King's Private Secretary, consulted Lord Esher, that extraordinary confidant of royalty and so many others, about candidates for the Order. Esher suggested Randall Davidson, the Archbishop of Canterbury, and while Lord Stamfordham expressed surprise that Esher had neglected Sir Edwin Lutyens in the 'Arts' category. Lord Esher replied that Randall Davidson had done more for Christian philosophy than had the late Lord Morley (a founder O.M., 1902) in pagan philosophy. Lord Esher waxed lyrical within the theme of the Order's statutes: 'You can define Science, but not Literature or Art. Would Cicero have qualified? Or Demosthenes? Or Tillotson? Or Cranmer? Bridges* is venerable. If you wait for genius you make few appointments.'[13]

George V appointed thirty-five members of the Order of Merit, including the histo-rian, G.O. Trevelyan (whose son was later an O.M.). There was the composer, Sir Edward Elgar; Admiral of the Fleet Sir Arthur Knyvet Wilson, a bachelor who had won the V.C.; Sir Joseph Thomson (the discoverer of the electron, who developed the ionic theory of electricity and the electrical theory of inertia of matter); Sir Archibald Geikie, the British geologist; Henry James, the distinguished novelist, appointed in January, but dead by 28 February 1916; Admiral of the Fleet Earl Jellicoe, victor of Jutland; Earl Haig, the Field Marshal; and Earl Beatty, the Admiral of the Fleet.

He also found Sir James Barrie, creator of *Peter Pan*; the reclusive philosopher Francis Herbert Bradley[†]; Sir Charles Sherrington (the English physiologist, and expert on the brain and nervous system, who lived to be 94); Sir James Frazer (the anthropologist and author of *The Golden Bough*; Sir Ernest Rutherford (the physicist who won the Nobel prize for work on radioactivity); and Sir Charles Parsons, the first engineer to receive the Order.

The others were Sir George Grierson, the oriental scholar; Robert Bridges, the poet; John Galsworthy, author of *The Forsyte Saga*; Samuel Alexander, the philosopher;

---

*   Robert Bridges (1844-1930), Poet Laureate, created O.M. 1929.
†   Bradley was a short-lived holder of the O.M. Because of a violent inflammation of the kidneys in 1871, he was forced to live quietly in Merton College (where he was a Fellow) and never taught, though he remained in college and continued his philosophical studies. He was given the O.M. on 3 June 1924 (the King's birthday), but died on 18 September. The only illustration of him is a posthumously executed portrait by R.G.Eves, inspired by a passport photograph. It is a photograph of this portrait by which his features are recorded in the album of mem-bers of the Order of Merit.

Montague Rhodes James (the Provost of Eton, and English scholar, who wrote critical works on the Bible and also some celebrated ghost stories); the historian G.M. Trevelyan; Wilson Steer (the artist, noted for delicacy of colour in his portraits and landscapes); Sir William Bragg, the mathematician; Dr J.W. Mackail (one of the finest classical scholars of his day, married to a daughter of Sir Edward Burne-Jones); John Masefield, the Poet Laureate; Ralph Vaughan Williams, the composer; Sir F. Gowland Hopkins (the English biochemist who worked on proteins and vitamins); and Field Marshal Sir Philip Chetwode, whose many distinctions included being the father-in-law of John Betjeman.

In December 1935, a month before his own death, King George V altered the statutes of the Order as follows, that it should include: 'such persons, being subjects of Our Crown, as may have rendered exceptionally meritorious service in the Crown services of Our Empire, or have rendered exceptionally meritorious service towards the advancement of the Arts, Learning, Literature and Science'.[14]

King Edward VIII made no conferments in his short reign. When Alec Hardinge was Private Secretary to King George VI, he found himself having to defend the King's control of the Order of Merit on several occasions. He wrote:

> One of the duties that interested me most was finding suitable candidates for the Order of Merit – the only Order (other than the Victorian Order) which the King then gave without any recommendation from the Prime Minister. I noticed that covetous eyes were occasionally cast on this Order from 10 Downing Street, but we fortunately had strong written evidence, as well as precedent, to support our case. It was my ambition only to make suggestions to the King that would maintain the very high standard of this Order, and I naturally took a lot of outside advice before suggesting anybody. During my time I put forward the names of Augustus John, Lutyens, Gilbert Murray, and Adrian, among others, and I do not think that any of these could be said to have let the standard down. Since my day it has been given to several octogenarians, which I think a pity, and was certainly contrary to the practice in Lord Stamfordham's time, when it was held – and I think rightly – that if a man had ever been worthy of the O.M. he would have got it when in his prime, i.e. long before he was eighty.[15]

King George VI's first appointment was the founder of the Boy Scouts, Lord Baden-Powell. Then he chose H.A.L. Fisher (the English historian, and also a minister, responsible for the Education Act of 1918).* The next two members were Sir Arthur Eddington and Sir James Jeans. They were rivals in the scientific field. Sir Arthur was an astrophysicist and one of the ablest mathematical astronomers of his day. Sir James was a theoretical physicist and popular expositor of physical science and astronomy. Around 1917 meetings of the Royal Astronomical Society reverberated with scientific controversy between the two men on the subject of stellar structure.

---

* Fisher's theory of history was not one of 'a plot, a rhythm, a predetermined pattern', but of 'one emergency following upon another as wave follows upon wave'. [H.A.L. Fisher, *A History of Europe* (Edward Arnold, 1936) p.v]

Marshal of the Royal Air Force Lord Newall was appointed at the beginning of the war. He had presided over the development of the Royal Air Force which was to play such an important role in the Second World War (most of which he spent as Governor-General of New Zealand). The civil appointments were Professor Gilbert Murray (at last), the famous Greek scholar and translator of Greek poets, a man keen on women's emancipation; Sir Edwin Lutyens, the architect who designed Government House, Delhi and the Cenotaph; Augustus John, the portrait painter*; Lord Adrian, the physiologist who won the Nobel Prize (with Sir Charles Sherrington) in 1932†; and Sir William Holdsworth, the lawyer and Oxford historian, who enjoyed the honour for exactly a year.

In September 1943 (on the fourth anniversary of the outbreak of war) Admiral of the Fleet Sir Dudley Pound was given the O.M. as he approached death (on Trafalgar Day, 21 October). At King George VI's request, Winston Churchill called on the Admiral in the Royal Masonic Hospital and placed the insignia into his hands. Pound, the victim of two severe strokes, was unable to speak but grasped the Prime Minister's hand.[16]

The next O.M.s were Lord Passfield, better known as Sidney Webb, the English sociologist, founder of the *New Statesman*, leading economist and mainstay of the growing Labour movement; Sir Henry Dale, the physiologist-pharmacist, Sir Giles Scott, the architect, who designed Waterloo Bridge and the Anglican Cathedral at Liverpool; and Professor Alfred Whitehead, the philosopher who developed the trend of modern metaphysical thought in his philosophy of organism: *The Concept of Nature*.

After the war the King gave an honorary O.M. to General Eisenhower, who later became President of the United States. In 1947 he gave an honorary O.M. to the Hon. John Winant, the US Ambassador, who died aged 58 on 3 November that year.

In the 1946 New Year Honours, Churchill received the honour. He explained his delight to a friend, expressing the same sentiments with which he would accept the Garter from Queen Elizabeth II: 'The O.M. comes from the King alone and is not given on the advice of Ministers. This renders it more attractive to me.'[17] Marshal of the RAF Lord Portal of Hungerford was chosen in the same list. That June there were two more war leaders, Field Marshal Lord Alanbrooke and Admiral of the Fleet Lord Cunningham of Hyndhope, and the Earl of Halifax, a favourite of the King, chosen for his services in America during the war§.

In 1947 there came two Commonwealth Prime Ministers – Field Marshal Smuts, visited by the King on his successful South African Tour, and Mackenzie King, Prime Minister of Canada, who came to Britain for the present Queen's wedding. In 1948

---

* Augustus John was one of the Order's more bohemian members. His wife would not countenance the idea of him accepting a knighthood, which depressed him, so the offer of the O.M. was eagerly accepted, and he chose to see this as a deal made direct between him and the King. His biographer tells us that some 'deplored the old anarchist accepting recognition from the State. His response to all criticism was that people should be allowed to do whatever they liked ...' [Michael Holyroyd, *Augustus John Volume II* (Heinemann, 1974) p.178]

† Adrian was involved in the way the nervous system might generate electrical rhythms, and conducted long studies concerned with the sense of smell.

§ Lord Halifax had been appointed Ambassador in Washington, partly as a way of removing him from the political scene in Britain.

the King appointed the poet T.S. Eliot, and in 1949 the chemist Sir Robert Robinson, and the philosopher and social reformer, Bertrand Russell. In 1961 Russell took part in the mass sit-down in Trafalgar Square protesting against nuclear arms and was sentenced to two months in prison.*

Towards the end of 1950 King George VI intimated to Sir Alexander Cadogan that he wished to appoint him to the Order. He was the first ever civil servant to receive it, the man who had been Head of the Foreign Office from 1938 to 1946, advisor to three Foreign Secretaries, and who had accompanied Churchill on his wartime visits to the great conferences. The honour was gazetted in the New Year List of 1951. Anthony Eden congratulated him, pointing out that it was not only for his contribution during the difficult war years but 'for a brilliant record of service'.[18]

In 1951 the King chose Marshal of the Royal Air Force Lord Trenchard, who had served as a kind of universal roving ambassador to the RAF during the war, and later that year the philosopher Professor G.E. Moore, a shy man whose acceptance of the Order was therefore considered remarkable.

In November 1951 the King appointed Clement Attlee to the Order. He gave it following Attlee's defeat at the Polls as a mark of respect for eleven years service as a minister, for six of which he was his Prime Minister.

QUEEN ELIZABETH II

The Queen has to date appointed some sixty-seven holders (including three honorary ones). The first was Wilder Penfield, the distinguished neurosurgeon (who for some reason eluded the D.N.B.). Then came the much loved poet, Walter de la Mare, and in 1955 the Queen gave an honorary O.M. to Dr Albert Schweitzer. In 1956 the distinguished Indian civil servant, Lord Hailey (who lived to be 97), was appointed and the following year Sir John Cockcroft, the nuclear physicist, who considerably developed the possibilities of radar.

Another of the Order's invalids to receive it literally at the last moment was Viscount Waverley, the former Home Secretary, Sir John Anderson. In November 1957, the Prime Minister, Harold Macmillan, wrote to him asking him to accept it as 'a tribute to your long service to the nation in many fields'.[†19] When Sir Michael Adeane, the Queen's Private Secretary wrote to offer it formally, he noted with pleasure that Lord Waverley qualified for the Order both for long service to the Crown, and for his contributions to the arts and learning. But Waverley was already very sick and so Macmillan asked Adeane if the appointment could be announced at once in December rather than in the New Year honours. The Queen agreed immediately and on her own initiative despatched Sir Michael Adeane to the hospital that very afternoon to present Waverley with the insignia on her behalf. An excuse was made that the Queen did not wish him to interrupt his convalescence abroad in the spring to

* Due to his advanced age (88) and relative ill health, he was only detained a week. His O.M. was never in jeopardy of being removed from him for going 'inside' as is sometimes the case with other Orders.
† The Queen had consulted her Prime Minister about the bestowal of this O.M. although the award of the O.M. remained the 'unfettered gift of the Sovereign independent of Ministers'.

receive the Order. Waverley, though weak, was delighted. But he was dead by 4 January 1958, so he was an O.M. for less than a month.

Sir Macfarlane Burnet was appointed in 1958. He was Australia's leading biologist and the most distinguished authority on viruses in the Commonwealth. He also made important contributions to immunology. Viscount Samuel, appointed later that year, was a statesman, administrator, philosopher of the 'common sense school' and one of the last survivors of Campbell-Bannerman's Liberal Government. In 1960 the Queen selected three men: Field Marshal Earl Alexander of Tunis, an outstanding wartime leader, then Governor-General of Canada and later still Minister of Defence; Sir Cyril Hinshelwood, the chemist, President of the Royal Society and a man of great intellect who bridged the gap between science and the humanities; and thirdly, the artist Graham Sutherland, the first holder of the Order to have been born this century.

In 1962 came Sir Geoffrey de Havilland, the aircraft engineer and designer and the creator of the de Havilland Moths, Comets, Rapides, and Mosquitos. And with him was Sir Basil Spence, the architect responsible for Coventry Cathedral.

Sir Owen Dixon (1963) was Chief Justice of Australia for many years; G.P. Gooch was the eminent historian, and Henry Moore the famous sculptor. In June 1963 the Queen gave an honorary O.M. to Dr (formerly Sir) Sarvepalli Radhakrishnan, then President of the Republic of India, on the occasion of his state visit to Britain. He was followed by Benjamin Britten, the composer, in 1965, and the senior living holder, the chemist and Fellow of Somerville College, Oxford, Professor Dorothy Hodgkin.

When Lord Mountbatten received his Order of Merit in a private audience with the Queen on his retirement as Chief of the Defence Staff in 1965, he described it as 'an absolutely wonderful gesture on her part'[20]. He believed he was following in the footsteps of Rudyard Kipling and Thomas Hardy, thought it only the second time it had been given to a sailor for work in peacetime, and thought himself only the seventh sailor to have ever received it. As his biographer, Philip Ziegler, pointed out: 'Mountbatten's historical exposition was off the mark. Kipling refused the O.M., and eleven sailors had received it before him, seven of them for work in peacetime.'[21] Appointed with Mountbatten was Lord Florey, the scientist who led the team that developed the use of penicillin.

In 1967 Lord Blackett was chosen. He was a physicist, and political and military strategist. And with him was the composer, Sir William Walton, responsible for so much of the 1953 coronation music. The next two (in 1968) were Ben Nicholson, the internationally renowned abstract painter (once married to Dame Barbara Hepworth), and Lord Zuckerman, President of the Zoological Society of London and Chief Scientific Advisor to the Government. Then, on his 47th birthday, the Queen gave the civil division of the Order to the Duke of Edinburgh.

E.M. Forster, the novelist and writer of books such as *A Passage to India* and *Howard's End*, received his badge in his rooms at King's College, Cambridge, from Sir Michael Adeane, an honour to mark his 90th birthday, which coincided with 1 January 1969. He died in June 1970. There were four more O.M.s that year: Malcolm MacDonald, son of Ramsay MacDonald, and a distinguished Commonwealth statesman, Lord Penney, Rector of Imperial College and a molecular phycisist, Sir Geoffrey Taylor, a highly original scientist who applied the mechanics of solids and fluids to

FAR LEFT: *Dame Veronica Wedgwood, O.M. by Tim Rukavina.*

LEFT: *Sir Isaiah Berlin, O.M. by John Ward.*

meteorology, aeronautics, and many branches of engineering, and Dame Veronica Wedgwood (the historian, C.V. Wedgwood).

Professor John Beaglehole was a short-lived holder, appointed in 1970 and dead in 1971. He was Professor of British Commonwealth History at Victoria University, Wellington, New Zealand. He was followed in 1971 by Lester Pearson, another short-lived holder, and Prime Minister of Canada from 1963 to 1968. The Queen also appointed Sir Isaiah Berlin, the Oxford historian and philosopher.

In 1971 Sir George Edwards, the aeronautical engineer, was chosen, and two years later, Professor Sir Alan Hodgkin, the physiologist, and Paul Dirac, the mathematician and phycisist. In 1976, at the age of 82, Harold Macmillan became an O.M., some years after refusing the Garter, and some years before accepting the Earldom of Stockton. Lord Hinton of Bankside, the chemist and mechanical engineer, Kenneth (Lord) Clark, the distinguished art historian, and Sir Ronald Syme, the historian, were also chosen.

There were four appointments in 1977: Lord Todd, Lord Franks, Sir Frederick Ashton, the distinguished choreographer, and the writer, J.B. Priestley. In 1981, the first ever actor, Lord Olivier, was selected together with the medical scientist and Nobel prize winner, Sir Peter Medawar, and Group Captain Lord Cheshire, V.C., founder of the Cheshire Homes. In 1983 there were another four: the Rev. Owen Chadwick, the ecclesiastical historian; Sir Andrew Huxley, the physiologist; Sir Sidney Nolan, the Australian artist; and Sir Michael Tippett, the composer. The most recent honorary O.M. was that given to Mother Teresa by the Queen in November 1983 during her state visit to India.

The late Graham Greene, the novelist, joined the Order in 1986 with Dr Frederick Sanger, the biochemist, and Air Commodore Sir Frank Whittle, the aeronautical engineer who developed jet propulsion.

Of the above-mentioned, Dorothy Hodgkin, the Duke of Edinburgh, Dame Veronica Wedgwood, Sir Isaiah Berlin, Sir George Edwards, Sir Alan Hodgkin, Lord Todd, The Rev. Owen Chadwick, Sir Andrew Huxley, Sir Michael Tippett, Frederick Sanger, and Sir Frank Whittle are the present living holders as are the others mentioned below.

ABOVE: *Dr. Max Perutz, O.M., by Michael Noakes.*

CENTRE: *The Rev. Owen Chadwick, O.M. by Thomas Phillips.*

RIGHT: *The Baroness Thatcher, O.M. by John Edwards.*

Lord Menuhin, the violinist and founder of the Menuhin schools, was chosen in 1987, and was joined in 1988 by Sir Ernst Gombrich, the Viennese born art historian and philosopher, and Professor Max Perutz, the molecular biologist. There were two appointments in 1989: Dame Cicely Saunders, the hospice pioneer, and Lord Porter of Luddenham, the chemist.

The decision to appoint Mrs Thatcher to the Order of Merit was clear indication of the Queen's appreciation of her long years of service as Britain's first woman Prime Minister, and the appointment coming so soon after her ousting from power was a signal mark of the Queen's respect and gave great pleasure to Mrs Thatcher's many admirers, shocked at her sudden downfall.

The Queen appointed Dame Joan Sutherland in November 1991 and presented her with her O.M. at Admiralty House, Sydney, during her Australian tour in February 1992. Francis Crick, another molecular biologist, was also appointed in November 1991.

There are not many people given awards of great distinction at an extremely advanced age, but Dame Ninette de Valois was appointed at the age of 94 on 17 November 1992. Appointed with her was Sir Michael Atiyah, the mathematician, and President of the Royal Society.* Then in 1993, the politician, Lord Jenkins of Hillhead and the controversial artist, Lucian Freud were appointed.

The Order of Merit has developed in its relatively brief history, the military element disappearing, as was inevitable in a prolonged period of peace. And it has included certain figures who were perhaps primarily performers in the world of art and music, for example Dame Joan Sutherland. But its members comprise some of the most interesting figures of the twentieth century, and the main concern of the Order's redoubtable Secretary and Registrar, Sir Edward Ford, is that he hopes there is no unsung hero being overlooked.

* Some say that to be President of the Royal Society brings the Order of Merit automatically. This is not the case, though the last of six Presidents have held the Order. This is more due to the wisdom of choosing the very best scientists to be President of the Royal Society.

HOLDERS OF THE ORDER OF MERIT[*]

Edward VII

Founder Members

Field Marshal the Earl Roberts of Kandahar,
    V.C. (1902) (Mil.)
Field Marshal the Viscount Wolseley (1902)
    (Mil.)
Field Marshal the Earl Kitchener of Khartoum
    (1902) (Mil.)
The Lord Rayleigh (1902)
The Lord Kelvin (1902)
The Lord Lister (1902)
Admiral of the Fleet Hon. Sir Henry Keppel
    (1902) (Mil.)
The Viscount Morley of Blackburn (1902)
W.E.H. Lecky (1902)
Admiral of the Fleet Rt Hon. Sir Edward
    Seymour (1902) (Mil.)
Sir William Huggins (1902)
G.F. Watts (1902)

Field Marshal Sir George White (1905)
Admiral of the Fleet the Lord Fisher (1905) (Mil.)
Sir Richard Jebb (1905)
Sir Lawrence Alma-Tadema (1905)
George Meredith (1905)
William Holman Hunt (1905)
The Earl of Cromer (1906)
The Viscount Bryce (1907)
Sir Joseph Hooker (1907)
Miss Florence Nightingale (1907)
Professor Henry Jackson (1908)
Alfred Wallace (1908)

George V

Sir William Crookes (1910)
Thomas Hardy (1910)
Rt Hon. Sir George O. Trevelyan (1911)
Sir Edward Elgar, Bt. (1911)
Admiral of the Fleet Sir Arthur Knyvet
    Wilson, V.C. (1912) (Mil.)
Sir Joseph Thomson (1912)
Sir Archibald Geikie (1914)
Field Marshal the Earl of Ypres (1914) (Mil.)
The Viscount Haldane (1915)
Henry James (1916)
Admiral of the Fleet the Earl Jellicoe (1916) (Mil.)
The Earl of Balfour (1916)

Admiral of the Fleet the Earl Beatty (1919) (Mil.)
Field Marshal the Earl Haig (1919) (Mil.)
The Earl Lloyd George of Dwyfor (1919)
Sir James Barrie, Bt (1922)
Francis Herbert Bradley (1924)
Sir Charles Sherrington (1924)
Sir James Frazer (1925)
The Lord Rutherford of Nelson (1925)
Hon. Sir Charles Parsons (1927)
Sir George Grierson (1928)
Robert Bridges (1929)
John Galsworthy (1929)
Samuel Alexander (1930)
Montague Rhodes James (1930)
G.M. Trevelyan (1930)
Admiral of the Fleet Sir Charles Madden, Bt
    (1931) (Mil.)
Philip Wilson Steer (1931)
Sir William Bragg (1931)
Dr John William Mackail (1935)
John Masefield (1935)
Ralph Vaughan Williams (1935)
Sir F. Gowland Hopkins (1935)
Field Marshal the Lord Chetwode (1935) (Mil.)

King George VI

Rt Hon. Herbert Laurens Fisher (1937)
The Lord Baden-Powell (1937) (Mil.)
Sir Arthur Stanley Eddington (1938)
Admiral of the Fleet the Lord Chatfield
    (1939) (Mil.)
Sir James Hopwood Jeans (1939)
Marshal of the RAF the Lord Newall (1940)
    (Mil.)
Professor Gilbert Murray (1941)
Sir Edwin Lutyens (1942)
Augustus John (1942)
The Lord Adrian (1942)
Sir William Holdsworth (1943)
Admiral of the Fleet Sir Dudley Pound (1943)
    (Mil.)
The Lord Passfield (1944)
Sir Henry Dale (1944)
Sir Giles Gilbert Scott (1944)
Professor Alfred Whitehead (1945)
Rt Hon. Sir Winston Churchill (1946)
Marshal of the RAF the Viscount Portal of
    Hungerford (1946) (Mil.)

[*] The styles given are the later styles of all holders. Some were not so styled when given the O.M.

The Order of Merit luncheon at Buckingham Palace in July 1992. Back row (left to right): Professor Francis Crick, Lord Porter, Sir Ernst Gombrich, Sir Sidney Nolan, Sir Andrew Huxley, Dame Joan Sutherland, Rev. Prof Owen Chadwick, Sir Michael Tippett, Frederick Sanger, Sir Yehudi Menuhin, Dr Max Perutz and the Secretary, Sir Edward Ford.

Front row: Baroness Thatcher, Lord Todd, Sir Isaiah Berlin, Prof. Dorothy Hodgkin, The Queen, Prince Philip, Lord Zuckerman, Sir George Edwards, Group Captain Lord Cheshire, and Dame Cicely Saunders.

Field Marshal the Viscount Alanbrooke (1946) (Mil.)
Admiral of the Fleet the Viscount Cunningham of Hyndhope (1946) (Mil.)
The Earl of Halifax (1946)
Field Marshal Rt Hon. Jan Christiaan Smuts (1947)
Rt Hon. William L. Mackenzie King (1947)
T.S. Eliot (1948)
Sir Robert Robinson (1949)
The Earl Russell (1949)
Rt Hon. Sir Alexander Cadogan (1951)
Marshal of the RAF the Viscount Trenchard (1951) (Mil.)
Professor G.E. Moore (1951)
The Earl Attlee (1951)

Queen Elizabeth II

Wilder George Penfield (1953)
Walter de la Mare (1953)
The Lord Hailey (1956)
Sir John Crockcroft (1957)
The Viscount Waverley (1957)
Sir Macfarlane Burnett (1958)
The Viscount Samuel (1958)
Field Marshal the Earl Alexander of Tunis (1959) (Mil.)

Sir Cyril Hinshelwood (1960)
Graham Sutherland (1960)
Sir Geoffrey de Havilland (1962)
Sir Basil Spence (1962)
Sir Owen Dixon (1963)
G.P. Gooch (1963)
Henry Moore (1963)
The Lord Britten (1965)
Dorothy Hodgkin (1965)
Admiral of the Fleet the Earl Mountbatten of Burma (1965) (Mil.)
The Lord Florey (1965)
The Lord Blackett (1967)
Sir William Walton (1967)
Ben Nicholson (1968)
The Lord Zuckerman (1968)
H.R.H. the Duke of Edinburgh (1968) (Civil)
E.M. Forster (1969)
Rt Hon. Malcolm Macdonald (1969)
The Lord Penney (1969)
Sir Geoffrey Ingram Taylor (1969)
Dame Veronica Wedgwood (1969)
John Beaglehole (1970)
Rt Hon. Lester Pearson (1971)
Sir Isaiah Berlin (1971)
Sir George Edwards (1971)
Sir Alan Hodgkin (1973)
Paul Dirac (1973)

The Earl of Stockton (1976)
The Lord Hinton of Bankside (1976)
The Lord Clark (1976)
Sir Ronald Syme (1976)
The Lord Todd (1977)
The Lord Franks (1977)
Sir Frederick Ashton (1977)
J.B. Priestley (1977)
The Lord Olivier (1981)
Sir Peter Medawar (1981)
Group Captain the Lord Cheshire, V.C. (1981)
Rev. Professor Owen Chadwick (1983)
Sir Andrew Huxley (1983)
Sir Sidney Nolan (1983)
Sir Michael Tippett (1983)
Graham Greene (1986)
Frederick Sanger (1986)
Air Cdre Sir Frank Whittle (1986)
The Lord Menuhin (1987)
Professor Sir Ernst Gombrich (1988)
Dr Max Perutz (1988)
Dame Cicely Saunders (1989)
The Lord Porter of Luddenham (1990)
The Baroness Thatcher (1990)
Dame Joan Sutherland (1991)
Professor Francis Crick (1991)

Dame Ninette de Valois (1992)
Sir Michael Atiyah (1992)
The Lord Jenkins of Hillhead (1993)
Lucian Freud (1993)

Honorary Members

Field Marshal Prince Yamagata (1906)
    (Hon. Military)
Field Marshal Prince Oyama (1906) (Hon.
    Military)
Admiral Count Togo (1906) (Hon. Military)
Field Marshal (Marshal of France) Ferdinand
    Foch (1918) (Hon. Military)
Marshal of France Jacques Joffre (1919)
    (Hon. Military)
General of the Army Dwight Eisenhower
    (1945) (Hon. Civil)
The Hon. John Gilbert Winant (1947)
    (Hon. Civil)
Dr Albert Schweitzer (1955) (Hon. Civil)
Dr Sarvepalli Radhakrishnan (1963)
    (Hon. Civil)
Mother Teresa (1983) (Hon. Civil)*

Total: 162 members.

---

*   Mother Teresa's real name is Agnes Gonxha Bojaxhiu.

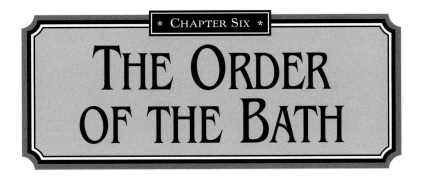

CHAPTER SIX

THE ORDER OF THE BATH

F ROM SAXON TIMES until the coronation of King Charles II a 'degree of Knighthood' was conferred in England with great ceremony, and according to a variety of myths it was called the Knighthood of the Bath. This Knighthood was not an 'Order' like that of the Garter with a chapel, statutes, seal and officers, but simply a 'degree of Knighthood', greatly esteemed owing to the distinction of the persons on whom it was conferred and to the solemnity of the various Ceremonies connected with the creation of the Knights.

Princess Alice, Duchess of Gloucester in the robes of the Order of the Bath, outside Westminster Abbey.

The reference to the 'Bath' was symbolic of the preparation for knighthood undergone by the recipients. They bathed as a symbol of spiritual purification, not unlike the sacrament of baptism. Some forty-six knights were created in 1399 at the time of the coronation of Henry IV, involving considerable fees paid to the heralds. The last such knights were created for the coronation of King Charles II.

The Order of the Bath has been a rather different order from 1725 onwards. There has always been a certain humour in the name, foreigners finding difficulty 'in not associating it with some form of personal ablutions'. Indeed, as the Order's formidable historian, James Risk, has pointed out: 'The designation, 'Companion of the Bath', has been known to arouse broad humour of a kind unacceptable in Victorian England.'[1].

On 11 May 1725, King George I created a military Order of Knighthood to be thereafter known as the Order of the Bath, and by later statutes laid down the ordinances which were to be observed within the Order. These statutes ordained that the candidates appeared in the Prince's Chamber of the palace of Westminster, accompanied by two esquire supporters. The new Knight took his bath and was put to bed, wearing a robe of russet, before a long night of vigil in the Henry VII Chapel, Westminster Abbey. In due course he was fortified with wine and spices, and after his vigil, was allowed a snooze from which he was awakened by the trumpet's call.

Adorned in the crimson robes of the Order, the new Knight was then ready to be installed. If subsequently promoted to the Garter, Knights of the Bath were meant to relinquish the junior order as, in those days, it was rare to belong to more than one

Order.* As with nearly all the Orders, there is a riband and star, collar and badge. The star has three crowns surrounded by the motto 'Tria Juncta in Uno', and the riband is red. The collar consists of crowns and knots interlinked with the badge suspended from it. The robes are of bright red silk, with the badge on the left breast. There are slight differences between the badges of the civil and military divisions.

In May 1725 the first investiture was held, at which twenty-eight new Knights were created in the Royal Closet of St James's. At that time the Order consisted of the Sovereign, a senior Prince of the Blood Royal[†], and the Great Master, the first of whom was John, Duke of Montagu[§]. A magnificent installation ceremony was held in Westminster Abbey in June.

The Order appealed very much to the Prime Minister of the day, Robert Walpole, who saw it as a means of bestowing patronage, and a stepping stone towards the Order of the Garter. His son, Horace Walpole, described it as 'an artful bank of thirty-six Ribbands to supply a fund of favours in lieu of places'[2]. In those days of course, Orders tended to be bestowed on the grandees of the country more for who they were than for any personal achievement. This latter concept only developed somewhat later on.

It was also traditional for Knights to wear their sashes at all times, rather as Frenchmen wear the buttonhole ribbon of the Legion of Honour these days. One poor knight, Sir William Morgan of Tredegar, had his badge stolen by a burglar who literally cut it off him. This gave the future Lord Chesterfield the chance to deride the Order and Robert Walpole in a wicked poem, a snatch of which went:

> 'Twas one of the toys
> Bob gave the boys
> When first the chits were knighted.[3]

At the coronation of George II, the Knights of the Bath were given seats, the precedence of which annoyed the judges, who refused to take the seats ascribed to them.

Gradually the Order began to become more military, largely because between 1770 and 1815 England was invariably at war. Stalls were granted to the Knights in the Henry VII Chapel at Westminster Abbey, and in 1797, the Order's most famous Knight, Admiral Nelson, was invested by George III in London.[¶]

As with all Orders, there existed the means to remove an unworthy Knight. Degradation was effected if 'a Knight had been convicted of Heresy, High Treason, or had fled from the field of battle'[4]. There were two such cases, one in 1814 and another in 1816**, besides the much later case when a foreign head of state was removed from the Order for hostilities against Britain.

From 1725 a good record of the members of the Order was preserved in the stall-plates in the Henry VII Chapel, Westminster Abbey, but these memorials were discontinued

Henry VII Chapel, Westminster Abbey, the chapel of the Order of the Bath.

---

* The Duke of Wellington, some years later, was reluctant to hand over his Bath when given the Garter.
† The infant Prince William, later Duke of Cumberland, of Battle of Culloden fame, was appointed to the Order.
§ Fees payable by new Knights earned the Duke some £9,500 between 1725 and his death in 1749. To become a Knight of the Bath cost about £510 in the currency of the time.
¶ The Admiral was in London because he had lost his arm. He refused to pay any expenses, declaring 'I cannot think of being at one sixpence expense'.
** Lord Cochrane was the first. His banner was kicked out of the door of the Abbey. He was later readmitted by the Prince Consort. The second was General Sir Eyre Coote.

for a century in 1812. On 1 June that year the last installation ceremony took place until 1913.

At the conclusion of the war in 1814 the Order was enlarged and, instead of one class of Knights, two more were added, Knights Commanders, and Companions, and subsequently in 1847 changes were made in the constitution of the Order to bring it in line with the altered state and circumstances of society.

In 1815 the first civil G.C.B. was created and in 1820 the custom of creating new Knights of the Bath before the coronation was revived. Interestingly Queen Victoria's first ceremonial function after her accession in 1837 was to bestow the Order of the Bath on the Earl of Durham. At Waterloo dinners, the Duke of Wellington used to wear his G.C.B. instead of the Garter, a custom also adopted by King George IV and King William IV, but Queen Victoria did not like to wear anything other than her blue Garter riband.

The Order's Great Master from 1837 until his death in 1843 was the Duke of Sussex, sixth son of George III. He was succeeded by the Prince Consort, who took as constructive an interest in the Order as in all things that concerned him. He managed to turn the Order into a useful machine to reward services to the crown. After his death, Queen Victoria refused to replace him and later in the reign Disraeli succeeded in getting the distribution of all honours, including the Bath, into the hands of the Prime Minister. Only at the time of her Diamond Jubilee did Queen Victoria appoint the Prince of Wales Great Master. To mark the occasion, the Prince gave a dinner for the G.C.B.s at St James's Palace.

In 1912 there was an appeal for funds and members of the various grades of the Order produced enough money to create stalls for forty-six Knights Grand Cross in the Henry VII Chapel. The next year King George V intimated his intention of restoring the ceremony of installation which had been omitted for so many years. This was largely due to the considerable interest shown in the Order by the Great Master, the Duke of Connaught. On 22 July some forty-six Knights Grand Cross were installed, and the custom of erecting banners and stall-plates in the Chapel of the Order, the Henry VII Chapel was revived.

The King processed to Westminster Abbey from the House of Lords, and in the words of James Risk: 'The outdoor procession from the Lords to the Abbey permitted the citizens of London to enjoy the splendour of the crimson, gold and waving plumes as they had been accustomed to do in the eighteenth century.'[5]

There was a particularly impressive installation service in 1928, recorded by the painter Frank O. Salisbury, at which the King was present. Amongst the Knights Grand Cross present was Admiral the Hon. Sir Edmund Fremantle, and the order of service records that he had 'leave from the Great Master to remain in King Henry VII's Chapel during the Service'[6], as well he might have done, having been born in 1836, and therefore then aged nearly 92. Other great men present in the Abbey that day were: Field Marshal Lord Methuen, Viscount Esher, General Sir Bindon Blood, the Marquess of Reading, General Sir Ian Hamilton, Admiral of the Fleet Lord Beatty, Lord Stamfordham, and Sir Frederick Ponsonby. Field Marshal Viscount Allenby and Admiral of the Fleet Earl Jellicoe were among the ten Knights Grand Cross installed that day.

Owing to the increase in the number of Knights of the Order, it is now impossible to assign a stall to each Knight. So Knights Grand Cross have to be particularly senior before they are installed, although they can all take part in the Bath processions wearing their mantles. Today there are twenty-six military stall-holders and eight civil ones.

On 24 May 1951, King George VI installed his brother, the Duke of Gloucester, as Great Master. The King loved all such ceremonies, and this was the only Bath ceremony he ever attended and the last such grand ceremony at which he was present. According to Sir Ivan de la Bere: 'he was, to the great distress of all present, particularly the officers of the Order who were attending him, obviously ill and in such pain that the procession had to be considerably curtailed in an endeavour to spare him fatigue'.[7] The King had a temperature, and soon afterwards was in the hands of his doctors.

It is the Queen's custom to give the Grand Cross of the Order of the Bath to presidents who come to Britain on state visits. This has meant that there have been some somewhat controversial holders of the year. Mussolini was appointed an honorary G.C.B. by King George V in 1923 and demoted from the order in World War Two. President Ceausescu of Romania was given it on his state visit to Britain in 1978, and had it removed from him by order of the Sovereign in December 1989, just before his capture and shooting by the Romanian army.

The Queen installed President Gustav Heinemann of the Federal Republic of Germany in a ceremony at Westminster Abbey on 26 October 1972. American presidents do not accept honours, but General Eisenhower was an honorary G.C.B., General Marshall can be seen wearing the robes of the Order at the Queen's coronation in 1953, and a year after he left office, President Ronald Reagan was given an honorary G.C.B. (1989) by the Queen, on the personal recommendation of Margaret Thatcher. Former President George Bush was similarly honoured in 1993.

Since 1971 ladies have been admissible to the Order. Princess Alice, Duchess of Gloucester is the only Dame Grand Cross, but the President of Iceland, Vigdis Finnbogadottir, was made an honorary G.C.B. on the Queen's State Visit in the summer of 1990. There are two ladies who are Dame Commanders (D.C.B.): Dame Mildred Riddelsdell (1972), 2nd Permanent Secretary DHSS, and Dame Anne Mueller (1988), Second Permanent Secretary to the Treasury.

Princess Alice took part in the 1975 ceremony at which the Prince of Wales was installed Great Master in succession to her late husband, the Duke of Gloucester. At that service, there were representativees of the Order of St John, the British Empire. the Royal Victorian Order, the Saint Michael and Saint George, the Thistle and the Garter. Princess Alice has never been installed as such.

The senior Knight present was General Sir Frederick Pile, born in 1884 and a G.C.B. since 1945. Other previously installed Knights included General Sir Richard O'Connor, K.T., Lord Harding of Petherton, Earl Mountbatten of Burma, Sir Gerald Templer and Lord Sherfield. Amongst the newly installed Knights were Sir Dermot Boyle, Sir Francis Festing and the present senior Knight, Air Chief Marshal Sir Harry Broadhurst.

There have been services of the Order roughly every four years since then, sometimes presided over by the Queen and sometimes by the Prince of Wales.

KNIGHTS GRAND CROSS

GREAT MASTER: H.R.H. the Prince of Wales (1975)

Extra Dame Grand Cross: H.R.H. Princess Alice, Duchess of Gloucester (1975).

The insignia of the Order of the Bath - the star and badge of the Grand Cross (Military).

Air Chief Marshal Sir Harry Broadhurst (1960)
The Lord Sherfield (1960)
Field Marshal Sir James Cassels (1961)
Sir Alexander Johnston (1962)
A.C.M. Sir Edmund Hudleston (1963)
Sir Harold Kent (1963)
Sir William Murrie (1964)
Admiral Sir Charles Madden, Bt (1965)
Sir Thomas Padmore (1965)
Admiral of the Fleet Sir Varyl Begg (1965)
Admiral Sir Desmond Dreyer (1967)
Marshal of the RAF Sir John Grandy (1967)
General Sir John Hackett (1967)
Sir Richard Powell (1967)
General Sir Charles Harington (1969)
Sir James Dunnett (1969)
Admiral Sir John Bush (1970)
General Sir Geoffrey Musson (1970)
Admiral of the Fleet the Lord Hill-Norton (1970)
Field Marshal the Lord Carver (1970)
A.C.M. Sir Brian Burnett (1970)
The Lord Allen of Abbeydale (1970)
Admiral of the Fleet Sir Michael Pollock (1971)
General Sir Desmond Fitzpatrick (1971)
Marshal of the RAF Sir Denis Spotswode (1971)
Sir George Godber (1971)
Sir Edmund Compton (1971)
Admiral Sir Horace Law (1972)
General Sir John Mogg (1972)
General Sir Anthony Read (1972)
A.C.M. Sir Frederick Rosier (1972)
Sir Arnold France (1972)
A.C.M. Sir Christopher Foxley-Norris (1973)
The Lord Croham (1973)
General Sir Harry Tuzo (1973)
Admiral of the Fleet Sir Edward Ashmore (1974)
Sir Charles Cunningham (1974)
Admiral Sir Anthony Griffin (1975)
General Sir Cecil Blacker (1975)
A.C.M. Sir Neil Wheeler (1975)
General Sir Frank King (1976)
Admiral of the Fleet the Lord Lewin (1976)

Field Marshal Sir Roland Gibbs (1976)
General Sir John Gibbon (1977)
Admiral Sir David Williams (1977)
Lt-General Sir David House (1977)
A.C.M. Sir Douglas Lowe (1977)
The Lord Hunt of Tanworth (1977)
The Lord Charteris of Amisfield (1977)
General Sir Jack Harman (1978)
Marshal of the RAF Sir Michael Beetham (1978)
Sir William Pile (1978)
Admiral of the Fleet Sir Henry Leach (1978)
Field Marshal the Lord Bramall (1979)
The Lord Bancroft (1979)
General Sir Patrick Howard-Dobson (1979)
General Sir Peter Whiteley (1979)
A.C.M. Sir David Evans (1979)
Rt Hon. Sir Frank Cooper (1979)
General Sir David Fraser (1980)
Sir Douglas Wass (1980)
Admiral Sir James Eberle (1981)
General Sir Robert Ford (1981)
A.C.M. Sir Rex Roe (1981)
Rt Hon. Sir Patrick Nairne (1981)
General Sir Richard Worsley (1982)
Field Marshal Sir John Stanier (1982)
Marshal of the RAF Sir Keith Williamson (1982)
Sir Peter Carey (1982)
Admiral Sir Desmond Cassidi (1983)
General Sir Michael Gow (1983)
A.C.M. Sir Peter Terry (1983)
The Lord Armstrong of Ilminster (1983)
General Sir George Cooper (1984)
Sir Brian Cubbon (1984)
The Lord Moore of Wolvercote (1984)
Admiral of the Fleet Sir William Stavely (1984)
Marshal of the RAF the Lord Craig of Radley (1984)
Sir William Fraser (1984)
A.C.M. Sir Thomas Kennedy (1985)
Field Marshal Sir Nigel Bagnall (1985)
Sir Kenneth Stowe (1986)
Admiral Sir Nicholas Hunt (1987)
General Sir Roland Guy (1987)
Marshal of the RAF Sir Peter Harding (1988)

Sir Brian Hayes (1988)
Field Marshal Sir John Chapple (1988)
Sir Clive Whitmore (1988)
Admiral of the Fleet Sir Julian Oswald (1989)
A.C.M. Sir Patrick Hine (1989)
Sir Peter Middleton (1989)
Sir Derek Oulton (1989)
Rt Hon. Sir William Heseltine (1990)
Admiral Sir David Benjamin Bathurst (1991)
Sir Michael Quinlan (1991)
General Sir Brian Kenny (1991)

A.C.M. Sir David Parry-Evans (1991)
General Sir Peter Inge (1992)
Rt Hon. Sir Terence Heiser (1992)
Admiral Sir John Slater (1992)
A.C.M. Sir Brendan Jackson (1992)
Sir Robin Butler (1992)
General Sir David Ramsbotham (1993)
A.C.M. Sir Michael Graydon (1993)
Admiral Sir John Kerr (1993)
Sir Christopher France (1994)

The military division of the Order of the Bath is of a straightforward nature. In the Navy all the admirals of the fleet are Knights Grand Cross, as are the more senior admirals. Most, but not all, serving vice-admirals are Knight Commanders. In the Army, all the field marshals are G.C.B.s*, likewise the senior generals, while the other generals and most of the lieutenant-generals are K.C.B.s. The same pattern exists in the Royal Air Force, with all the marshals of the RAF as G.C.B.s, and one serving air chief marshal. The other air chief marshals and almost all the air marshals are K.C.B.s.

The exception to all three of the above groups is that H.R.H. Prince Philip, Duke of Edinburgh, who is the senior Admiral of the Fleet, Field Marshal and Marshal of the RAF, is not in the Order of the Bath, presumably by his own choice.

At present the military division includes eight admirals of the fleet, twelve admirals, seven field marshals, twenty-two full generals, one lieutenant-general, six marshals of the Royal Air Force, and fifteen air chief marshals. It has been given more or less automatically in order of seniority, as and when vacancies occur, but John Major's recent stipulations about the Honours List are likely to reduce the number of G.C.B.s appointed.

The civil division is rather more interesting, though again most of its members are civil servants and thus predictable in appointment. Of the senior civil servants, Sherfield, Croham, Wass and Middleton were at the Treasury; Johnston, France, and Pile were Inland Revenue; Sir Harold Kent was Treasury Solicitor; Murrie and Fraser were at the Scottish Office; Padmore was Transport; Powell was Board of Trade; Dunnett, Cooper, Whitmore and France were Ministry of Defence; Lord Allen, Cunningham and Cubbon were Home Office; Godber was Chief Medical Officer at various departments; Sir Edmund Compton was Parliamentary Commissioner for Administration, best known as 'The Ombudsman'; Lord Hunt and Lord Armstrong were Cabinet Secretaries, and Sir Robin Butler is the present holder of that post; Lord Bancroft was Head of the Civil Service; Nairne and Stowe were at the DHSS; Hayes was at Trade and Industry; Sir Derek Oulton was Clerk of the Crown in Chancery and Head of the Lord Chancellor's Office; Quinlan was at Employment; and Heiser at the Department of the Environment. Other than them, Lord Charteris, Lord Moore and Sir William Heseltine were Private Secretaries to the Queen.

* H.R.H. the Duke of Kent, appointed a Field Marshal in 1993, is not a G.C.B., nor is Field Marshal Sir Richard Vincent, who is G.B.E., K.C.B..

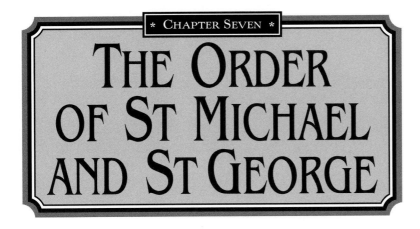

CHAPTER SEVEN

THE ORDER OF ST MICHAEL AND ST GEORGE

HE ORDER OF ST MICHAEL AND ST GEORGE is the Order of diplomacy, given to those who serve this country as ambassadors overseas, or in the Foreign, Commonwealth or Colonial services in London. It is given to Governors and Governors-General. The Order was originally founded a few years after George III assumed sovereignty over the island of Malta in 1814, and a new Order was required. It was used to honour those who served in the Mediterranean area.

It was the Prince Regent who founded the Order on behalf of George III with three grades, the Knights Grand Cross, the Knight Commanders and the Companions. In Corfu a palace was erected to honour the Order in 1819, as a place where ceremonial occasions could take place. The Throne Room there contains a copy of the portrait of George IV by Lawrence, and the ceiling is covered with the emblems of the Order. It also contains a painting of St George attacking a papier-mache dragon and a copy of Guido Reni's St Michael. The Palace, which still stands today 'faintly mottled by time and tribulation, grey or glowing according to the disposition of the weather'[1], remained the symbolic home of the Order until 1864.

The Order changed emphasis over the years and by the statutes of 1868 was remodelled in its present form to honour those British subjects serving in foreign countries overseas. During the First World War it was used to recognise military service overseas as a kind of junior Order of the Bath. Nowadays there is a maximum of 100 G.C.M.G.s, 355 K.C.M.G.s, and 1,435 C.M.G.s. Certain members of the Royal Family and foreign princes or republicans can be added as extras, and there have been Dames Grand Cross, Dame Commanders and lady Companions since 1965. Queen Salote of Tonga, who so bravely wore her G.B.E. robes in the soaking coronation procession of 1953, was the first lady G.C.M.G. appointed in 1965. She died on 15 December that year.

The chapel of the Order is in St Paul's Cathedral and there are some banners of the Grand Crosses hanging there. It was consecrated in 1904. There used to be an annual

King Edward VII, the Prince of Wales (later King George V) and the Duke of Connaught in the robes of the Order of St Michael and St George in their stalls at the service of consecration of the Order's chapel in St. Paul's Cathedral in 1904.

111

*The Queen
attending a service
of the Order of St
Michael and St
George in 1968.*

service during which the Grand Crosses processed through the body of the Cathedral in robes of Saxon blue and scarlet silk, but this now takes place every other year. The banners of deceased holders are borne from the chapel by squires and the banners of new Knights are duly affixed in their place. At a later point in the Service of Thanksgiving there is a roll call of deceased Companions, Knights and Dame Commanders and Grand Crosses. The Duke of Kent as Grand Master of the Order presides, and from time to time the Queen attends as Sovereign, wearing the mantle of the Order.

Like the other Orders there is a collar (a mixture of lions and and Maltese crosses) from which is suspended the badge – a star of seven rays of silver surmounted by the cross of St George, and in the centre a blue circle bearing the motto in gold, 'Auspicium Melioris Aevi' (Token of a better age). In the middle of the blue band is a representation of the Archangel St Michael holding a sword and trampling on Satan. The riband of the Order is blue, red, blue in equal stripes.

From 1981 the Order's Registrar was Sir Charles Johnston, G.C.M.G. (1971), former High Commissioner in Australia. He was also a translator of Pushkin, a poet and a diarist. He wrote that the 1979 service did not impress him, and he confessed that he only went because he was lunching afterwards with the Duke of Kent:

> It was not a religious service at all, but a brassy celebration of the British Empire. It was a manifestation of an official Imperial cult, as it might be of Augustus or Claudius; the commemoration of the deified Victoria. Personally I find our Empire something touching, and, on the whole, beneficent. But on this occasion it was on parade in its most blaring and aggressive form; one could well understand what made the Irish and the Indians and the Egyptians hate it so much. The pompous vulgarity of the whole thing disgusted me particularly: whether it was the brass of the Grenadiers thumping out the Grand March from Athalie, the most pompier thing Mendelssohn ever wrote – more like Meyerbeer – or Elgar's March Imperial; and the poor old imperial relics, my contemporaries, tripping, or, more like, stumping up and down the aisle in a series of ridiculous processions from which they were clearly deriving a deep emotional satisfaction – all this under the hideous neo-Byzantine decoration of the dome and squinches. Among the Knights Grand Cross was one particularly incongruous pair: G. Templer* glaring furiously straight ahead, while beside him Gladwyn† was smirking and bowing right and left like a rather experienced and self-confident bride.
>
> A less grotesque and comical, in fact rather a macabre note was struck by Sammy Hood§ pacing meditatively along: mantled, starred, abstracted, enormously tall but elongated and distorted à la Greco – it was Count Orgaz walking in his own funeral procession[2]

Two years later Lord De L'Isle persuaded Johnston to become Registrar and he was duly received in audience by the Queen. Then came the next service:

---

*   Field Marshal Sir Gerald Templer.
†   Lord Gladwyn (born 1900), now the senior G.C.M.G.
§   Viscount Hood (1910-1981), Deputy Under Secretary of State, Foreign and Commonwealth Office, and former Minister in Washington.

On Tuesday at the Michael and George service in St Paul's I made my first public appearance as Registrar, parading in a scarlet robe at the rear of the procession, beside Michael Palliser, and just in front of Bill De L'Isle and the Duke of Kent. There were no actual cat-calls from the nave, but I think there must have been a certain amount of astonishment at my appearance in this role.[3]

In 1983 Sir Charles was still critical of the proceedings:

I ambled up and down in my scarlet mantle, near the tail of the procession – behind the blue-mantled Grand Crosses and just ahead of Chancellor De L'Isle and his banner. I have a split attitude about the occasion. *Au fond* I despise this sort of thing, and think it's a lot of flummery. As a romantic Victorian reconstruction of medieval chivalry, the order of St M. and St G. is only one degree less bogus than the Order of St John of Jerusalem – which was thrust on me, unsought, because I was Ambassador in Amman, and with which I have had no communication for years.

But, unlike St J. of J., M. and G. is also a sort of club for old sweats from all of the three overseas services – Foreign, Commonwealth, and Colonial – and to be an officer of it is a sign of respectability and recognition. For years a lot of my old colleagues have looked askance at me, partly because of my books about Jordan and Aden ('Why was he allowed to write them?') and partly because of my rather flamboyant City career. Now, all of a sudden, here I am in a red dressing gown, at the very centre of the Establishment.[4]

Sir Charles Johnston, G.C.M.G. with Valerie Hobson.

It took the presence of the Queen herself in 1984 to bring a more lyrical description of the proceedings from Sir Charles:

In St Paul's we had the normal flim-flam of parading in our robes; but this time even I was moved: processing down the aisle, as we approached the West Door I saw the massed plumes of the Queen's Bodyguard and the Tudor magnificence of the Yeomen, and sensed an electric thrill: the Queen was coming to the service, for the first time in seven or eight years, and here, waiting for her arrival, was the Apparat of the Monarchy with a capital M. The great doors are thrown open, jockey-capped state trumpeters blow a fanfare, bishops bow until their mitres practically fall off, and here, advancing on the enormous officers of the Order (all of us six foot or over), and somehow dwarfing us is this tiny, brilliant, numinous figure. I get that irresistible smile and 'Hello Ch. . .' – I suppose 'Charles', and still more 'Charlie', might sound rather out of place. Her page – the eldest son of Jamie and Sasha [the Duke and Duchess of] Abercorn – is rather taller that she is. At various points in the service I find myself placed quite near her; she sits there calmly, with her thick spectacles on – glittering quietly away.[5]

To belong to an Order, such as the St Michael and St George, is to accept a certain responsibility rather like being the member of a club. That is why the giving of an honour has sometimes been a method used by the Establishment to tame a difficult character. People are only as important as they may consider themselves in their wildest dreams when they are in trouble. The classic newspaper-stand headline 'Famous Actress Dies' invariably signifies a small paragraph about a former soap star whose name is very far from familiar.

In the Order of St Michael and St George was Sir Peter Hayman, K.C.M.G. (1971), a civil servant and diplomat, whose last appointment had been High Commissioner in Canada. Unfortunately Sir Peter had a weakness for pornography which landed him in the tabloids. When he died the task of writing his obituary fell to another member of the Order, Lord Greenhill of Harrow, G.C.M.G. (1972). He wrote in the *Independent*:

> Few things are sadder than the spectacle of an active and distinguished public career ruined by self-inflicted disgrace. This was the case with the diplomat Sir Peter Hayman. Enough publicity has been given to his involvement in a Paedophiliac Information exchange, revealed by documents left on a bus. A subsequent offence of gross indecency added to the shame.[6]

Lord Greenhill then outlined his career in its more positive aspects. He may not have known that when the offences were first made public, the officers of the Order of St Michael and St George assembled to discuss whether or not to recommend to the Queen the removal of Sir Peter's name from the list of K.C.M.G.s.

It was following Sir Peter's second offence that the officers met at the request of the King of Arms, Lord Saint Brides*. The general view was that Sir Peter had served an honourable war, followed by a distinguished and unblemished diplomatic career, that he had not been convicted of paedophilia, and that the officers should not recommend what they called 'a stripping'. However, it was unanimously agreed that the Prelate should have a meeting with Sir Peter, and issue him with a stern warning about the consequences of further trouble. This warning was duly given, and Sir Peter died a Knight some years later.

The Queen attended the service of St Michael and St George again in 1992. On years when there is no service, a cocktail party is held.

KNIGHTS AND DAMES GRAND CROSS

GRAND MASTER: H.R.H. the Duke of Kent
CHANCELLOR: The Lord Carrington

The Lord Gladwyn (1954)	Sir Hilton Poynton (1964)
The Lord Sherfield (1955)	Sir Garfield Barwick (1965)
The Earl of Listowel (1957)	Sir John Paul (1965)
The Earl of Selkirk (1959)	Sir Richard Luyt (1966)
Sir Robert Black (1962)	Sir John Stow (1966)
Sir Richard Turnbull (1962)	Sir Evelyn Shuckburgh (1967)
Sir Frank Roberts (1963)	Sir John Rennie (1968)
Sir Patrick Dean (1963)	Sir Patrick Reilly (1968)
The Lord Grey of Naunton (1964)	Sir Bernard Burrows (1970)

* Lord Saint Brides (1916-1989), a former diplomat, Morrice James, who succeeded Sir Charles Johnston as High Commissioner in Australia. He was then resident in the South of France.

Sir Robert Foster (1970)
Sir Banja Tejan-Sie (1970)
Sir Denis Wright (1971)
The Lord Greenhill of Harrow (1972)
Sir William Nield (1972)
Sir Ellis Clarke (1972)
Sir Ramon Osman (1973)
Sir Stewart Crawford (1973)
Sir Edward Peck (1974)
The Lord Brimelowe (1975)
Sir Edward Tomkins (1975)
Sir Vincent Evans (1976)
Sir Michael Walker (1976)
Rt Hon. Sir Michael Palliser (1977)
Sir Tore Lokoloko (1977)
Rt Hon. Sir John Gorton (1977)
Sir Nicholas Henderson (1977)
Sir Donald Maitland (1977)
Rt Hon. Sir Zelman Cowen (1977)
Sir John Johnston (1978)
Hon. Sir Peter Ramsbotham (1978)
Sir David Scott (1979)
Sir Paul Scoon (1979)
Sir Penitala Teo (1979)
Sir Alan Campbell (1979)
Sir John Killick (1979)
Sir Sydney Gun-Munro (1979)
Sir Gerald Cash (1980)
Rt Hon. Sir Antony Duff (1980)
Sir Donald Tebbit (1980)
Sir Baddeley Devesi (1980)
Sir Michael Wilford (1980)
Hon. Sir David Beattie (1980)
Sir Oliver Wright (1981)
Rt Hon. Sir Harry Gibbs (1981)
Sir Florizel Glasspole (1981)
Sir Clive Rose (1981)
Sir Howard Smith (1981)
Sir Wilfred Jacobs (1981)
Sir Reginald Hibbert (1982)
Sir Anthony Parsons (1982)

Rt Hon. Sir Ninian Stephen (1982)
Sir Curtis Keeble (1982)
Rt Hon. Ratu Sir Kamisese Mara (1983)
Hon. Sir Kingsford Dibela (1983)
Sir Percy Cradock (1983)
Sir Hugh Cortazzi (1984)
Sir James Craig (1984)
Sir Clement Arrindell (1984)
Dr Dame Minita Gordon (1984)
Sir Hugh Springer (1984)
Sir Michael Butler (1984)
Sir John Thomson (1985)
Sir Joseph Eustace (1985)
Most Rev. Paul Reeves (1985)
Sir John Graham (1986)
Hon. Sir Veerasamy Ringadoo (1986)
Sir Antony Acland (1986)
Sir Tupua Leupena (1986)
Sir Julian Bullard (1987)
Sir John Fretwell (1987)
The Lord Bridges (1988)
The Lord Carrington (1988)
Sir George Lepping (1988)
Sir Crispin Tickell (1989)
Sir Patrick Wright (1989)
Dame Nita Barrow (1990)
Rt Hon. Sir Toaripi Lauti (1990)
Dame Catherine Tizard (1990)
Rt Hon. Sir Michael Somare (1990)
The Lord Wilson of Tillyorn (1991)
Sir David Jack (1991)
Sir David Goodall (1991)
Sir Howard Cooke (1991)
Sir Wiwa Korowi (1991)
Sir John Whitehead (1992)
Sir Stanislaus Anthony James (1992)
Sir Michael Alexander (1992)
Sir Reginald Palmer (1992)
Sir Ewen Fergusson (1992)
Sir Rodric Braithwaite (1994)
Sir David Gillmore (1994)

All the above have served either as governors or governor-generals, or in the Foreign and Commonwealth or Colonial Office. Usually to be a senior ambassador brings a G.C.M.G..

For example Lord Gladwyn was Ambassador in Paris, Lord Listowel was Governor-General of Ghana, Lord Grey of Naunton was Governor of the Bahamas, Sir Florizel Glasspole was Governor-General of Jamaica, and the Most Rev. Paul Reeves was Primate of New Zealand.

* CHAPTER EIGHT *
THE ROYAL VICTORIAN ORDER

HE ROYAL VICTORIAN ORDER was founded on 21 April 1896 by Queen Victoria as a way of rewarding outstanding personal service to her. As this is still the Queen's Order, it is held in particularly high esteem. The Order is given by Her Majesty to members of her family, her household and others. It is sometimes given to British ambassadors after a state visit she has paid to the country where they are *en poste*, and it is often given to foreign royals and members of foreign courts. (It is thus not surprising to find a Japanese chamberlain adorned with the riband of the Grand Cross in Tokyo). Progression within the order is said to be as certain as death.

Queen Victoria wanted to have an Order which was entirely in her control, and her Prime Minister saw the advantages of this. He stipulated that no government expense should be involved in this. Thus the awards to the Royal Victorian Order, and the giving of the insignia, are paid for by the Sovereign. The Order takes precedence before the Order of the British Empire. Associated with it is the Royal Victorian Medal, but entirely separate from it is the Royal Victorian Chain. Queen Victoria made sparing appointments − to close family and courtiers.

The Order has five classes, now known as G.C.V.O., K.C.V.O. or D.C.V.O., C.V.O., L.V.O. and M.V.O.. Originally the L.V.O.s or Lieutenants were M.V.O.s fourth class, because 'O.V.O.' was considered an unsuitable award. There are three grades of the medal, silver-gilt, silver and bronze, and these are given to royal servants for long service.

Edward VII was particularly fond of the Order and decided to boost its numbers. He thought nothing of distributing it almost as some kind of a tip. When he visited Chatsworth in January 1907, he decided to give it to his host, the 8th Duke of Devonshire, a man intensely bored by honours. Indeed he had once enraged the King by wearing his Garter upside down. The Duke was far from thrilled to hear of his new honour. As Sir Frederick Ponsonby put it: 'Anyone less anxious to receive an Order I had never seen, and I had to explain that the King looked upon his personal Order as a high honour, but the Duke seemed to think it would only complicate his dressing'.[1]

Princess Margaret, Princess Alice, the late Princess Marina and the Duchess of Kent and the 1966 Opening of Parliament. The first three princesses wear the riband of the G.C.V.O.

117

The Duke agreed to wear the G.C.V.O. at dinner, with Garter star and Garter.*

Sir Frederick Ponsonby had many other tales connected with the Order, which seemed to cause particular trouble on state visits overseas, when foreign decorations of little merit were distributed like confetti, often in the hope of getting the Royal Victorian Order in exchange. Nevertheless, examples of the Order can be found spread far afield. There is a G.C.V.O. riband and star in the museum of the Royal Palace in Cetinje, given to King Nicholas of Montenegro, amongst a great deal of other multi-coloured orders on show to the public.

Lord Hardinge of Penshurst (Viceroy of India) described King Edward's approach to orders: 'King Edward had rather foreign ideas about decorations. He liked people to be plastered with them and could not understand anybody thinking otherwise.'[2] The King never forgave Sir Edward Grey, a man who heartily disliked Orders, for refusing the G.C.V.O. 'The King's annoyance was extreme', wrote Hardinge.[3] George V elevated the Order to a position of high esteem, as 'a unique prestige, as a high honour and a valuable personal gift from the monarch'.[4] Ladies were first admitted during the reign of King Edward VIII, by the revised statutes of 28 May 1936, one of the few changes in orders that he made, and Queen Mary was appointed the first Dame Grand Cross at that time. This was Edward VIII's only appointment. After his accession George VI gave the Order to one or two of those who had helped the abdicated King in his trauma.

George VI was particularly interested in the Order, appointing his wife, Queen Elizabeth as the first Grand Master, and giving the G.C.V.O. to his surviving aunt, Queen Maud of Norway, and to his surviving great-aunts, Princess Louise, Duchess of Argyll and Princess Beatrice amongst others. He selected the Chapel of the Savoy to be the chapel of the Order, and ordained that escutcheons of the arms of the Knights and Dames Grand Cross be displayed there. He presented silver altar plate to the chapel in 1939. Services of the Order were held there in 1946, 1949 and 1958.

King George VI, who loved all Orders, actually conferred the G.C.V.O. in person on two of his physicians, when they were on their sick-beds: Sir Maurice Cassidy shortly before his death in October 1949, and in 1950 Sir Morton Smart, who survived until 1956. The present Queen attended the dedication of some treasures given to the Chapel of the Savoy to mark the seventh century of the Duchy of Lancaster in 1965. When the Governor of Windsor Castle, Sir David Hallifax, was about to retire due to ill health in 1992, the Queen called on him and invested him with the K.C.V.O..

The riband of the Order is particularly distinctive, dark blue, with a border of three thin stripes – red, white and red. The robes are dark blue silk, edged with red satin and lined in white silk. The collar comprises rectangular pieces bearing inscriptions relating to Queen Victoria, from which is suspended the badge, a Maltese cross of eight points with Queen Victoria's monogram, surrounded with a royal blue band and the word 'Victoria', the whole surmounted by the imperial crown. When the medal is

---

*   On another occasion King Manoel of Portugal gave the Duke the Order of the Tower and Sword. Soon after this the Duke of Portland, a man similarly honoured, visited him at Chatsworth to be greeted by the Duke with the words: 'How do you do, brother of the Order of the Elephant and Castle. For that is the name of the Order we've both been given, isn't it?' The Duke of Devonshire wore it at dinner, but drawing one bad hand after during their post-prandial bridge, declared: 'I believe this damned Elephant and Castle is bringing me bad luck. If I have another poor hand I shall throw the wretched thing into the fire.' [The Duke of Portland, *Men, Women and Things* (Faber & Faber, 1928) pp.189-90]

given to servants abroad on state visits, the riband bears a thin white line in the middle, to differentiate it from the medals given to the Queen's employees in England for what is sometimes a lifetime of service.

Since 1978 there have been services of the Royal Victorian Order every three years at St George's Chapel, Windsor.* The first one took place on 7 December 1978. Amongst the Knights Grand Cross present and robed that day were Sir John Kerr (the controversial Governor-General of Australia), the Duke of Beaufort and Lord Mountbatten. There was a good royal attendance, the Queen Mother wearing the Royal Victorian Chain on her coat, Princess Anne, Princess Margaret, Princess Alice, Duchess of Gloucester and the Duke of Gloucester. Until the last moment 95 year old Princess Alice, Countess of Athlone, the last grand-daughter of Queen Victoria, was expected but she did not appear. Nor did the Duchess of Kent.

The Queen and Prince Philip[†] arrived together, and at the end of the service as they left the Chapel, Prince Philip turned to the Queen and said: 'Well you wouldn't have got all that lot in the other chapel.'[§] The whole of St George's Chapel was full of members of the different grades of the Order, and apart from the Knights and Dames Grand Cross walking in the procession, the various grades were mixed up together in the nave, a G.C.V.O. next to an M.V.O. etc.. The service was magnificent, and at the opening of the recessional hymn, 'All People that on Earth do dwell. . .', there was a blast of trumpets and the procession began to wend its way down the nave aisle.

The insignia of a Dame Commander of the Royal Victorian Order.

In 1983 the service was held in April and was followed by a reception for holders of the Order of all ranks in the State Apartments of Windsor Castle. The Queen was particularly delighted with the success of the service: 'Now isn't that just the sort of service you like?'[6] She also commended its brevity. It lasted forty minutes. Amongst those who took part were Sir Paul Hasluck (also a Knight of the Garter), the former Governor-General of Australia, Ratu Sir George Cakobau, the Governor-General of Fiji and Sir Baddeley Devesi, the Governor-General of the Solomon Islands. There was another service in 1987, and to date the most recent is that held in April 1991. There were some interesting features about that service, notably the arrival of a man in a raincoat wearing the Royal Victorian Chain, who turned out to be Roland Michener, the 91-year-old former Governor-General of Canada (who died that summer). 'Yes, I'm Michener', he said on his way in.[7]

But the most ancient attender was the Earl of Southesk, K.C.V.O. (1923), then aged 97. He had been present at the 1983 service, striding in gamefully, shoes-a-sparkle, with no hint of his then 89 years. This time he was somewhat frail, but he insisted on sitting near the Royal Family as was his right as the widower of Princess Maud, the grand-daughter of King Edward VII. Interestingly he had to sit below Sir Angus Ogilvy, who had been appointed a K.C.V.O. some sixty-three years after the doughty Earl.[¶] A future member of the Royal Family was seated discreetly in the nave:

---

* For a description of the 1983 rehearsal in St George's Chapel, see the Introduction.
[†] Prince Philip is not a member of the Order.
[§] Prince Philip was referring to the Queen's Chapel of the Savoy, the official chapel of the Royal Victorian Order.
[¶] There was some concern, expressed by the Earl himself before he arrived, that he might not be able to stay in his seat throughout the entire service on account of his advanced years. An emergency strategy was set up, but the Earl took his full part in the service without the slightest problem. He died the following February at his home, Kinnaird Castle, near Brechin, at the age of 98.

Commander Timothy Laurence, M.V.O., R.N., seated not far from a line of royal protection officers.

Members of the Royal Household advance through the Order, being upgraded about once every eight years, depending on their jobs. There is a committee that sits to advise the Queen on who should get what and at what time. The most extraordinary example of non-advancement was that of Sir Anthony Blunt, who was a K.C.V.O., but retired as Surveyor of the Queen's Pictures in 1972. He was given the title Surveyor Emeritus, but significantly he was not advanced to G.C.V.O.. Later, of course, following his exposure in the House of Commons in 1979, he was stripped of his knighthood. That he did not become a G.C.V.O. gives evidence that certain members of the Queen's Household did know of his spying activities. His successor, Sir Oliver Millar, was appointed G.C.V.O. on his retirement as Surveyor.

KNIGHTS AND DAMES GRAND CROSS:

GRAND MASTER: Her Majesty Queen Elizabeth the Queen Mother (G.C.V.O. 1937).
CHANCELLOR: The Lord Chamberlain (The Earl of Airlie)

H.R.H. Princess Alice, Duchess of Gloucester (1948)
H.R.H. the Princess Margaret, Countess of Snowdon (1953)
H.R.H. the Duke of Kent (1960)
H.R.H. Princess Alexandra (1960)
H.R.H. the Duke of Gloucester (1974)
H.R.H. the Princess Royal (1974)
H.R.H. the Duchess of Kent (1977)
H.R.H. the Duchess of Gloucester (1989)

The Lord Gladwyn (1957)
Sir Frank Roberts (1965)
Sir Roderick Barclay (1966)
The Earl of Snowdon (1969)
The Lord Grey of Naunton (1973)
Sir Fred Warner (1975)
The Lord Charteris of Amisfield (1976)
The Hon. Sir Peter Ramsbotham (1976)
The Earl Waldegrave (1976)
Sir Seymour Egerton (1977)
Sir Oliver Wright (1978)
The Earl of Dalhousie (1979)
Rt Hon. Sir Zelman Cowen (1980)
The Duchess of Grafton (1980)
Hon. Sir David Beattie (1981)
Major-General Lord Michael Fitzalan-Howard (1981)
Rt Hon. Sir Ninian Stephen (1982)

Sir Tore Lokoloko (1982)
Sir Baddeley Devesi (1982)
Sir Penitala Teo (1982)
The Lord Moore of Wolvercote (1983)
Sir Florizel Glasspole (1983)
The Earl of Airlie (1984)
Sir Robin Mackworth-Young (1985)
Dr Dame Minita Gordon (1985)
Sir Gerald Cash (1985)
H.E. Sir Clement Arrindell (1985)
Sir Wilfred Jacobs (1985)
Sir Joseph Eustace (1985)
Sir Hugh Springer (1985)
H.E. Sir Paul Scoon (1985)
The Duke of Norfolk (1986)
Most Rev. Paul Reeves (1986)
Lt-Col Sir John Johnston (1987)
Lt-Col Sir John Miller (1987)
Marshal of the RAF Sir John Grandy (1988)
Rt Hon. Sir William Heseltine (1988)
Sir Oliver Millar (1988)
Patricia, Viscountess Hambleden (1990)
Major-General Sir George Burns (1990)
Sir Antony Acland (1991)
Sir Ralph Anstruther (1991)
Sir Ewen Fergusson (1992)
Rear-Admiral Sir Paul Greening (1992)
Sir Christopher Mallaby (1992)

It is quite easy to explain the reason why the above have the Grand Cross, as they fall into select groups very easily. First, there are the members of the Royal Family. The Queen normally gives this Order to the ladies of the Royal House, and in earlier times, more of them would have it, and more would have it sooner. It is interesting that Prince Philip does not have the Order, nor do either the Prince or Princess of Wales. Lord Snowdon received his for arranging the investiture of the Prince of Wales at Caernarvon Castle.

Then there are the high officers of the Queen's Household: The Earl Marshal, the Duke of Norfolk; the Lord Chamberlain, Lord Airlie; the Mistress of the Robes, the Duchess of Grafton; former Private Secretaries: Lord Charteris, Lord Moore, and Sir William Heseltine; the former Lord Warden of the Stanneries, Lord Waldegrave; the Queen Mother's former Lord Chamberlain, Lord Dalhousie, and two senior members of her court, Lady Hambleden and Sir Ralph Anstruther; the former librarian at Windsor, Sir Robin Mackworth-Young; the former Comptroller of the Lord Chamberlain's Office, Sir John Johnston; the former Crown Equerry, Sir John Miller; the former Surveyor of the Pictures, Sir Oliver Millar; and the Master of the Household, Sir Paul Greening.

There are some who have served the Queen closely in other ways: the retiring Marshal of the Diplomatic Corps, Lord Michael Fitzalan-Howard, now Colonel of Life Guards, who sits with her on the rostrum at the trooping; likewise Sir George Burns, former Colonel of Coldstream Guards; and Sir John Grandy, the retired Governor of Windsor Castle. There is her banker, Sir Seymour Egerton, after his retirement as Chairman of Coutts Bank. And the Queen gave it to Lord Grey of Naunton when he ended his time as Governor of Northern Ireland.

The others are governors, governors-general or ambassadors to whom the Queen has paid official or state visits: Gladwyn (Paris); Roberts (Germany); Barclay (Belgium); Warner (Japan); Ramsbotham (Washington – following the Queen's Bicentennial visit); Wright (Germany again); Cowen (Governor-General of Australia – the Queen opened the new High Court in Canberra); and Beattie (New Zealand).

The Queen distributed four G.C.V.O.s during her visit to Australia and other Commonwealth countries in October 1982: Stephen (Australia), Lokoloko (Papua New Guinea), Devesi (the Solomon Islands), and Teo (Tuvalu). In February 1983 she went to Jamaica and gave it to the Governor-General, Sir Florizel Glasspole. And there are seven surviving G.C.V.O.s from a tour of the West Indies in October 1985: Gordon (Belize), Cash (the Bahamas), Arrindell (St Christopher and St Nevis), Jacobs (Antigua and Barbuda), Eustace (St Vincent and the Grenadines), Springer (Barbados), and Scoon (Grenada).

The Queen gave it to Paul Reeves, Primate of New Zealand, on her visit of 1986; to Sir Antony Acland Ambassador during her state visit to George Bush in 1991); and to Sir Christopher Mallaby (Ambassador, during her visit to West Germany in 1992).

Patricia, Viscountess Hambleden, a Lady in Waiting to the Queen Mother from 1937, was given the honour in celebration of the Queen Mother's 90th birthday.

The Royal Family also includes a few K.C.V.O.s, H.R.H. Prince Michael of Kent receiving it in 1992 on his 50th birthday, and the Hon. Sir Angus Ogilvy in the New Year Honours of 1989. Captain Mark Phillips was given a C.V.O. in 1974, following the kidnap attempt in the Mall, and the Duke of York and Prince Edward were similarly honoured on their 25th birthdays.

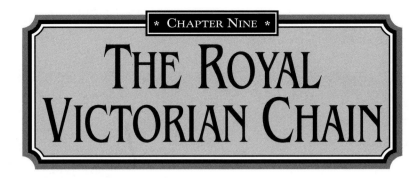

CHAPTER NINE

THE ROYAL VICTORIAN CHAIN

HE ROYAL VICTORIAN CHAIN is a rare and special honour in the gift of the Sovereign. It is sparingly given. Like the Order of Merit, it was founded by King Edward VII in 1902, and carried with it no rank or precedence. The Chain is worn around the neck by men and spread on a ribbon and bow by women (admitted since 1937).

The Royal Victorian Chain, as worn by ladies (above) and gentlemen (below)

Edward VII intended to keep the Order for royal personages and for certain eminent British subjects. Its concept came from the Continent where there existed certain chains used exclusively as family Orders. At the time of his coronation, the King gave the Chain to his brother, the Duke of Connaught, his son the Prince of Wales, and to other royal visitors and family members: King Frederick VIII of Denmark, King Haakon VII of Norway, Prince Henry of Prussia, the Duke of Argyll (husband of Princess Louise), the Grand Duke of Hesse, Prince Christian of Schleswig-Holstein (another brother-in-law), and his son-in-law, the Duke of Fife. The King also gave it to the Archbishop of Canterbury, Dr William Temple. Later in the year, he gave it to the Kaiser, and to King Carlos I of Portugal. An interesting later choice in the King's reign was Abbas Hilmi, Khedive of Egypt in 1905.

At present there are only nineteen holders, including the Queen, who never wears the decoration. It is held by two members of the British Royal Family, the Queen Mother and Princess Margaret. The former, given it by the King in the year of his Coronation, has worn it only at a ceremony of the Royal Victorian Order, the first one in December 1978. As worn by ladies it does not quite work. It looks a little ugly, the chain, spread out across the ribbon and bow of the Royal Victorian Order ribbon. Princess Margaret was given hers at Balmoral in August 1990 on the occasion of her 60th birthday. She appears to like wearing this Order, and wears it on state occasions in lieu of the riband of G.C.V.O..

Eleven of the holders are foreign royals, who have received it in connection with state visits. The Queen often gives it to a royal head of State when he or she comes here. Then she gives the Garter when they next meet officially for the return state visit.

*The Queen and the
President of
Germany during
her State Visit to
Germany in
October 1992. Dr.
von Weizsacker
wears the Royal
Victorian Chain,
and the Queen
wears the Order of
Merit of the
Federal Republic,
given to her in
London in 1958.*

The following fall into this category:

Princess Juliana of the Netherlands	1950
The King of Thailand	1960
The Crown Prince of Ethiopia	1965
(on the Queen's State Visit to Emperor Haile Selassie, his father)	
The King of Jordan	1966
The King of Afghanistan	1971
The Queen of Denmark	1974
The King of Nepal	1975
The King of Sweden	1975
The Queen of the Netherlands	1982
The King of Spain	1986
The King of Saudi Arabia	1987

Queen Margrethe of Denmark and Queen Beatrix of the Netherlands already had the
G.C.V.O. and have worn both G.C.V.O. and Royal Victorian Chain at the same time.
Princess Juliana, the Queen of Denmark, the King of Sweden, Queen Beatrix of the
Netherlands, and the King of Spain all received the Garter later. The other Kings were
not Christians and thus not eligible for the Garter.

Of the other holders, former Archbishops of Canterbury are usually given this honour when they retire. Lord Coggan received it in 1980, and Lord Runcie in 1991. There were many who felt that Lord Charteris of Amisfield might qualify for the Order of the Garter. There were certain problems about this, however. First he is of a Scottish family, so the Thistle might have been more appropriate, even though most of his activities were in the South of England. His elder brother, the Earl of Wemyss, is a Knight of the Thistle already, and it would have been odd (though not impossible) had the Queen given the younger brother a senior honour. No private secretary had ever been given the Garter, and the press, speculating about this, dreamed up the line: 'The Queen does not give the Garter to servants'. But Martin Charteris had gone on to give excellent service as Chairman of the Trustees of the National Heritage Fund, and Provost of Eton. He received the Royal Victorian Chain following his retirement from an extended public career in 1992.*

The other three members are General Antonio Eames (1985), President of Portugal from 1976 to 1986, and President Mitterand of France, given the Chain during the Queen's state visit to Paris in 1992, and the Federal President of Germany, Dr Richard von Weizsacker, given the Chain on the Queen's state visit to Germany in the autumn of 1992.

There is no evidence to suppose that the late Lord Mountbatten put in a bid to be given the Royal Victorian Chain, but he might well have received it on his 80th birthday, which would have fallen the summer after his murder. A great expert on Orders and decorations, he would not have been oblivious to the fact that it was the only additional honour that the physical frame could have borne. We shall never know.

The Royal Family after the 1978 Royal Victorian Order service. The Queen and Prince Philip with the Dean of Windsor, the Queen Mother on the extreme left, wearing the Royal Victorian Chain. Back left is Sir John Johnston (now a G.C.V.O.), and on the extreme right the present author (in his capacity as Lay Steward of St George's Chapel).

* Lord Charteris wears the Chain previously held by Lord Adeane, another private secretary so honoured.

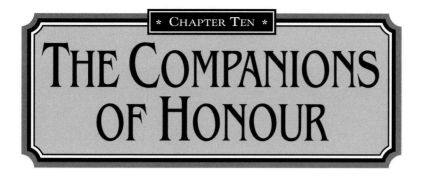

THE ORDER OF THE COMPANIONS OF HONOUR was founded by King George V on 4 June 1917, consisting of ordinary members and certain honorary ones. The Order was limited to fifty, with precedence before the Order of the British Empire.

The persons eligible were delineated as follows:

The badge of a Companion of Honour.

> Such persons, male or female, being subjects of Our Crown, and such Native Princes and Chiefs of India and such subjects of Native States of India, as may have rendered conspicuous service of National importance, and that the persons to be admitted as Honorary Members shall be Foreign Princes and Persons upon whom We may think fit to confer the honour of being received into this Order.[1]

This statute stands to this day.

A good story is told in Sarah Bradford's biography of Sir Sacheverell Sitwell concerning the efforts needed to obtain this order for a worthy candidate. As Sitwell neared his 80th birthday in 1977, his friends began to put their heads together to obtain an honour for him. Foremost amongst these were Sir Edward Ford, Secretary of the Order of Merit, and Christian, Lady Hesketh. Sir Edward and Raymond Mortimer composed a letter to Downing Street, pointing out that Sir Sacheverell was the only one of the three Sitwells unhonoured.* The letter was signed by Kenneth Clark, Hugh Casson and others, but was unsuccessful.

Sarah Bradford believed that the mysterious Maecenas Committee (which advises on honours in the field of the arts) had blocked the honour. Approaches for honorary degrees were also made to several universities, resulting in a sole honorary doctorate from Sheffield University.

Later Sir Edward Ford again approached Downing Street, this time occupied by Mrs Thatcher. His link was the Cabinet Secretary, Sir Robert Armstrong. She turned

---

* Sir Osbert Sitwell was created C.B.E. in 1956 and C.H. in 1958. Edith Sitwell was created a Dame of the Order of the British Empire in 1954.

the idea down. But finally, in 1984, when Lord Gowrie was Minister of Arts, the award of Companion of Honour was granted. Gowrie said that Sitwell's 'original and influential contributions to connoisseurship'[2] must be recognised. Sitwell was then 86.

The Order has occasionally been used as a reward for ministers of the crown either removed from office or retiring. This practice was started by Harold Macmillan, who assuaged his conscience by giving it to people like Selwyn Lloyd, dismissed in the 'Night of the Long Knives'. Lord Kilmuir, Viscount Mills, John Maclay, Harold Watkinson (the Minister of Defence, who wanted to go back to private business), Lord Eccles, Charles Hill, and Selwyn Lloyd were victims of the Prime Minsiter's knife.

Selwyn Lloyd was the one who was taken by surprise. He had no wife, no other life, no business. He refused a peerage. After his meeting with the Prime Minister, Macmillan told his Principal Private Secretary, Tim Bligh, to telephone him 'and say that in the emotion of our talk I had forgotten to offer him a C.H. Would he like it?'[3] Lloyd accepted it. David Watkinson 'went quietly'[4] with a C.H. for comfort. The incident was summed up by Jeremy Thorpe: 'Greater love hath no man than he lay down his friends for his life'.[5]

In this category can be put Lord Cledwyn of Penrhos (the former Cledwyn Hughes), Lord Carrington, who resigned as Foreign Secretary over the Falklands, Lord Tebbit (whose services in the 1987 Election campaign were highly successful and came after his near tragic involvement in the Brighton bomb of 1983); Lord Thorneycroft, Chairman of the Parliamentary Conservative Party and master-minder of Mrs Thatcher's first election victory in 1979; and the Labour minister, Lord Healey. The departing Ministers after the 1992 Election were likewise honoured: Kenneth Baker, Tom King and Peter Brooke.

There are other politicians: Lord Eccles, a long-serving politician, Lord Ashley of Stoke (the blind MP Jack Ashley); Lord Aylestone (the former Herbert Bowden, a politician, who was later Chairman of the IBA); Lord Glenamara (the former Ted Short, Labour Lord President of the Council); and Lord Joseph (the former Keith Joseph).

Lord Houghton of Sowerby is a notable holder, being Britain's oldest peer at the age of 95. He was a Labour politician, and was still active in the Lords in the summer of 1993, voting in the Maastricht debate.

Rt.Hon. Sir Keith Joseph, C.H.

Lord Goodman received his C.H. in 1972 from Edward Heath following his successful missions to and from Rhodesia. Heath hinted that if this was not good enough, something else would be made available. 'I could not think of anything better, so I agreed with alacrity,' wrote Goodman.[6] He was given his honour in private audience with the Queen: 'It was a tremendous privilege, and compared to lining up with hundreds of others in order to receive some trivial award like a knighthood, the conferment of the C.H. stands out as something of special quality and considerable pleasure.'[7]

Lord Hailsham and Lord Whitelaw received their C.H.s in the 1974 resignation honours list, but went on to serve Mrs Thatcher for many years.

Several holders of the C.H. have gone on to receive the Order of Merit – Professor Max Perutz, Sir Michael Tippett, Dr Frederick Sanger and Dame Ninette de Valois. Sir Edward Ford noted that it was important that the Queen's choice of O.M.s was not frustrated by the Prime Minister suddenly giving a C.H.. Indeed, the Companions of Honour are likely to provide good candidates for the senior Order.

The Queen has given it to several former Commonwealth prime ministers – to John Gorton and Malcolm Fraser (former Prime Ministers of Australia); to Pierre Trudeau (a rare British honour for a Canadian); to David Lange (Prime Minister of New Zealand); to Sir Brian Talboys (New Zealand's Minister for Foreign Affairs); and to the first ever Prime Minister of Papua New Guinea, Sir Michael Somare.

Art is represented by Victor Passmore, Lucian Freud and Sir Hugh Casson; literature by Anthony Powell, V.S. Pritchett and Sir Steven Runciman; architecture by Sir Philip Powell; the theatre by Sir John Gielgud*; science by Professor Sir Karl Popper, Sydney Brenner and Joseph Needham; academia by George Rylands; and music by Janet Baker.

James Jones (better known as Jack Jones), was the Secretary of the Transport and General Workers' Union, and Professor Stephen Hawking is the extraordinary mathematician, whose book, *A Brief History of Time*, has been such a long-term bestseller. David Astor received it for public and charitable work and Sir John Smith for conservation and heritage work.

There are two honorary Companions: Lee Kuan Yew, former Prime Minister of Singapore, and Dr Joseph Luns, former Secretary-General of NATO.

Sir Hugh Casson, C.H.

COMPANIONS OF HONOUR
The Viscount Watkinson (1962)

The Lord Houghton of Sowerby (1967)
Rt Hon. Sir John Gorton (1971)
The Lord Goodman (1972)
The Lord Hailsham of St Marylebone (1974)
The Viscount Whitelaw (1974)
The Lord Ashley of Stoke (1975)
The Lord Aylestone (1975)
Prof. Max Perutz (1975)
The Lord Cledwyn of Penrhos (1976)
The Lord Glenamara (1976)
Rt Hon. Malcolm Fraser (1977)
Sir John Gielgud (1977)
James Jones (1977)
Rt Hon. Sir Michael Somare (1978)
The Lord Healey (1979)
The Lord Thorneycroft (1979)
Sir Michael Tippett (1979)
Victor Pasmore (1980)
Frederick Sanger (1981)
Rt Hon. Sir Brian Talboys (1981)
Rt Hon. Douglas Anthony (1982)
Dame Ninette de Valois (1982)
Prof. Sir Karl Popper (1982)
The Lord Carrington (1983)
Lucian Freud (1983)
Sir Hugh Casson (1984)

The Viscount Eccles (1984)
Sir Philip Powell (1984)
Hon. Sir Steven Runciman (1984)
Rt Hon. Pierre Trudeau (1984)
Sydney Brenner (1986)
The Lord Joseph (1986)
Anthony Powell (1987)
George Rylands (1987)
The Lord Tebbit (1987)
Prof. Stephen Hawking (1989)
Rt Hon. David Lange (1989)
Rt Hon. Kenneth Baker (1992)
Rt Hon. Peter Brooke (1992)
Rt Hon. Tom King (1992)
Joseph Needham (1992)
Sir Victor Pritchett (1992)
Charles Sisson (1993)
Dr Elsie Widdowson (1993)
Hon. David Astor (1994)
Dame Janet Baker (1994)
Sir John Smith (1994)

Honorary Members
Lee Kuan Yew (1970)
Dr Joseph Luns (1971)

* Surely a candidate for the Order of Merit.

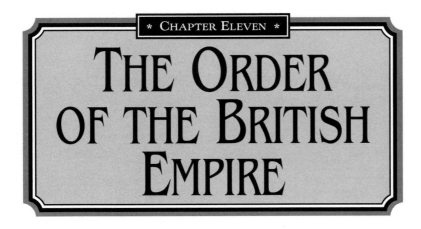

CHAPTER ELEVEN

THE ORDER OF THE BRITISH EMPIRE

THE ORDER OF THE BRITISH EMPIRE was founded in 1917. Of all the Orders it is the one most widely used to decorate British citizens in the two honours lists each year.

Before the the First World War, Lord Esher had proposed a new civilian order 'for persons connected with the Territorial Forces, charitable work of all kinds, missionary work overseas'.[1] George V duly established this new Order of Chivalry, in order that honours could be given more widely to deserving citizens for their war work. There was then no suitable decoration for the more junior ranks in the armed services, working back at headquarters, or in the camps and hospitals. And there was no suitable honour for women, who were suddenly liberated in the First World War, and played such a strong part in both the military and civilian endeavours of that time. While the Imperial Service Order took care of civil servants, there was no other Order for those ineligible for it, being outside the civil service.

At one point there was a scheme to enlarge the Orders of the Bath and Saint Michael and Saint George by adding a fourth and a fifth class, but this was rejected. It was clear to the King that a new honour should be instituted to provide a suitable award for people of every rank in the community, and in this respect the new Order was unlike the existing orders of chivalry. The others were basically reserved for those of high social standing. And they did not include women at that time, which the Order of the British Empire did.

It was also agreed that this new Order could be given to foreigners who helped the British war effort, and it was also open to members of the permanent civil service who had performed valuable war work. After its initial wartime role was fulfilled, the King wanted to use it to reward services to the state over a wide field, including those from the worlds of science, the arts and literature, and voluntary social and charitable workers. Members of the armed forces were equally eligible, if they had performed particularly hazardous work.

The badge and star of a civil Knight Grand Cross of the Order of the British Empire.

131

There was much discussion about the name to be given to the new Order. Rejected ideas included the Order of George and Mary, the Patriotic Service Order, the Order of the United Empire, the Order of the Imperial Crown, and the War Service Order. There were even plans to call it the Order of Saint Martin, the Order of Saint Lewis, the Order of the Golden Rose, or the Order of Mars. In the end the King decreed that it was to be called the Most Excellent Order of the British Empire, with five classes, and a medal.

At first the King intended that the first two classes should not carry knighthoods, and should rank immediately after Knights Bachelor; and there was even a suggestion that knighthood in these classes should be optional. But this quickly proved impracticable. Interestingly at this time a style had to be invented for ladies. 'Madame' had inappropriate connotations, 'lady' was too vague, so the rather awesome title of 'Dame' was adopted. It is interesting that the style of Dame only dates back to 1917, though it had unofficial usage in earlier times.

The King appointed the Prince of Wales as the Order's first Grand Master. He appointed the Duke of Connaught and Queen Mary in 1917, and Queen Alexandra in 1918. Later that year he appointed Princess Christian, Princess Louise and Princess Helena Victoria. In 1919 he appointed Princess Marie Louise. And another early Dame Grand Cross was the Empress Eugenie of France, who received it just before her 93rd birthday.

But despite this, the Order experienced all sorts of difficulties in its early days, some maintaining they deserved a higher honour. The O.B.E. came in for much criticism, especially as no limit on numbers was enforced. George Robey apparently appeared on stage wearing O.B.E. trousers, and Kenneth Rose records the Duke of Devonshire reading out a letter in the House of Lords from an honours tout with a knighthood for sale. The Duke added: 'not of the British Empire, no nonsense of that kind, but the real thing'.[2] There were cases of people recommending themselves. Gradually as the years went by, there were fewer appointments, the numbers were restricted, and the Order started to grow in general esteem.

The original riband was coloured purple, and when the Order was divided into civil and military in 1918, the military division was marked by a scarlet stripe down the centre. In 1937, when Queen Mary succeeded her son as Grand Master, the riband was changed to pink edged with pearl grey. The military division was thereafter distinguished by a narrow grey stripe down the centre. The motto of the Order is 'For God and the Empire'.

The original badge had the figure of Britannia in the centre, holding a trident and seated beside a shield bearing the Union Jack. Under a statute of 9 March 1937, this design was replaced by gold effigies of King George V and Queen Mary. This, evidently, led one man to complain in 1953 'on the grounds that it was bad enough to be using stocks of the medal so old that Queen Elizabeth the Second's grandparents were still shown; but far worse, that the riband was so old that it had faded from purple to pink'.[3]

Besides the different degrees of the Order, there was, until March 1993, the British Empire Medal, made of silver. John Major has effectively killed this now, though there were some appointments in the Commonwealth lists in June 1993. Gradually it will be phased out completely. On one side is Britannia and the motto of the Order, and the

The Queen leaving St Paul's Cathedral in the distinctive robes of the Sovereign of the Order of the British Empire.

words 'For Meritorious Service'. On the reverse is the royal cipher of the Sovereign and 'Instituted by King George V'. Bars could be attached to the medal by a person who has rendered services deserving additional recognition.

In 1960 the new chapel of the Order was dedicated in the crypt of St Paul's Cathedral, and there are services of the Order every four years in the Cathedral. The chapel was designed by Lord Mottistone and portrays likenesses of the founder and other sovereigns, and there hang the banners of the royal Grand Crosses, the Queen, Prince Philip, the Queen Mother, the late Princess Royal, the late Princess Marina, and Princess Alice, Duchess of Gloucester.

At the 1967 service, which celebrated the golden jubilee of the Order, the Queen and Prince Philip attended, along with the Duchess of Gloucester (Princess Alice), Princess Marina, Duchess of Kent and Princess Alice, Countess of Athlone. Forty-four Grand

133

Crosses walked in the procession, including seven distinguished Dames: Dame Helen Gwynne-Vaughan, the Dowager Marchioness of Reading, the Lady Spencer-Churchill, Dame Beryl Oliver, the Hon Lady Cripps, the Dowager Lady Freyberg, and the Countess Alexander of Tunis. Now, in 1993, there are only two non-royal Dame Grand Crosses.

The most recent service was in May 1992, at which only the actual holders of the different grades could be present – not their spouses – on account of the size of the Order. It was the 75th anniversary of the Order and to mark the occasion, the Queen gave permission for cuff-links, scarves and ties to be produced bearing the motif of the Order, so that these could be worn in rather the same way that Frenchmen wear the Legion of Honour in their buttonholes.

KNIGHTS AND DAMES GRAND CROSS

GRAND MASTER: H.R.H. the Duke of Edinburgh (GBE 1953)

Her Majesty Queen Elizabeth the Queen
    Mother (1927)
H.R.H. Princess Alice, Duchess of Gloucester
    (1937)
Dame Pattie Menzies (1954)
The Earl of Dalhousie (1957)
The Lord Cottesloe (1960)
Sir Colville Deverell (1963)
The Earl of Selkirk (1963)
Sir George Labouchere (1964)
Admiral Sir John Hamilton (1966)
The Lord O'Brien of Lothbury (1967)
Sir Robert Bellinger (1967)
General Sir Kenneth Darling (1969)
A.C.M. Sir David Lee (1969)
The Lord Benson (1971)
Sir Peter Studd (1971)
Sir Edward Howard (1972)
The Lord Shawcross (1974)
Sir Murray Fox (1974)
Sir Lindsay Ring (1975)
Admiral Sir Derek Empson (1975)
A.C.M. Sir Denis Smallwood (1975)
Sir Ronald Leach (1976)
The Lord Maclehose of Beoch (1976)
Sir Robin Gillett (1976)
Admiral Sir Peter White (1977)
Sir Robert Mark (1977)
Air Cdre the Hon. Sir Peter Vanneck (1977)
Rt Hon. Sir Roland Davison (1978)
A.C.M. Sir Peter Le Cheminant (1978)
Sir Yuet-Keung Kan (1979)
Sir Peter Gadsden (1979)
General Sir Hugh Beach (1980)

A.C.M. Sir Robert Freer (1981)
Sir Christopher Leaver (1981)
Admiral Sir Anthony Morton (1982)
General Sir Anthony Farrar-Hockley (1982)
Sir Francis Vallat (1982)
Sir Anthony Jolliffe (1982)
Admiral Sir William Pillar (1983)
Dame Mary Donaldson (Lady Donaldson of
    Lymington) (1983)
A.C.M. Sir John Gingell (1984)
Sir Alan Traill (1984)
General Sir Frank Kitson (1985)
Sir Allan Davis (1985)
Sir David Rowe-Ham (1986)
Sir Kenneth Newman (1987)
The Lord Plowden (1987)
Colonel Sir Greville Spratt (1987)
Sir Joshua Hassan (1988)
Sir Kenneth Berrill (1988)
Sir Christopher Collett (1988)
A.C.M. Sir David Harcourt-Smith (1989)
Sir Sze-yuen Chung (1989)
Rt Hon. Sir Thomas Eichelbaum (1989)
Admiral Sir John Woodward (1989)
Sir Hugh Bidwell (1989)
Field Marshal Sir Richard Vincent (1990)
Rt Hon. Sir Tasker Watkins, V.C. (1990)
Sir Alexander Graham (1990)
Admiral Sir Jeremy Black (1991)
A.C.M. Sir Patrick Hine (1991)
Sir Brian Jenkins (1991)
A.C.M. Sir Anthony Skingsley (1992)
Sir Francis McWilliams (1992)
Admiral Sir Kenneth Eaton (1994)

As will be seen from the above list, there are both military and civil holders. By and large the military ones are given to senior servicemen who are either not considered to merit the Grand Cross of the Order of the Bath, or they do merit a Grand Cross but there is none available. Of the existing ones, it will be seen that there are seven admirals, one field marshal, five generals, and eight air chief marshals.

Field Marshal Sir Richard Vincent was appointed a G.B.E. when it seemed that he had reached the peak of his profession as Vice-Chief of the Defence Staff, but he went further and became a Field Marshal.

Of the civil Grand Crosses, a great number of them are former lord mayors. It used to be the custom that the Lord Mayor of London was created a baronet, but that ceased in 1964, since which time each lord mayor (though not the present one) has become a G.B.E. instead. That accounts for twenty of them, including Dame Mary Donaldson, the only ever woman Lord Mayor of London.

Of the others, Dame Pattie Menzies (now 94) was the wife of the Australian Prime Minister; Lord Dalhousie was Governor of Rhodesia; Lord Cottesloe (now 93) was Chairman of the Tate Gallery; Sir Colville Deverell was Governor of Mauritius; Lord Selkirk was UK Commissioner for Singapore and South East Asia; and Sir George Labouchere was Ambassador to Spain. Lord O'Brien was Governor of the Bank of England; Lord Benson a senior Chartered Accountant and advisor to numerous boards; Lord Shawcros a barrister, and Chairman of the British Branch of the International Commission of Jurists. Sir Ronald Leach was another businessman and President of the Institute of Chartered Accountants; Lord Maclehose was Governor of Hong Kong, Sir Robert Mark and Sir Kenneth Newman were Commissioners of the Metropolitan Police; and Sir Roland Davison and Sir Thomas Eichelbaum were Chief Justices of New Zealand.

Sir Yuet-Keung Kan was Chairman of the Hong Kong Trade Development Council; Professor Sir Francis Vallat a Barrister and Member of the International Law Commission; Lord Plowden was Chairman of the Top Salaries Review Committee amongst other bodies; Sir Joshua Hassan was Chief Minister of Gibraltar; Sir Kenneth Berrill was Pro-Chairman of the Open University; Sir Sze-yuen Chung was Chairman of Hong Kong Polytechnic; and Sir Tasker Watkins, V.C., was Senior Presiding Judge for England and Wales.

General Sir Philip Christison, Bt, was the senior holder until his death on 21 December 1993. He was also the oldest living Grand Cross and reached his century on 17 November 1993. He was Allied Commander of Netherland East Indies after the war, and then G.O.C-in-C. Scottish Command and Governor of Edinburgh Castle. He was a keen ornithologist and published two books on birds.

CHAPTER TWELVE

THE IMPERIAL SERVICE ORDER

T HE IMPERIAL SERVICE ORDER was founded by Edward VII on 8 August 1902, the day before his coronation, in order to recognize 'more fully than had theretofore been possible the faithful and meritorious services rendered to Him by Members of the Civil Service of the various parts of His Empire'.[1] The Order was described as a new civil Order of Distinction.

The Imperial Service Order.

In 1954, the Queen changed the statutes slightly, confirming that 'Members of the administrative or clerical branches' of the civil services were eligible. There were to be no more than 887 Companions in all, with some extra ones having been appointed at the times of the coronations of George V, George VI and the present Queen. Of these 437 were for the home civil service, 200 for self-governing countries of the Commonwealth, and 250 for Colonies.

The Prime Minister or appropriate overseas Minister of State was to nominate recipients. And these recipients had to have given 'at least twenty-five years' meritorious service' (or in certain cases overseas, sixteen years). The Order was to rank next to the D.S.O. and holders had precedence immediately after O.B.E.s. The Order also had an imperial service medal for members of the civil service not eligible for appointment as Companions, in other words, lower Orders. The Secretary of the Order was the Permanent Secretary to the Treasury, and the Registrar the Secretary of the Central Chancery of Knighthood.

In 1959, the Queen increased the numbers to 930, with 480 in the home civil service. And in 1966, the Queen increased the number to 1,045, with 550 for home, 245 for the self-governing countries, and 250 for the Colonies.

The badge, which slightly resembled the 'E II R' as worn on a policeman's helmet, was surrounded by the motto 'For Faithful Service' and suspended from a red ribbon with a central blue stripe.

As part of his policy for doing away with almost automatic honours for the civil service, particularly for long service only, John Major abolished the Order in March 1993.

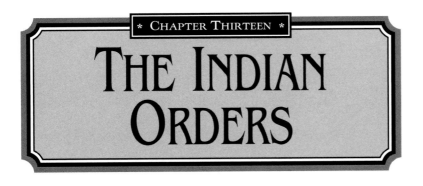

CHAPTER THIRTEEN

THE INDIAN ORDERS

HERE WERE THREE INDIAN ORDERS – the Most Exalted Order of the Star of India (created in 1861), the Most Eminent Order of the Indian Empire (created in 1868) and the Imperial Order of the Crown of India (1877). They were all short-lived as no conferments have been made since India was lost in 1947, and yet there have been some recent survivors and the Orders are still not entirely obsolete, partly due to the habit of giving them to members of the Royal Family, and maharajahs and maharanees at a youthful age.

The Begum of Bhopal, one of the rare ladies to be created a G.C.S.I. She wore the riband and star over the robes, which was not correct.

THE MOST EXALTED ORDER OF THE STAR OF INDIA (G.C.S.I.)

Queen Victoria instituted the Order of the Star of India on 23 February 1861, with the Governor-General of India or Viceroy as Grand Master. The first class of the Order were described as Knights Grand Commanders (rather than Crosses) in deference to non-Christian members. There were three grades, G.C.S.I., K.C.S.I., and C.S.I..

The G.C.S.I.s were either ruling princes or chiefs in India, or high officials in Britain who merited this degree of award for service in India. In 1911 King George V came to India with Queen Mary for the Delhi Durbar. One of the celebrations was the state investiture at which the Viceroy, Lord Hardinge of Penshurst, was present in the fabulous robes of the Grand Master. George V wanted to appear dressed as a G.C.S.I., but Hardinge felt that the King's robes would not then be as grand as his. The King finally agreed to wear Garter robes. Hardinge described the investiture of Queen Mary:

> The day before the investiture took place I suggested to H.M. that since the Queen was already a Knight of the Garter it would be very suitable to the occasion that she should also be made a Knight Grand Cross [Commander] of the Star of India, and he approved but wished it to be kept a surprise till the actual moment for investiture arrived, but naturally I made in advance all the necessary arrangements. As soon as all the official recipients of the G.C.S.I. had been invested I rose from my place on the King's right and having made a bow

to the Queen led her out of the tent to the great surprise of everybody, who could not imagine what was taking place. In the anteroom of the tent the Queen put on the robes of a Knight Grand Cross [Commander] and I then led H.M. back into the tent straight up to the King, who invested her with the insignia of the Order. The Queen's re-entry into the tent wearing the robes of the Order was very loudly cheered.[1]

Queen Mary was one of a very few ladies given the G.C.S.I.*

Lord Mountbatten was the last Grand Master, and his robes can be seen at Broadlands. The last surviving G.C.S.I. was Sree Varma, Maharajah of Travancore, a bachelor, who died on 19 July 1991. In *Burke's Peerage* in 1938, he was far from modest in his claims:

> Since his reign commenced, constitutional reforms, the construction of hydro-electric works in the High ranges and industrial expansion on a wide scale have been introduced. His benefactions include large sums of money for earthquake relief in Upper India and annual donations to several scientific bodies, and amongst his other charitable works he has established a Home for the Destitute and the Infirm. His Highness has given a special impetus to the development of the fine arts, for which the State has long been reputed, and he has founded a Picture Gallery at the capital in addition to the one he maintains in his own Palace. By a proclamation in 1936, His Highness threw open to all classes of Hindus without distinction (including those formerly known as untouchables) all temples under his control or that of the government. This act has been hailed as one of the greatest reforms made in India.[2]

The late Aga Khan in the robes of a G.C.S.I., leaving the Ritz in London for the Coronation of King George VI in 1937.

There could be a few surviving K.C.S.I.s – and there are certainly a few living holders of the C.S.I. A notable one is Vice-Admiral Sir Ronald Brockman, K.C.B., C.S.I., C.I.E., C.V.O., C.B.E., who served on Mountbatten's staff for many years, and is still active in the Royal Household as an Extra Gentleman Usher to the Queen. He rose through the ranks, with attendant orders from time to time as Mountbatten reached new heights.

The robes of the Order were sky blue satin with the star on the left side, and the collar was a valuable piece of bejewelled insignia, ornamented with many diamonds, consisting of the lotus of India, of palm branches, tied together, in saltier, and of the united white and red rose. The badge was an onyx cameo of Queen Victoria set in an oval, with the motto, surmounted by a star of diamonds, suspended from an imperial crown. The star used to be part of the design of the flag of India before Independence: a five pointed star, surrounded by the motto of the order 'Heaven's Light Our Guide', on rays of gold. The riband was sky blue edged in white.

The last time the insignia was worn conspicuously in public was by Lord Mountbatten at the Silver Jubilee celebrations of the present Queen in 1977.

---

* The Begum of Bhopal was appointed G.C.S.I. in 1872. Another Begum of Bhopal was appointed G.C.I.E. in 1904 and G.C.S.I. in 1910.

THE MOST EMINENT ORDER OF THE INDIAN EMPIRE (G.C.I.E.)

This Order was instituted by Queen Victoria on 2 August 1866, and given rather more freely than the Star of India. The G.C.I.E.s were people who had given distinguished service in India, meriting royal favour, or who were distinguished Eastern potentates. Like the Star of India, the holders have dwindled since the last appointments in 1947.

The badge of a Knight Grand Commander of the Order of the Indian Empire.

Again the Maharajah of Travancore was a G.C.I.E. and died in July 1991. The other most recent survivor was the Maharawal of Dungarpur, who was appointed in August 1947. He was born in 1908, and was a keen cricketer in his youth, who dreamed of playing at Lords until berated by the Viceroy for taking his sport too seriously. He was once present at a shoot in Bikaner where the bag was 4,000 grouse. He first married (to boost the state treasury) when he was 11, but was forbidden to sleep with his bride until he was 19. He added a second wife in 1928, soon after assuming ruling power. His father taught him to treat the Hindus and Muslims as one and the same, and he travelled widely around his state. In May 1947 he celebrated his Silver Jubilee, and was duly weighed against silver bars, the equivalent sum of which was distributed in rupees throughout the state for charity.

The Maharawal was actively involved in the difficult discussions about the handover of power in 1947. Mountbatten told the princes that the 'viable' states would survive. The Maharawal judged: 'This doctrine of viability ultimately slaughtered the Princes at the altar of Accession'.[3] He remained highly respected by local townspeople who garlanded him each birthday. The Maharawal accepted the loss of his power when Dungarpur merged with Udaipur and other states to form the Rajasthan Union. He was given his G.C.I.E. by Mountbatten the day before the transfer of power. He died on 6 June 1989.

There are several living K.C.I.E.s listed, and quite a large number of C.I.E.s, as this was the lowest grade of the Order and given quite freely to young people serving in India just before, during and after the war. Amongst the C.I.E.s, there are Air Marshal Sir Gerald Gibbs, Vice-Admiral Sir Ronald Brockman, K.C.B., C.S.I., C.I.E., C.V.O., C.B.E., again, and Alan Campbell-Johnston, the author, who wrote *Mission with Mountbatten*.

The Order's mantle was of imperial purple satin, with the star on the left side, and the collar was composed of elephants, lotus flowers, peacocks in their pride, and Indian roses, with an imperial crown in the centre, all linked with gold chains. From this was suspended the badge, an enamelled rose with Queen Victoria's head in the centre surrounded by the Order's motto 'Imperatricis Auspiciis' (Under the auspices of the Empress), surmounted by a gold imperial crown. The star was silver with a similar central piece to the badge, and the riband was of imperial purple.

THE IMPERIAL ORDER OF THE CROWN OF INDIA

This Order was for ladies and is rather attractive, being the royal cypher in a jewelled oval, surmounted by an heraldic crown and attached to a ribbon and bow of watered silk, pale blue in colour and edged in white. The Order was founded by Queen Victoria in 1877 and given to members of the Royal Family, ladies who were involved in Indian life, such as the wives of Viceroys, and some Maharanees. Receipt of the Order meant nothing more than that. It conferred no rank or title, though the ladies could use the letters 'C.I.' after their names. When India was lost in 1947, the Order became defunct to the degree that no further conferments were made.

Not surprisingly there are few survivors. Queen Elizabeth the Queen Mother (now 93) received it in 1931, and used to wear it as Duchess of York. It can thus been seen in certain portraits of her, but she has not worn it since she became Queen consort in 1937.

The present Queen received it in 1947. When the King realised that India was going he very quickly gave it to his two daughters, the first decorations they received. The Queen wore it occasionally in the late 1940s, and most notably when she received her Commonwealth Prime Ministers at the time of the Coronation. But since then she has not worn it. She wore it regularly as a medal when in Guards uniform at the annual Birthday Parade (or Trooping the Colour, as it is wrongly known), and she has not worn it since she gave up riding in the Parade in 1986.

Princess Alice, Duchess of Gloucester received it in 1937 at the time of George VI's coronation. She used to wear it in evening dress, but being 92 no longer attends full-dress evening occasions.

Princess Margaret received it on the same day as her sister, and she too sometimes wears it, though she sometimes prefers just to wear the Royal Victorian Chain. Both Princess Alice and Princess Margaret wear it as a medal when in uniform.

The other listed survivor is the Maharani of Travancore, who was given it in King George V's birthday honours list, 3 June 1929. Her name is still listed each year in *Whitaker's Almanack* and she was certainly alive in 1984, at the age of 89. By then she had been the matriarch of the family for many decades.

The Maharani's story is rather a fascinating one. She was born in 1895, and succeeded the Maharajah of Travancore, a man described by Pierre Loti as 'of cultivated and defined tastes and a most amiable Prince'.[4] He was born in 1857, became Maharajah in 1885 and died in 1924. So respected was he that he was allowed a twenty-one gun salute, rather than the allocated nineteen.

Setu Lakshmi Bai was not the mother of the new Maharajah. The succession laws in Travancore are rather odd. The Maharajah is succeeded by whichever male of the family is the senior in age, be it a younger brother of the old Maharajah or the son of one of his sisters. In this case it was a nephew, then too young.

Her Highness Sri Padmanabha Sevini Vanchi Dharma Vardhini Raja Rajeswari Maharani Setu Lakshmi Bai (to giver her her full title) served as Regent until 1931, when the last Maharajah, a G.C.S.I. and G.C.I.E. as mentioned above (1912-1991) assumed power.

Originally she was adopted by the then Senior Maharani in 1900 when she was 4. The idea was that in the fullness of time she might produce a new Maharajah. Every day she had to prostrate herself before the family deity. Meanwhile she lived with the Senior Maharani at the Sundervilas Palace. At the age of 10 she was taken to a window to look down on a prospective bridegroom, one of two brothers from a branch of the Kilimanoor family. She chose the younger of the two, Rama Varma Valia Koil Tampurau.[5] She was married in 1906 at the age of ten, and thereafter her husband visited her for exactly an hour each day. The marriage was not consummated until she was 14. Instead they played hopscotch, or he read fairy tales to her. She was particularly fond of *Little Red Riding Hood.*[6]

The Maharani occupied a semi-divine status. During her regency, visitors would bow and place their gifts of flowers and fruit in a bowl in front of her as they could not touch her. Even her brothers and sisters called her 'Your Highness'. As late as in the 1940s, every time the Maharani came into the courtyard of her palace, the Satelmond Palace in Trivandrum, South India, forty or fifty *pattakers* (attendants) bowed seven times to the floor.

Of more recent holders of the order, a notable lady was Doreen, Lady Brabourne, who died as a result of the explosion in which Lord Mountbatten was murdered in Ireland in August 1979.

CHAPTER FOURTEEN

THE ROYAL FAMILY ORDERS

THERE IS EVIDENCE that King George IV gave out a Royal Family Order, among others, to his sister, the Princess Royal, married to the King of Wurttemberg, and to his niece, Augusta, Grand Duchess of Mecklenburg-Strelitz (Queen Mary's aunt), and both these decorations exist in the Royal Collection at Windsor. Then on one of the few times the future Queen Victoria met her uncle, he gave her his image suspended from a ribbon.

Unlike other Orders, these are given out privately and informally by the Sovereign of the day to the ladies of the Royal Family. Nowadays they are only worn in full evening dress with other decorations (or occasionally on their own). There have been occasions when brides of the Royal House, or brides marrying into the Royal House, have worn the Royal Family Order on their wedding dresses.

The Queen and Princess Margaret had the Orders of their father and grandfather as little girls and wore both at the 1937 coronation. Princess Anne got hers in 1969.

There have been times when these decorations have been worn with day dress. The present Queen and all the Royal ladies wore the Royal Family Order of King George VI at his funeral in 1952, and interestingly at the coronation luncheon at Guildhall in London in June 1953, they all wore their Royal Family Orders on short day dress.

In relatively recent times, the ladies of the Royal House wore long dresses and coats with hats and orders at Royal Weddings. Ribands, stars, and Royal Family Orders were thus displayed at the present Queen's wedding in 1947. But at Princess Margaret's wedding in 1960, the dresses were still to the floor, but the Orders had been put away.

Princess Alice, Countess of Athlone, the last grand-daughter of Queen Victoria, photographed by Lord Snowdon for her 95th birthday. She wears the Royal Family Orders of the Queen and George V, and the badge of the Order of Victoria and Albert. Her riband and star are the G.C.V.O.

QUEEN VICTORIA
The Royal Order of Victoria and Albert

Queen Victoria created her own Order, the Order of Victoria and Albert, which was founded on 10 February 1862, and given to Princesses of the Blood Royal and other ladies favoured by the Queen. She wore a decoration with a badge on which the Prince Consort's head was cut in front of hers. All the others were the other way round. The Order was a cameo of the Queen's head, suspended on a bow of white moiré silk, and worn on the left shoulder.

*Queen Victoria,
founder of the
Order of Victoria
and Albert and the
Order of the Crown
of India, wearing
both Orders with a
foreign order above.*

The Order was divided into four classes, and the last creations, shortly after the Queen's death in 1901, were: Princess Patricia of Connaught (later Lady Patricia Ramsay) (1902), and Princess Ena of Battenburg (later Queen of Spain). Lady Patricia wore it at the 1953 Coronation, and Queen Ena wore it in Europe in her old age.

Several holders of the Order survived into the present reign: Queen Mary (died 1953) and Queen Wilhelmina of the Netherlands (died 1962) were both First Class holders; Queen Elisabeth of the Hellenes (died 1956), Princess Marie Louise (died 1956), Princess Alice, Countess of Athlone (the last survivor – died 1981), and Princess Alfonso of Bourbon (died 1966) were all in the second class.

KING EDWARD VII

King Edward VII created a Family Order similar to the Order of Victoria and Albert, but it was not registered as an order in the same way. It showed the King's head suspended on a narrow blue ribbon edged in white and red.

The King gave out his Royal Family Order to: Queen Alexandra, the Princess of Wales, the Princess Royal, Princess Victoria, Queen Maud of Norway, his sisters Princess Christian, Princess Louise, Duchess of Argyll and Princess Beatrice, his sister-in-law, the Duchess of Albany, to his grand-daughters, Princess Arthur of Connaught and Princess Maud (later Countess of Southesk), and to Princess Alice, Countess of Athlone.

It has not been possible to obtain a full list.

KING GEORGE V

King George V's Royal Family Order is his image suspended from a moiré silk bow of pale blue. The King gave his Royal Family Order to Queen Mary, Queen Alexandra, Princess Mary, the Princess Royal (Princess Louise), Princess Arthur of Connaught, Princess Maud, Princess Victoria, Queen Maud of Norway, the Duchess of Connaught, the Duchess of Albany, Princess Christian, Princess Louise, the Duchess of Argyll, and Princess Beatrice.

Later he gave it to the Duchess of York (now Queen Elizabeth the Queen Mother), the Duchess of Kent (the late Princess Marina), the Duchess of Gloucester (now Princess Alice, Duchess of Gloucester), to his sister-in-law, Princess Alice, Countess of Athlone, and to his grand-daughters, Princess Elizabeth and Princess Margaret.

It has not been possible to obtain a full list.

George V's Royal Family Order.

KING GEORGE VI

As King Edward VIII did not have time to create a Royal Family Order, the next monarch to give them out was King George VI. His order showed an image of himself suspended from a pink moiré silk ribbon.

George VI gave his Order to Queen Elizabeth, Queen Mary, Princess Elizabeth, Princess Margaret, the Princess Royal, the Duchess of Gloucester, the Duchess of Kent, Queen Maud of Norway, Princess Louise, Duchess of Argyll, Princess Beatrice, and Princess Alice, Countess of Athlone.

He gave the Order to Princess Alexandra of Kent in 1951.

Today it is worn by the Queen, the Queen Mother, Princess Margaret, Princess Alice and Princess Alexandra.

George VI's Royal Family Order.

QUEEN ELIZABETH II

At the beginning of the reign, the present Queen also created a Royal Family Order, which depicts her image as in an early Dorothy Wilding portrait, and it is worn on a bow of pale yellow moiré silk. The Queen gave her Royal Family Order to Queen Elizabeth the Queen Mother, the late Queen Mary, Princess Margaret, the late Princess Royal, Princess Alice, Duchess of Gloucester, the late Princess Marina, Duchess of Kent, Princess Alexandra and the late Princess Alice, Countess of Athlone.

Later the Queen gave it to the Duchess of Kent, Princess Anne (1969), the Duchess of Gloucester and the Princess of Wales (1981).

She has not given the Order to the Duchess of York or Princess Michael of Kent.

Elizabeth II's Royal Family Order.

There are also a series of lesser versions of Royal Family Orders, but which look very similar, and these are the badges of the Queen's Mistress of the Robes, and Ladies-in-Waiting in their varying degrees. These are quite widely worn, even when the Queen is not wearing Orders, for the purpose of easy identification by officials.

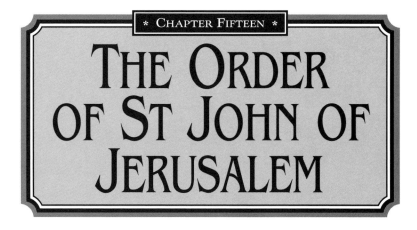

HIS ORDER IS not quite like the other ones in that it is not recognised in the same way. Its history is very ancient and it claims to be a revival of an Order founded by Queen Elizabeth I in 1559. But its origins also go back to the Hospitallers founded in 1092, and introduced into England in about AD1100. The Order of St John received a royal charter from Queen Victoria on 14 May 1888. It is an independent ecumenical Christian Order of Chivalry, and its members have to be profess-ing Christians. Further royal charters were granted later and it received the title 'Venerable' in 1926. At the same time the Order was expanded as the result of an amend-ing Royal Charter and subsequent new statutes. By these the Order acquired five grades, like the other Orders of Chivalry, including the new grade of Bailiff or Dame Grand Cross. It also acquired the ancient Gatehouse of the old priory of St John at Clerkenwell, and from here the various branches of the British Order are administered.

The Queen is Sovereign Head of the Order and the Grand Prior is always a mem-ber of the Royal Family. Currently it is H.R.H. the Duke of Gloucester, who is an active participant in the affairs of the Order and has travelled abroad on its behalf. His father also served as Grand Prior until his death in 1974. Some members of the Royal Family are Knights and Dames of the Order, nominated by the Sovereign Head. There is a Lord Prior, currently Lord Vestey, and a Prelate, currently the Rt Rev. Michael Mann, the former Dean of Windsor.

The various grades of the Order are as follows. All Knights or Dames are styled 'of Grace'. To be a Knight or Dame of Justice requires certain genealogical or armorial qualifications. There is a Chapter-General, there are 'Original Knights of Justice', and Representative Senior Knights. The Bailiffs Grand Cross and Dames Grand Cross are the senior grade and this is very much a promotion, and a restricted one. The Bailiffs Grand Cross include the five Great Officers and twelve other knights with records of distinguished service to the Order. (Two of these are nominated by the Priories: Scotland, Wales, Canada and so on.) The Dames Grand Cross number seven (one of whom is a Priory nomination).

The next grade consists of the Knights of Justice, Knights of Grace, Dames of Justice and Dames of Grace. Then come the chaplains and Commanders. Grade four are the Officers, grade five the Serving Brothers or Serving Sisters, and Grade six the Esquires. (Knights nominate the Esquires, a Knight of Justice can appoint two, a Knight of Grace one). The star and badge of the Order are eight-pointed crosses, and the riband is of black moire silk.

The purpose of the Order is to encourage and promote ambulance, hospital and other charitable work. Obviously it is closely associated with St John Ambulance Brigade, branches of which are spread throughout the Commonwealth and indeed the world.

St John's Day is celebrated at the end of June. The Order has a service at St Paul's Cathedral, and in 1993 the Lord Mayor gave a luncheon afterwards.

There are a number of other Orders of St John in the world and the relationship between them is complex. Nevertheless on 14 December 1987, the heads of the five different Orders issued a joint declaration explaining their purpose as to 'provide a Christian answer to the problems of a troubled and materialistic world. They have a common devotion to a historical tradition and a unique vocation: the lordship of the sick and poor. They strive to realize their aim by mutual collaboration as well as by their own works'.[1]

In 1926, when the Order was enlarged, most of the Royal Knights and Dames were promoted to the senior grade.

Princess Margaret in the robes of a Dame Grand Cross of the Order of St John.

CHAPTER SIXTEEN

COMMONWEALTH ORDERS AND DECORATIONS

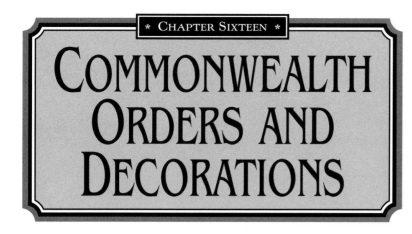

Australia

A USTRALIA'S RELATIONS WITH the British honours system is almost as complicated as their relationship with the Queen as head of state. That most ambitious of politicians, Mr Paul Keating (re-elected to serve as Australia's Prime Minister in a surprise vote in March 1993), has declared that he intends to hold a referendum on the Queen's continuance as head of state, with the aim of establishing a republic by the year 2001. This controversy still rages.

At the time of the Queen's most recent visit to Australia in February 1992, Keating attained world headlines by putting his arm around the Queen, a gesture about which he proceeded to make jokes at the Adelaide Festival a few weeks later. Mr Keating saw the opportunity of diverting the Australians from their economic problems by attacking Britain's role in the last war, a few days after the Queen left. This again achieved world headlines. In the ensuing discussions, Mr Malcolm Fraser, a former Prime Minister, gave his opinion that in such a referendum, the Australians would vote 60-40 in favour of retaining the Queen. Mr Keating made the republican question an issue in his electioneering in the Spring of 1993, and after his victory was quoted as saying that the Queen had not been in touch to congratulate him. In September 1993 he vistited Balmoral to inform the Queen in person of his wish to turn Australia into a republic by the year 2001. Interestingly, he was not supported by the socialist Govenor-General, Bill Hayden, who, during his term of office, came to see the advantages of a constitutional monarchy over untried alternatives.

When the referendum question was raised on the BBC Radio 4 programme, *Any Questions*, on 26 February 1993, all the panellists agreed meekly that it was an obvious

The Queen with her Commonwealth Heads of Government

progression for a new country to want to have its own president, and that the British should not interfere in the question.

In a statement issued on 19 October 1992, Mr Keating announced that Australian governments, both federal and state, would no longer recommend citizens for British honours. This announcement had the Queen's approval. It confirmed a policy that dated back to 1989, the last occasion when the Queensland government submitted recommendations for British awards. The various other governments had ceased making such recommendations some time earlier.

Mr John Paul, from the University of New South Wales, pointed out in the *Spectator* (21 November 1992) that this simply meant that neither the federal or state governments in Australia would recommend citizens for imperial honours. He made it clear that the Queen had retained her prerogative to appoint whom she pleased to the Garter, Thistle, the Order of Merit and the Royal Victorian Order. Whereas certain Canadians have lately been appointed Companions of Honour, this Order is not listed in the order of precedence of honours in Australia. The only holder in Australia now is Rt Hon. Malcolm Fraser, appointed in Silver Jubilee Year, 1977.

Australians were appointed to the Garter – the late Lord Casey in 1969, and the late Sir Paul Hasluck in 1979 (both were former Governor Generals). The Queen gave the Thistle to Sir Robert Menzies, Prime Minister of Australia 1939 to 1941 and 1949 to 1966. In 1992 the Queen invested Dame Joan Sutherland with the Order of Merit at Admiralty House, Sydney (the Governor General's residence). She also knighted David Smith, Official Secretary to the Governor General, appointing him a K.C.V.O. in 1990.

Mr Paul made the further point that Australians residing in the United Kingdom are not debarred from accepting imperial honours, and that 'Australian citizens resident in Australia may be admitted to Imperial honours in an honorary capacity for services to Britain'[1].

The whole question of British honours in Australia predates the recent antics of Mr Keating by some twenty years. When Gough Whitlam became Prime Minister of Australia in December 1972, he immediately initiated moves to scrap the system of British honours in Australia.

Whitlam declined to be sworn of the British Privy Council on the grounds that he did not wish to be beholden to a British prime minister, who would have to make the recommendation.* He also took to heart what Pierre Trudeau, the Prime Minister of Canada, had to say – that he did not wish to find a conflict between his oath to the Queen of Canada and the Privy Councillor's oath to the Queen of the United Kingdom.[†]

The Privy Council in particular irked Whitlam. Sir Robert Menzies had favoured many appointments, which federal ministers enjoyed because they became 'Right Honourable'. But under Malcolm Fraser, with the support of Wilson and Callaghan, there were as many Australian privy councillors appointed in two years as under the sixteen of Menzies. Likewise certain governor-generals were appointed – Sir John

---

* Previously only Alfred Deakin (1856-1919), who first became Prime Minister of Australia in 1903, had declined to become a Privy Councillor.
† For example in the Vietnam War, the Queen of Australia and New Zealand was at war, while the Queen of Great Britain and Canada was not.

Kerr and Sir Zelman Cowen – while a popular earlier governor-general, Sir William Slim, was not. High Court judges in Australia also liked being appointed to the Privy Council as they could then sit on its Judicial Committee. According to Whitlam, in 1935, old Chief Justice Gavan Duffy, then aged 83, was refusing to retire in the hope that Lyons and Menzies would get him into the Privy Council, when they visited England. They failed to do this but his successor, John Latham, had to wait in suspense for a year.

The Order of St Michael and St George and the Order of the British Empire were the two Orders that flourished in Australia. Whitlam, as a Labour man, was against both and most particularly against knighthoods, while the Liberal Party were for them.*

There are obviously a considerable number of survivors of holders of British honours in Australia. The Order of St Michael and St George flourishes there, with many recipients making a point of attending the annual service at St Paul's Cathedral each July. In 1992 when Lord Carrington was visiting Melbourne, a dinner was held, at which he presided as Chancellor and which was attended by many holders of the Order. Australians in that Order often coincide their annual visits to London in order to attend the annual service of the Order in St Paul's Cathedral.

There are a few Dames of the Order of the British Empire, notably Dame Pattie Menzies, G.B.E. (born 1899), widow of the Prime Minister; Dame Elisabeth Murdoch, D.B.E. (born 1909), mother of the newspaper publisher, Rupert Murdoch; Hon. Dame Roma Mitchell, D.B.E. (born 1913), Governor of South Australia; Dame Mary Durack, D.B.E. (born 1913), the novelist; Dame Beryl Beaurepaire, D.B.E. (born 1923), Convenor of National Women's Advisory Council, Australia; and Dame Joan Sutherland, O.M., D.B.E. (born 1926), the famous opera singer.

The Queen normally created the Governor-General a G.C.V.O., and gave a state governor a K.C.V.O. after she had stayed with him.[†]

Gough Whitlam admitted that he had been responsible for a great number of knighted justices of the High Court, having recommended in 1955 that if they were to be knighted this should happen the moment they were appointed. That great anglophile and lover of honours, Sir Robert Menzies, instantly adopted the idea and knighted each new appointment on the spot.[§] Whitlam refused to confer any honours, and after the 1974 when the Governor-General, Sir Paul Hasluck, told him that he had not sent off the recommendations of his predecessor, and asked him if he would like it

* The only Labour recommendation for a civilian knighthood was for Frederick Shedden, Secretary for the Department of Defence. He received a K.C.M.G. in 1943. Sir Isaac Isaacs, the first ever Australian Governor-General, was already a Knight when the Labour Prime Minister, James Scullin, persuaded George V to appoint him (after a long battle with the King). The second Australian Governor-General, W.J. McKell, was not knighted on recommendation by the Labour Party, but later by Sir Robert Menzies.

Similarly Labour premiers did not ask the British Government to knight their state governors, with one or two exceptions. The best case of breach of Labour rules occurred in Tasmania, when, in 1947, the Premier, the Hon. Robert Cosgrove (1884-1969), requested a D.B.E. for his wife, a K.B.E. for Chief Justice Burbury in 1958, and a K.C.M.G. for himself in 1959. All were granted.

† The later cession of recommending honours inevitably meant that some people missed out. The Queen was going to stay with the Governors of Southern Australia and Western Australia in 1974, but had to return home early to England because of the uncertainties of the February General Elections. But as the Australians were not recommending anyone for honours, she was not going to knight them. Prince Philip toyed with the idea of a K.C.V.O. for Australia's National Director of the Duke of Edinburgh's Award Scheme, but settled for a C.V.O..

§ Previously some had waited as long as twenty years.

sent, Whitlam said he would not.* Indeed the only such honour that Whitlam ever conferred was a spoof one, but one that is widely known. He appeared at the end of the film, *Barry McKenzie holds His Own* in a cameo role, to greet Mrs Edna Everage on her return to Australia. He embellished the script by adding the words 'Arise Dame Edna', and Barry Humphries' creation has been Dame Edna ever since.[†]

Whitlam dreamed up the idea of the Order of Australia in May 1967 when he asked the Prime Minister, Harold Holt, in Parliament, if he did not think that the Order of the British Empire was not 'so archaically named' and as such caused embarrassment to Australian diplomats and servicemen in South East Asia. Referring to the recently instituted Order of Canada, he asked for a similar system in Australia. What appealed to him was the Canadians' 'long-standing and bipartisan' practice of having an honour that did not include any titles.[2]

It all took some time as Harold Holt was drowned, and his successors, John Grey Gorton and William McMahon, did not take up the idea. But in Whitlam's time, it did happen, and they were fortunate to have the advice of Karl Lachlan, Secretary of the Order of Canada, whose services were made available to them by Pierre Trudeau. Thus in 1975, the Order of Australia was founded.

In 1991, the Governor-General, Bill Hayden, issued a booklet about the Australian Honours System, explaining that since 1975 Australia had been moving towards its own system of honours, awards and decorations, allowing for 'official recognition of outstanding and meritorious service to the community, exceptional acts of bravery in war or peace and notable and long service in particular fields of endeavour'[3]. The Australian system of honours began with the introduction of the Vietnam Medal in 1968. The Order of Australia followed in 1975, then various other decorations and medals.

It now consists of the Victoria Cross for Australia (1991), continuing from the British Victoria Cross, originally founded in 1856, and identical to it; four Bravery Decorations: Cross of Valour (1975), Star of Courage (1975), Bravery Medal (1975), and Commendation for Brave Conduct (1975); the Order of Australia; three levels of Gallantry Decoration, founded in 1991: Star of Gallantry, Medal for Gallantry, and Commendation for Gallantry; three levels of Distinguished Service Decoration, also founded in 1991: Star, Medal and Commendation; two Conspicuous Service Decorations, founded in 1989: Conspicuous Service Cross, and Conspicuous Service Medal.

Then there are several other medals:

Nursing Service Cross (1989) for nursing duties in both operational and non-
    operational situations by members of the Defence Force and others
The Public Service Medal (1989)
The Australian Police Medal (1986)
The Australian Fire Service Medal (1988)
The Antarctic Medal (1987) – for Australian Antarctic expeditions.

---

* Johannes Bjelke-Petersen, the Premier of Queensland, tried to recommend a larger quota for imperial honours after that, but after discreet discussions between Government House, Australia, Buckingham Palace and Harold Wilson, nothing came of it.
† This reveals Whitlam's further ignorance of the honours system, of course, as Dames are not dubbed in the same way as Knights.

Australian Active Service Medal (1988)

Australian Service Medal (1988)

The Vietnam Medal (1968) – for service in Vietnam

The Police Overseas Service Medal (1991)

Defence Force Service Medal (1982)

Reserve Force Decoration (1982)

Reserve Force Medal (1982)

The National Medal (1975) – for 15 years diligent service by members of the
   Defence Force

The Champion Shots Medal (1988) for Defence Force shooting contests

Finally, there are Unit Citations to recognise gallantry in action or outstanding service in warlike operations (1991): Unit Citation for Gallantry, and Meritorious Unit Citation.

The honour with the widest scope is the Order of Australia.

THE ORDER OF AUSTRALIA

The concept of the Order of Australia was presented to the Queen by Gough Whitlam in December 1974 and founded on 14 February 1975 as 'an Australian society of honour for the purpose of according recognition to Australian citizens and other persons for achievement or for meritorious service'[4]. At its foundation it was made clear that the Queen might still occasionally give out the Royal Victorian Order, that appointments to the Order of Australia would be made on her birthday and that she would hold the first investiture at a later date.* It took a few years to get it balanced correctly and there were a number of early amendments and changes. Originally the order had a 'Civil' and 'Military' division. In 1976 'Civil' was widened to 'General'. Until 1986 there were Knights and Dames of the Order, but that level was removed and the senior grade are now known as Companions. This means that the Prince of Wales, appointed in 1981, is a Knight, while his father, the Duke of Edinburgh, appointed in 1988, is a Companion.

There are few surviving holders of the former grade of Knight. These are:

Rt Hon. Sir Zelman Cowen (1977)   Hon. Sir Charles Court (1982)

H.R.H. the Prince of Wales (1981)   Rt Hon. Sir Ninian Stephen (1982)

Sir Roden Cutler, V.C. (1981)   Sir Douglas Wright (1983)

Rt Hon. Sir Garfield Barwick (1981)   Sir Gordon Jackson (1983)

Of these, Cowen and Stephen are former Governors-General, Cutler was Governor of New South Wales from 1966-1982, Barwick was Chief Justice of Australia, Court was Premier of Western Australia 1974-82, Wright was Chancellor of Melbourne University, and Jackson a senior businessman dedicated to charitable work. The last two are the only two men in the world who are 'Sirs' and not part of the British knightage system.

There was only ever one Dame of the Order, Dame Alexandra Hasluck, appointed in 1978, the wife and lately the widow of the former Governor-General, Sir Paul

---

* This turned out to be 1977, in her Silver Jubilee visit to Australia.

The Sovereign's badge of the Order of Australia,

Hasluck. She was the author of many books – biographies and philanthropic works (such as a history of the Guide Dogs for the Blind Movement in Australia), and was a leading lady in the National Trust of Western Australia, who contributed to the Australian Dictionary of National Biography. Dame Alexandra died not long after her husband, in June 1993. Like the Knights of the Order of Australia, she was the only lady to be a Dame who was not part of the British system.

The above recipients wear a neck badge (or shoulder badge in the case of Dame Alexandra) and can also wear a Breast Badge. Their honour gives them the right to be called 'Sir' or 'Dame', and they can add the letters A.K. or A.D. after their names.

Today the Order's Sovereign is the Queen, while the Governor-General is Chancellor, and the Prince of Wales has precedence immediately after him. There is a council which consists of the Chief Justice of Australia, the Vice-President of the Federal Executive Council, the Secretary to the Department of Administrative Services, the Chief of the Defence Force, and fifteen others (selected variously by the Governor-General or nominated in other ways). The council considers nominations to the order, which are then sanctioned by the Governor-General, the Sovereign always giving her approval.

This is the major difference between the Order of Australia and the old imperial honours system. No more can politicians procure honours. They can recommend them, but they cannot grant them. It is the council that decides in its own turn.

Both the general and military divisions have three grades and a medal. The general division is also open to members of the Defence Force, and to people who are not Australians. The military division is obviously only open to members of armed forces.

COMPANIONS OF THE ORDER

This is now the senior grade and appointments in the general division are made 'for eminent achievement and merit of the highest degree in service to Australia or to humanity at large'[5]. Only twenty-five people are appointed in the general division each calendar year, and in the military division the entire number of appointments in any grade must not exceed 'one-tenth of 1 percent of the average number of persons who were members of the Defence Force on each day of the immediately preceding year'[6]. Of these the appointments of Companions must not exceed 5 percent of the above. The citation for military appointments reads 'for distinguished service in responsible positions'[7].

There are some well known characters in the list (as at June 1991) and selected at random: the late Dame Judith Anderson (1991), Australian by birth and best remembered as Mrs Danvers in the Hitchcock film of *Rebecca*; Sir Donald Bradman (1979), the cricketer; H.R.H. the Duke of Edinburgh (1988); Rt Hon. Malcolm Fraser (1988), former Prime Minister; Hon. Robert Hawke (1979), former Prime Minister; Rt Hon. Sir William Heseltine (1988), former Private Secretary to the Queen; the late Sir John Kerr (1975), former and controversial Governor-General; Hon. Dame Roma Mitchell (1991); Dame Elisabeth Murdoch (1989) and her son, Rupert Murdoch (1984); the late Sir Sidney Nolan (1988), the artist; Mr Kerry Packer (1983), the newspaper magnate;

Lord Shackleton (1990); Dame Joan Sutherland (1975); Barry Tuckwell (1992), the horn player; and Hon. Gough Whitlam (1978), former Prime Minister.

The Companions wear a neck badge on a riband. They use the letters A.C. after their names.

OFFICERS OF THE ORDER

Officers are appointed for 'distinguished service of a high degree to Australia or to humanity at large'[8] in the general division, and 'for exceptional service or performance of duty'[9] in the military. Only 100 are appointed each year in the general division, and the number of military officers must not exceed 20 percent of the allocated number each year. Inevitably the names of the officers are less well known generally, but glancing down the list, one finds: Alan Bond (1984) the now disgraced financier; L. Gordon Darling (1989), who succeeded in setting up the National Portrait Gallery of Australia in the Old Parliament House in Canberra; Stuart Devlin (1988) who designed most of the medals and insignia; David Malouf (1987), the novelist; June Mendoza (1989), the artist; Lady Potter (1988), supporter of the Australian ballet; John Truscott (1985), Director of the Melbourne Festival; and the late Brett Whiteley (1991), the artist.

The officers wear neck badges or shoulder badges, and are called A.O..

MEMBERS OF THE ORDER

Members in the general division are chosen for 'service in a particular locality or field of activity or to a particular group'. 225 can be appointed each year. In the military division they are chosen for 'exceptional service or performance of duty'[10]. Their insignia is more like a medal, and they use the initials A.M. after their names.

MEDAL OF THE ORDER

This is given in the general division for 'service worthy of particular recognition'[11] and in the military division for 'meritorious service or performance of duty'[12]. The Medal is a less impressive version of the members' insignia, worn as a medal.

As with the new arrangements within the British honours system, any person or organisation can submit a recommendation for an honour in the general division. The military recommendations come from the Minister of Defence. The Order of Australia has no religious affiliation. Recipients can surrender the honour if they wish by writing to the Governor-General, and their appointments can be terminated by ordinance.

The insignia of the order is the emblem – a single flower of mimosa, in the form of a convex disc. This is ensigned with the crown of St Edward, and in the centre of the convex is a blue circlet inscribed with the word 'Australia' in gold and two sprigs of mimosa, also in gold. This hangs from a riband of moiré royal blue silk, with a central band containing scattered mimosa blossoms of various sizes. The military division is differenced by a gold band on each side of the riband. The Order is given either by the Sovereign or the Chancellor (the Governor-General), and if people are given the Order in both general and military divisions, they can wear both insignia.

New Zealand

New Zealand also has two Orders – the Queen's Service Order, the garish medal of which adorns the breast of H.R.H. the Duke of Edinburgh, when in uniform, and like-wise H.R.H. the Prince of Wales, and the Order of New Zealand.

THE QUEEN'S SERVICE ORDER

The Order was instituted by the Queen on 13 March 1975, and comprises the Sovereign and one level of recipient only – Companions. These are chosen in two divisions: 'For Community Service' and 'For Public Service', and only thirty may be appointed each year. The criterion for appointment is that the recipients have either rendered valuable voluntary service to the community, or 'meritorious and faithful ser-vice' to the Crown. The recipients can place the letters Q.S.O. after their names, and in New Zealand they take precedence after O.B.E.s. Thus they are not relatively as important as Companions of the Order of Australia, or indeed of Canada. There are two ex-officio officers of the Order: The Governor-General, who serves as Principal Companion, and the Clerk of the Executive Council of New Zealand, who is the Order's Registrar and Secretary.

The badge of the Order is worn as a medal on the left breast by men, and from a bow by women. The badge itself is circular with five large petals and five small ones in frosted silver, representing the Manuka, an indigenous flower of New Zealand. In the centre is an effigy of the Queen, surrounded by the appropriate designation of award, and surmounted by St Edward's crown. The ribbon is a zigzag of whites and blacks in the centre with an ochre strip each side, a traditional Maori pattern. It produces a very noticeable effect when worn, perhaps lacking the discreet subtlety of other medal ribbons.

Princes and princesses can be made Extra Companions, for example the Duke of Edinburgh, and the Prince of Wales. And certain foreigners can be appointed hon-orary Companions.

Amongst its members, we find three former private secretaries to the Queen, Lord Charteris of Amisfield (1978), Lord Moore of Wolvercote (1986), and Sir William Heseltine (1990). Lord Charteris was much involved with the setting up of the Order. The Order is meant to be confined to New Zealanders. The Private Secretaries were given it in their capacity as servants of the Queen of New Zealand.

THE ORDER OF NEW ZEALAND

This is a particularly exclusive order, founded by the Queen as recently as 6 February 1987. It comprises only twenty ordinary members at any one time, and certain honorary ones. The ordinary members are people who have 'rendered outstanding service to the Crown and people of New Zealand in a civil or military capacity'[13]. They put O.N.Z. after their names, and men wear the badge suspended from their necks, while women wear it on a

The Queen and Prince Philip, wearing the Queen's Service Order of New Zealand. The Queen also wears the Order of the Garter. Prince Philip wears the Garter Collar, the Garter and Thistle star, the Thistle riband, and the badge of the Order of Merit at his neck. His uniform is that of Admiral of the Fleet.

bow on the left shoulder. There can be a few additional members appointed to commemorate special occasions, and the honorary members are basically non-New Zealanders.

The badge is gold, oval shaped and contains the Royal Arms of New Zealand, surrounded by a Kowhaiwhai pattern. The ribbon is ochre with a narrow white stripe near each edge. The insignia must be returned on the death of the holder. Again the Registrar is the Clerk of the Executive Council of New Zealand.

OTHER MEDALS

New Zealand also has the Queen's Service Medal, associated with the Queen's Service Order, and numerous other medals for acts of bravery, etc..

159

Canada

As with Australians, Canadians are entitled to accept certain British honours. But for some years, these have been much more restricted. No Canadians have been appointed Knights of the Garter or Thistle, and the only senior holder of such an Order, now living, is Rt Hon. Pierre Trudeau (former Prime Minister), appointed a Companion of Honour in 1984. The former Governor General, Rt Hon. Roland Michener was given the Royal Victorian Chain in 1973 and attended the service of the Royal Victorian Order in April 1992, dying the following August aged 91. Canada specifically recognises that the Queen gives out the three lower awards of the Royal Victorian Order, the C.V.O., the L.V.O., and the M.V.O..

In times gone by, the Canadian premier, W.L. Mackenzie King, accepted the Order of Merit from King George VI in November 1947, and Lester Pearson, Prime Minister of Canada from 1963 to 1968, accepted it from the Queen in May 1971 not long before his death in December 1972.

There exist special arrangements for the wearing of British decorations and medals received prior to 1 June 1972. In practice very few have been given since the 1930s.

Canada gave up the honours system as a sign of a move towards a more egalitarian state, but the Canadians soon realised that it was essential to have some way of rewarding public service, and so they invented their own Order. In 1967, they established the Order of Canada, and added the Order of Military Merit in 1972. Interestingly, unlike the British Orders which have strong religious connections, most having their own chapel, none of the recognised Canadian Orders has any such orientation.

Ladies' badge of the Order of Canada

THE ORDER OF CANADA

The Order of Canada was established on 1 July 1967, to mark the 100th anniversary of the Confederation. Its motto 'desiderantes meliorem patriam' means 'They desire a better country'. Originally the Order had only Companions and what they called a Medal of Service. But in 1983 it was expanded to its present form. The Order is now divided into three grades, Companion, Officer and Member, and the holders are allowed to use the initials, C.C., C.O., or C.M. after their names. The Order is defined as follows: 'It is a fraternity of merit, not a society of the elite . . . The three levels of membership are designed to embrace a spectrum of achievement and service in fields as diverse as agriculture and ballet, medicine and philanthropy. Those who strive for the betterment of their immediate communities or devote their talents to special causes stand with people who have gained high distinction on the national or international scene.'[14]

The Queen is Sovereign of the Order and the Chancellor and Principal Companion is the Governor General. The Chief Justice of Canada is the Chairman and he presides over the affairs of the Order, assisted by an advisory council. It is their job to assess the relative merits of those to be appointed and to recommend them to the Chancellor.

Any Canadian can be appointed to any rank, though there are only 150 Companions at any time (and the Governor General and his or her spouse, and likewise any previous Governor General and his or her spouse). Only 46 officers and 92 members can be appointed each year. Any Canadian can submit a name for recommendation, and then twice a year, just before New Year's Day or before 1 July, the new recipients are listed in the Canada Gazette. Later there is an investiture and reception at Government House. Members and officers can be promoted within the Order, but this rarely happens within five years of a previous appointment.

The Badge of the Order is 'a stylized snowflake bearing the crown, a maple leaf and the Latin motto'[15]. The designer was given only a short time to submit his design, and the story goes that he was observed dodging shoppers in an outdoor walkway of a somewhat exclusive shopping mall in Ottawa, trying to catch snowflakes and determine the best shape for his design.[16]

Male Companions and officers wear their badges suspended from a ribbon (white, edged in red) round the neck. Members wear theirs like a medal. Female recipients wear all three on a ribbon and bow. There are miniatures for all degrees and also a series of lapel buttons and brooches which can be worn at any time with street clothes.

There are three ways that membership of the Order of Canada ceases. The most usual is by death, but members can resign by writing to the Governor General. The third way is by 'the termination of his appointment to the Order by Ordinance'.

Each year the Lieutenant Governor of the province gives a reception for members of the Order in his province. In 1992, there were celebrations to mark the Order's 25th anniversary, which (in Toronto) included a gala at the Theatre Royal Alexandra and a dinner at Ed's Warehouse afterwards, both establishments owned by Mr Edwin Mirvish (known in Britain for his connection with the Old Vic Theatre).

The list of recipients of the Order stretches to some 82 pages, and for purely English eyes most of the names are unfamiliar. It is perhaps permissible to select the following for special attention: the Hon. Conrad M. Black, P.C., Officer of the Order 1990, and Robertson Davies, the eccentric author, Companion (1972), who was one of the sponsors of the festivities in Toronto. Rt Hon. Lester Pearson (who died in 1972) was appointed Companion in 1968, and le très honorable Pierre Trudeau, former Prime Minister, was appointed Companion in 1985. In the Order too is Leonard Cohen, the Canadian poet and singer, appointed Officer in 1991. Many children of the late sixties listened in rapt and mournful mood to his sad songs about love and separation, enjoyed his summons to 'Suzanne's' riverside retreat, sang along as he bade farewell to 'Marianne' and as he reminisced about long bedtime encounters in the Chelsea Hotel. Cohen is noted for his wry humour. In a recent album, he sang with splendid absence of tunefulness: 'I was born with the gift of a golden voice. . . .', and observed 'I ache in the places where I used to play'. A resident of Los Angeles, he is perhaps the most unlikely man to be an Officer of the Order of Canada.

THE ORDER OF MILITARY MERIT

The Order of Military Merit was founded on 1 July 1972, and is restricted to those serving in the Canadian Armed Forces, both Regular and Reserve. It has three levels of membership, almost the same as the Order of Canada, except that the senior grade are Commanders. It is awarded to those 'who have distinguished themselves through long-term, outstanding meritorious service in various duties'[17]. The Chief of Defence Staff is Principal Commander.

The Order has a complicated system of limiting its numbers. The constitution limits appointments to one-tenth of 1 percent of the average number of persons serving in the Canadian forces the year before. 6 percent of these can be Commanders, 30 percent officers and 64 percent members. There is no overall maximum membership. Nominations are published twice a year.

The badge is a cross with a red maple leaf on white, surrounded by the motto 'Merit. Merit. Canada', the whole surmounted by a crown. It is suspended from a dark blue ribbon, edged in orange.

Beyond this, the Canadian honours system consists of five decorations: the Cross of Valour, the Star of Courage, the Medal of Bravery, the Meritorious Service Cross, and the Special Service Medal (basically for bravery). Then there are six further medals representing exemplary service.

The Cross of Valour (C.V.) takes precedence over all other honours and is awarded for 'acts of the most conspicuous courage in circumstances of extreme peril'. It is not limited to Canadians, but there must be a Canadian connection.

The Star of Courage (S.C.) is for 'acts of conspicuous courage in circumstances of great peril'. The Medal of Bravery (M.B.) is for 'acts of bravery in hazardous circumstances'.[18]

Those invested with the Order of St John of Jerusalem are allowed to wear the insignia of that order in Canada, alongside other Canadian decorations, but members of the Order of Saint Lazarus of Jerusalem, which has operated a Grand Priory in Canada since 1962 are not meant to wear their insignia. At present efforts are being made to 'nationalize' the St Lazarus in Canada.

OTHER COMMONWEALTH COUNTRIES
Papua New Guinea

Interestingly Papua New Guinea still recognises the British honours system, and awards are announced in the Commonwealth section of the British honours list each January and June. Papua New Guinea used to be a colony of Australia, itself a colony of Great Britain. There had been discussions about Papua New Guinea becoming independent as early as 1963, at which time Gough Whitlam predicted they would become a republic. However, in the 1970s, Sir Martin Charteris, the Queen's Private

Secretary, received a representation to the effect that Papua New Guinea would like to have the Queen as Queen of Papua New Guinea for a decade or so, for the following reasons:

1   They loved and admired the Queen.
2   They appreciated that the Queen was above politics.
3   They wanted to continue to receive British honours.

As it has turned out, the Queen is still their Queen today, despite their independence from 16 September 1975, and the honours are still given. Indeed, when the Prince of Wales came to Papua New Guinea to represent the Queen at the Independence Day celebrations, he breakfasted at Government House and invested John Guise (the Governor-General designate), with the G.C.M.G., exhorting him: 'This is from Mother.'[19]

Gough Whitlam was surprised that the Papua New Guineans did not become a republic, but he acknowledged: 'The Somare Government*, however, came to regard the Queen as a symbol of continuity and consolidation. This could be done without maintaining Australian control because, on independence, she would act on the advice of the Prime Minister of P.N.G..'[20]

THE OTHER COUNTRIES

The only other Commonwealth countries to bestow imperial honours besides New Zealand and Papua New Guinea are Fiji, the Solomon Islands, Tuvalu, the Bahamas, Barbados, Grenada, St Lucia, the Cook Islands, Antiqua, Barbuda, St. Christopher and Nevis and the Grenadines. These honours are announced as part of the British honours list at the New Year and on the Queen's Official Birthday. Although it is being phased out, there were even some appointments to the B.E.M. in the June 1993 honours list, from New Zealand, the Bahamas, Grenada, Papua New Guinea and the Solomon Islands.

Several Commonwealth countries also have their own honours, St Lucia, for example, having 'The Order of St Lucia' which even has the grade of Grand Cross.

---

*   Rt Hon. Michael Thomas Somare, C.H. (1978), P.C. (1977), the first Prime Minister of Papua New Guinea 1975-1980 and again from 1982–1986.

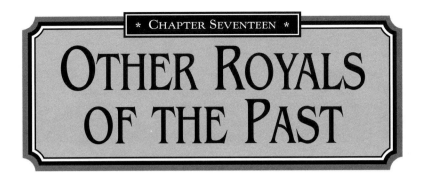

CHAPTER SEVENTEEN

OTHER ROYALS OF THE PAST

This section concentrates on members of the Royal Family who were alive in the present reign and also those children of Queen Victoria and King Edward VII who survived into living memory. The preoccupation with Orders of the three Kings, Edward VII, George V and George VI, which has been dealt with in detail earlier, is summarised here.

H.M. KING EDWARD VII
(1841-1910)

KING EDWARD VII'S attitude to Orders and decorations has already been made clear. He loved Orders and he liked to control who received them. He founded the Order of Merit, the Imperial Service Order and the Royal Victorian Chain. He was responsible for the distribution of a great number of the different degrees of the Royal Victorian Order.

He became a K.G. (1841), on his creation as Prince of Wales, but was not installed until 1858. He became an extra K.T. (1867) and an extra K.P. (1868) (being installed in Dublin on 18 April that year). He was appointed G.C.B. (1865), and served as Great Master of the Order of the Bath from 1897 to 1901. He was made K.S.I. (1861) (which became G.C.S.I.) in 1866, G.C.M.G. (1877), G.C.I.E. (1887), and G.C.V.O. (1896).

The King served as Grand Prior of the Order of St John, both before and after Queen Victoria's charter of 1888, becoming Sovereign of the Order in 1901. He was a Knight of Devotion in the Sovereign Order of Malta.

His elder son, Prince Albert Victor, Duke of Clarence (1864-1892), who died of influenza at Sandringham, was appointed K.G. (1883) and K.P. (1887). He served as Sub Prior of the Order of St John, under his father.

A house party at Knowsley in July 1907. In those days before the First World War, orders and decorations were worn more prominently and more often. King Edward VII is less adorned than his host, the Earl of Derby and the other guests. The King and Queen are seated in the centre, with Lord and Lady Derby either side of them. To Lord Derby's left is the bearded Earl Spencer ("The Red Earl") wearing the riband of the Garter. Behind Lady Derby is the Duke of Devonshire, K.G. Also in the picture is "the Blue Monkey" - the Marquis de Soveral, behind Queen Alexandra and Lord Derby.

165

H.M. QUEEN ALEXANDRA
(1844-1925)

*King Edward VII
and Queen
Alexandra.*

Queen Alexandra was the wife of King Edward VII and a Danish Princess in her own right, the daughter of King Christian IX of Denmark. Hailed by Lord Tennyson as 'The Sea King's daughter from over the sea', she arrived in Britain and was instantly beloved by the British people. She possessed beauty and elegance and, like all the most successful princesses in history, she loved to help the suffering. She established Alexandra Day when artificial wild roses were sold in aid of charity, and besides her care of humans, she was known as a great dog lover. Thus her place in the hearts of the British was assured.

As Princess of Wales, Queen Alexandra only received the V.A. and the C.I. like any of the other princesses. She was also a Lady of Justice of the Order of St John of Jerusalem (1876). But when he succeeded to the throne in 1901, Edward VII made her a Lady of the Garter, an honour that had not been given to a lady for over 400 years. She was appointed by special statute dated 12 February 1901. Then her son, King George V, appointed her a Dame Grand Cross of the Order of the British Empire on 1 January 1918.

Queen Alexandra was not known for punctuality, nor for her interest in Orders. Princess Marie Louise, the King's niece, recalled that on one occasion she arrived very late for a Court at Buckingham Palace. The King looked at her sternly and asked her why she was wearing the Garter star on the right side instead of the left. 'She merely smiled and answered that to wear it on the left side interfered with the arrangement of her jewels. According to her idea, it did not matter which side she pinned the Star!'[1]

H.M. KING GEORGE V
(1865-1936)

Like all members of the House of Windsor, King George V was a stickler for Orders and decorations, and would instantly spot one wrongly worn. In 1917 he founded the Order of the British Empire and the Order of the Companions of Honour.

Before coming to the Throne, George V was appointed K.G. (1884), P.C. (1894), P.C. (I) (1897), K.T. (1893), K.P. (1897), G.C.S.I. (1905), G.C.M.G. (1901), G.C.I.E. (1905), G.C.V.O. (1897), I.S.O. (1903), and he served as Grand Prior of the Order of St John of Jerusalem (1901-1910), becoming Sovereign of the Order that year. He received the Royal Victorian Chain in 1902.

H.M. QUEEN MARY
(1867-1953)

Her Majesty Queen Mary was born a Princess of Teck and though a descendant of King George III through her mother, Princess Mary Adelaide of Cambridge, she was only a Serene Highness. In her younger days she was short of money and relatively low of status, which partly explains why she adhered so strictly to such things in her later life. Queen Mary was engaged to the Duke of Clarence, a rather hopeless charac-

ter, who died before their wedding, at Sandringham in 1892. Queen Victoria was so disappointed at not having this perfect choice for future Queen that she arranged that she should then marry the next brother, the future King George V.

The wedding was celebrated in 1893. They became Prince and Princess of Wales in 1901, and succeeded Edward VII in 1910.

Queen Mary was a great lover of jewels, ceremonies and honours, and she wore them with immense dignity. Her ramrod back and majestic carriage belied a private sense of humour, but she could be fierce if things did not go to plan. Sir Ivan De la Bere, Secretary of the Central Chancery of the Orders of Knighthood, recalled a particular incident at the investiture of the present Queen as a Lady of the Garter at Windsor Castle in 1948. Normally the Garter ribands were hooked together tightly for an investiture so that they could not come unclasped. But as the King was being assisted by two Knights, he decided to have the riband placed over the new Knight by his assistants, and then he clasped it together himself. Sir Ivan, unaware of this plan until the ceremony was underway, had to work away surreptitiously on the tightly fastened clasps under the scrutiny of Queen Mary. He wrote: 'The look of disapproval which the author received from Queen Mary, who was sitting immediately next to the insignia table, at this apparently inexcusable mistake will never be forgotten.'[2] Only a year later did he get the chance to explain his crime, by which time Queen Mary was prepared to be amused.

Queen Mary was the holder of more British Orders than any other Queen Consort in history. She was appointed a Lady of the Order of Victoria and Albert by Queen Victoria, and likewise a Lady of the Order of the Crown of India in 1889. With these two Orders most British princesses had to be satisfied.

ABOVE: *Queen Mary, wearing the Garter riband and star, and the Royal Family Orders of George V and George VI. She also wears the Garter on her left arm.*

LEFT: *The Kings of Europe gathered for the funeral of Edward VII at Windsor. Back row, left to right: King Haakon VII of Norway, King Ferdinand of Bulgaria, King Manoel II of Portugal, Emperor William II of Germany, King George I of the Hellenes, and King Albert of the Belgians. Front row: King Alfonso XIII of Spain, King George V, and King Frederick VIII of Denmark. Amongst them are seven Knights of the Garter, and four holders of the Royal Victorian Chain.*

When George V came to the throne, he appointed her a Lady of the Garter (1910), and the following year she became a Lady Grand Commander of the Order of the Star of India to mark the Delhi Durbar in India. She was made a civil G.B.E. in 1917 on the founding of the Order of the British Empire and served as Grand Master from 1936, succeeding the Prince of Wales. She was also the first lady to be given the G.C.V.O. when the Order was opened to women by Edward VIII in 1936. In 1937 King George VI gave her the Royal Victorian Chain to mark his coronation.

Queen Mary was a Dame Grand Cross of the Order of St John of Jerusalem (1926) and R.R.C. (1910). She also held the Royal Family Orders of Edward VII, George V, George VI, and Elizabeth II. She normally wore the Garter riband and star (sometimes with the jewelled Garter itself on her left arm). She adorned this with the two Royal Family Orders of George V and George VI. Unfortunately she was too old to go out in public wearing Orders in the reign of the present Queen, into which she survived for but a year. Thus she was never photographed wearing the present Queen's Royal Family Order.

Queen Mary held certain foreign orders:

The Grand Cordon of the Legion of Honour, France
The Order of Al-Kamal, Egypt
The Order of Almar-i-Ala (1928), Afghanistan
Gold Chain of the Order of Saba, Ethiopia.

H.R.H. THE DUKE OF WINDSOR
(1894-1972)

The Duke of Windsor as King Edward VIII, wearing the Garter riband and star, the neck badge of St Michael and St George, and the Royal Victorian Chain.

The Duke of Windsor was no great lover of Orders and decorations, having suffered from being given too many of them for who he was and not for what he had actually achieved. He found it deeply embarrassing to have to wear medal ribbons on his uniform in the First World War, when his fellow soldiers were having to earn theirs at the cost of their lives. In this respect he was often in trouble, George V berating him for insulting foreign sovereigns by not wearing the Orders they had bestowed upon him.

In the middle of the war King George V wrote to him telling him to wear the ribbons of the French and Russian Orders which had been given to him. 'So get both the ribbons sewn on your khaki at once', wrote the King.[3] The young Prince replied: 'I feel so ashamed to wear medals which I only have because of my position, when there are so many thousands of gallant officers, who lead a terrible existence in the trenches and who have been in battles of the fiercest kind (many severely wounded or sick as a result) who have not been decorated.'[4] The Prince had a point.

When, as Prince of Wales, he travelled around Britain, he was inclined to send a message to his host seeking permission to dine in black tie, rather than full white tie and Garter insignia. This went down all right with Lord Harewood, who did not have the Garter (whereas his son did), and with Lord Fitzwilliam, but not with the Duke of Northumberland. He sent a message to the Prince to say that His Royal Highness could dine in his dinner jacket in the dining room but 'Buccleuch and I will dine in my rooms correctly dressed'.[5]

As Edward VIII, he distributed few honours, the most interesting being the appointment of his brother, the Duke of York, as a Knight of St Patrick, the last ever appointment in that Order. But he did open the Royal Victorian Order to women.

Following his abdication, there was a moment of real panic between the Duke and his future Duchess, at the thought that he might be demoted from the Order of the Garter.

In later life he was occasionally adorned with the Grand Cross of the Legion of Honour when he dined out officially in Paris.

The Duke's Orders and decorations are on display in the National Army Museum, Chelsea. They came there not long after his death at a time when the Duchess was still well enough to make decisions about such matters, and before her affairs were under the sole management of Maître Blum, the lawyer who 'protected' her during the long years of her illness.

Because he was King, the late Duke held the senior grade of all the British Orders. He was K.G., K.T., K.P., G.C.S.I., G.C.M.G., G.C.I.E., G.C.V.O. and G.B.E.. He was briefly Sovereign of the Bath and also held the I.S.O. and M.C..

As Prince of Wales, he automatically became a Knight of the Garter on 23 June 1910. He was invested and installed at Windsor the following year on 10 June 1911. His banner hung over the Prince's stall, then the Sovereign's stall, and finally as Duke of Windsor, he had yet a third banner over the third royal stall. There were certain occasions when the Duke wore his Garter star after the abdication, and in 1956 he was painted in Garter robes by Sir James Gunn.

The Duke's Garter insignia was Victorian, though parts were earlier still. The gold collar was made by John Edington of London in 1803/1804, the Garter itself by the same firm 1840/1841, and the Lesser George by William Culver of London 1864/1865. The star that was returned after his death was silver and enamel, of the Stuart pattern, and 'believed to have been reintroduced in 1946'. The riband as displayed in the National Army Museum shows signs of considerable wear, as well it might, having been worn intermittently between 1911 and 1972. It still possesses its bow.

He was given the G.C.M.G. on 21 October 1917, while serving as Captain 1st Battalion Grenadier Guards. Again there was only one badge interchangeable from riband to collar. He served as Grand Master until his accession.

In the same year he was made Knight Grand Cross of the newly formed Order of the British Empire, and again served as Grand Master until his accession (when Queen Mary assumed that role). His G.B.E. was of the old style, military, in other words a purple riband with central red stripe. He was appointed both G.B.E. and Grand Master on the day of the Order's foundation, 4 June 1917. He possessed just the riband, badge and star.

Thereafter honours came thick and fast. King George V made him a Knight Grand Cross of the Royal Victorian Order on 13 March 1920, the riband bearing no bow, and there being no collar issued.

He was given the two Indian Orders in 10 October 1921 just before he set off on his Far Eastern tour. The Duke's G.C.I.E. had only one badge, whereas the G.C.S.I. had a badge for both collar and riband. He received the Royal Victorian Chain on the day of his 27th birthday, 23 June 1921.

The Duke became a Knight of the Thistle on 24 June 1922. His Thistle collar, like that of the Garter, was made by Edingtons, in 1821/1822. The badge on the riband was made by Culver in 1867/1868, and the bow was removed.

He was appointed a Knight of St Patrick on 3 June 1927 (King George V's birthday). The St Patrick collar and badge was made by West & Son in Dublin 1887/1888.

Interestingly, despite becoming a Lieutenant-General in the Army in 1930, he did not hold the Order of the Bath until he became Sovereign. The first thing that King George VI did on 12 December 1936 was to appoint his brother a Knight Grand Cross of the Order. However the insignia of the Order were never issued to him. He was given the Imperial Service Order after the abdication on 1 January 1937, but the insignia were never issued to him.

The Duke was also a Bailiff Grand Cross of the Order of St John of Jerusalem. He became a Knight of Justice in 1917, served as Prior for Wales until 1926. He was also promoted to Bailiff Grand Cross in 1926. Only his riband and badge survive, the star having gone missing.

All these Orders and decorations he continued to hold as Duke of Windsor. The one he earned for himself was the Military Cross in 1916.

Like his brother, the Duke of Gloucester, the Duke thought the bows at the base of the ribands were effeminate, and he removed them.

The medals he wore with full-dress uniform were as follows:

Military Cross 1916
1914 Star (with one bar)
British War Medal 1914-1920
Allied Victory Medal 1914-1919 with one oakleaf
1939-45 Star
British War Medal 1939-45
Queen Victoria Diamond Jubilee Medal 1897
Edward VII Coronation Medal 1902
George V Coronation Medal 1911
George V Silver Jubilee Medal 1935
French Croix de Guerre 1915 with two oakleaves
Italian War Merit Cross 1919
Belgian Croix de Guerre 1918

The Duke was also awarded a great number of foreign Orders, which are listed below in order of gift:

Knight Grand Cross, House Order of Fidelity (1911) Baden
Order of Berthold (1911) Baden
Knight Grand Cross, House Order of the Golden Lion (1911) Hesse
Knight Grand Cross, House Order of the Wendian Crown (1911) Mecklenburg-Strelitz
House Order of the Principality of Hohenzollern (1913) Prussia
The Order of the Golden Fleece (1912) Spain*

170

* Retained at Windsor by Her Majesty the Queen.

Knight Grand Cross of the Legion of Honour (1912) France
Grand Cross, House Order of Duke Ernest the Pious (1913) Saxe-Coburg
Knight Grand Cross, Order of the Crown of Wurttemberg (1913) Wurttemberg
The Order of the Elephant (1914) Denmark
Grand Cross of the Order of St Olav with chain (1914) Norway
Memorial Medal (1914) Mecklenburg-Strelitz
The Order of the Annunziata (1915) Italy
Order of St Vladimir, 4th class, military division (1915) Russia
The Order of St George (1916) Russia
Military Order of Savoy, 5th class (1917) Italy
The Order of Leopold, military division (1918) Belgium
The Order of Michael the Brave, 5th class (1918) Roumania
Grand Cordon of the Supreme Order of the Chrysanthemum (1918) Japan
    (Collar presented 1921)
Order of the Royal House of Chakri, Siam
Grand Cordon of the Order of Mohamed Ali (1922) Egypt
Knight of the Order of the Seraphim (1923) Sweden
Knight Grand Cross of the Order of Carol I (1924) Roumania
Knight Grand Cross, Order of Merit, 1st class (1925) Chile (Grand Collar, Order of
    Merit (1931) Chile)
Knight of Order of El-Rafidain (1927) Iraq
Order of the Sun (1928) Afghanistan
Knight Grand Cross of the Order of the Sun (1931) Peru
Knight Grand Cross of the Condor of the Andes (1931) Bolivia
Civil Legion Star (1931) City of Vina dek Mar, Chile
Aeronautical Valour Cross, medal 1st class (1931) Roumania
Order of Christ and St Benedict of Aviz (1931) Portugal
The Order of the Southern Cross (1933) Brazil
Grand Cross of the Order of St Agatha (1935) San Marino
Token of Respect Award (1936) Tibet

These Orders were either given to the Prince of Wales on visits to German relations, or on overseas trips (such as the South American ones in the 1930s). Others were given on State Visits to Britain, notably the Carol I of Roumania, the Iraqi order, and the Afghanistan one.

The Duke received his Chrysanthemum on the visit to Britain of Prince Higashi Fushimo Yorihito on 21 September 1918, and was presented with the collar on the visit of Crown Prince Hirohito on 29 April 1921. Over fifty years later, after careers that neither Duke of Windsor or Emperor could have predicted, they met at the Duke's house in the Bois de Boulogne, during the Emperor's state visit to Paris, convergent worlds briefly re-united in old age. The Emperor's visit was the occasion for one of the very last public photographs of the Duke of Windsor, who died the following May.

The insignia of his British Orders were borne on cushions at his funeral. The Queen retained some of the Duke's insignia and Orders at Windsor.

THE DUCHESS OF WINDSOR
(1896-1986)

Interestingly in the Sotheby's sale of the Duchess of Windsor's jewels, a Silver Jubilee Medal (1977) was included.* Although the Duchess would have been too ill to recognise what it was, it is more than interesting that she was sent one. The Central Chancery's register records that she did indeed receive one in 1977.

One theory is that her lawyer, Maître Blum, would have insisted that the British Embassy sent one. However, the Ambassador of the time, Sir Nicholas Henderson, recalled that he was certainly not the person who caused it to be sent to her. It was sent via the Keeper of the Privy Purse.

The answer is that she was entitled to receive the medal, so the Palace sent her one without fuss or discussion.

H.M. KING GEORGE VI
(1895-1952)

King George VI loved honours and was as responsible as any of the present Royal Family for the ceremonies attendant on honours today. He particularly loved the Order of the Garter. Amongst his first acts as King was to confer the Garter on Queen Elizabeth, and to make plans for a Garter ceremony the following year. He also con-

---

* This Silver Jubilee Medal (Lot 104 in the sale) was sold with a Fashion Academy Award Medallion, inscribed on the reverse: 'Duchess of Windsor International Society', and various other pins and adornments. The estimate was 1,000-1,500 Swiss francs, and the price realised was 66,000 Swiss francs.

firmed the appointment of the Duke of Windsor as G.C.B. soon after the abdication. He revived the Garter ceremonies after the war, and managed on his own initiative to regain the Sovereign's right to appoint the Knights of the Garter and the Thistle.

During World War II the King bestowed the George Cross on the Island of Malta.

Before his accession, George VI was Duke of York. He was appointed K.G. (1916), K.T. (1923), K.P. (1936), P.C. (1925), G.C.M.G. (1926), G.C.V.O. (1921), and received the Royal Victorian Chain (1927). He was a Knight of Justice of the Order of St John (1917), promoted to Bailiff Grand Cross (1926).

In the last few days of his life, he was still preoccupied with the Garter, writing to Lord Halifax, the Chancellor, about the possibility of inventing some evening trousers that could take the Garter at the knee, instead of the need to wear breeches.

H.R.H. The Duke of Gloucester
(1900-1974)

H.R.H. Prince Henry was the third son of King George V and Queen Mary. A professional soldier, it was his dearest wish to command his regiment. This he was denied because of his royal duties. He served as Governor General of Australia from 1945 to 1947, but again the need to have the Regent Designate in Britain, when King George VI took his family to South Africa, meant that his term of office was foreshortened. In 1935, the Duke married Lady Alice Montagu-Douglas-Scott, and they had two sons, Prince William (1941-1972) and Prince Richard, the present Duke of Gloucester (born in 1944).

The late Duke of Gloucester was a man whose public duties involved the wearing of a great number of uniforms, and the late Stewart Perowne recalled the Duke taking the salute at a parade in connection with the enthronement of King Feisal of Iraq, in such broiling heat that the polish on his shoes blistered, while he remained resolutely at attention. As befitted a son of the Sovereign, a Field Marshal and Marshal of the Royal Air Force, the Duke held most of the British Orders. He was K.G., K.T., K.P., G.C.B., G.C.M.G. and G.C.V.O.. The Duke was given the Garter on his 21st birthday in 1921. He became a Knight Grand Cross of the Royal Victorian Order in 1922, a Knight of the Thistle in 1933, and a Knight of St Patrick in 1934.* This last appointment was made following a successful tour of the province of Northern Ireland. The Governor, the Duke of Abercorn, recommended him, with the approval of the Prime Minister, Lord Craigavon. The King reminded the Governor that appointments were made by him alone, and then gave it to his son. He was the penultimate Knight to be appointed and the last survivor in the Order. The Duke was made a G.C.M.G. in 1935 (following his attendance at the centenary celebrations of Melbourne, Australia). He received the Royal Victorian Chain in 1932.

He became a Knight Grand Cross of the Order of the Bath and the Order's Grand Master in 1942, following the death of his great-uncle, H.R.H. the Duke of Connaught. He was also a Bailiff Grand Cross of the Order of St John of Jerusalem (1930), and seved as Grand Prior from 1939 to 1974.

OPPOSITE: The Royal Family at the 1937 Coronation. From left to right: The Princess Royal and the Duchess of Gloucester, both wearing the G.B.E., the Duke of Gloucester in. Garter collar, Queen Mary with Garter riband, King George VI with Garter collar, Princess Margaret and Princess Elizabeth, Queen Elizabeth, the Duke of Kent with Garter collar, Princess Marina (the Duchess of Kent) with G.B.E. riband, and Queen Maud of Norway with G.C.V.O. riband.

---

*   The Duke was occasionally seen wearing the Order of St Patrick when inspecting Irish regiments as late as the 1960s. He was certainly the last Knight of St Patrick to wear the insignia in public.

The Duke was the holder of several foreign Orders:

Grand Cross of the Order of the Elephant (1924) Denmark
Grand Cross with chain of the Order of St Olav (1924) Norway
Grand Cordon of the Order of Leopold (1926) Belgium
Gold Collar of the Order of the Chrysanthemum (1929) Japan
The Order of the Seal of Solomon (1930) Ethiopia
The Order of El Rafidian (1933) Iraq
Grand Cross of the Order of Carol I (1937) Roumania
Grand Cross of the Legion of Honour (1939) France
The Order of the Royal House of Chakri (1940) Siam
The Order of the Redeemer (1942) Greece
The Order of Mohamed Ali (1948) Egypt.

The Duke took a great interest in uniforms, Orders and decorations. He detached the bows of the ribands he habitually wore. When he went to Ethiopia in 1958, he borrowed one of the Queen's smaller Garter stars to wear with evening tails.

The Duke began to suffer ill health in the mid 1960s. He last walked in the Garter Procession in 1965, though he attended the 1966 service, travelling to the chapel by car. Gradually he retired from public life, and then in 1968 a serious stroke deprived him of his powers of speech. He lived at Barnwell Manor, Northamptonshire until his death in 1974.

His Orders were carried in his funeral procession at Windsor, and this was the last time the Order of St Patrick was on public display.

H.R.H. PRINCE WILLIAM OF GLOUCESTER
(1941-1972)

The Duke's son, Prince William of Gloucester, did not live long enough to acquire many Orders. In his short career, he served in the Commonwealth Relations Office, was posted with the diplomatic service to Lagos, and then Tokyo, before returning to England on the instructions of the Queen to help look after his father's estates at Barnwell and to begin to take up normal royal duties. The Prince was killed in a flying accident while taking part in the Goodyear Air Race near Wolverhampton on 28 August 1972.

Prince William was a Knight of Justice of the Order of St John of Jerusalem (1968). There exists a photograph of him in the mantle of the Order at Buckingham Palace with the Queen in 1971.

H.R.H. THE PRINCESS ROYAL
(1897-1965)

The Princess Royal, only daughter of King George V and Queen Mary and aunt of the present Queen, was known in early life as Princess Mary and was held in great affection by the British people. Her image was a particular favourite amongst soldiers serving in the trenches in the Great War, to whom she sent gift parcels. Perhaps disappointingly, she did not make a glorious foreign match, but married the much older, weary-looking Earl of Harewood (then Viscount Lascelles). She spent much of her time at Harewood, though continued to take part in state occasions when it was necessary. Her bedroom at Harewood is open to the public and it is an uncomfortable proposition, where the bell pull can only be reached by climbing out of bed and crossing a draughty room to the fireplace.

There was an element of great modesty in this shy Princess, but this was laid aside when she donned her jewels and Orders. At the coronation of her brother, George VI, she was bedecked with splendid chokers, and again at that of the present Queen. The Princess used to wear a special star of the Order of the British Empire, set with over 350 brilliant-cut diamonds. This star was sold by her son, the Earl of Harewood, at Christie's on 7 October 1970 and was most recently sold again at Christie's for £20,000 on 14 March 1989.

The Princess Royal looked older than her years, dying suddenly of a heart attack at the age of 67, while walking with her son, Lord Harewood in the gardens of Harewood House. She was buried in the chapel in view of the house.

Normally, in full evening dress the Princess Royal wore the riband of G.C.V.O., and her diamond star of G.B.E. (though this was technically not correct as she should have worn the G.C.V.O. star instead). Then she wore the badge of the Crown of India, and three Royal Family Orders, given by the present Queen, King George VI and King George V.

The Princess Royal was a C.I., G.C.V.O., G.B.E., R.R.C., T.D., C.D., and G.C.St.J.. She was given the Order of the Crown of India in 1919, made a Dame Grand Cross of the Order of the British Empire in 1927, and became one of the first Dames Grand Cross of the Royal Victorian Order (when it was opened to women) at the time of the coronation of her brother, King George VI. She took a keen interest in nursing and was a Dame Grand Cross of the Order of St John of Jerusalem in 1926, and received the Royal Red Cross in 1953. She was also given the T.D. in 1951, and the Civil Defence Medal.

The Princess Royal does not appear to have held any foreign Orders at all. Her husband, the 6th Earl of Harewood, was K.G. (1922), G.C.V.O. (1934), D.S.O. (1918) and bar (1919), T.D. and a Knight of Justice of the Order of St John. Her son, the present Lord Harewood, has received no decorations for 'being royal' but was appointed K.B.E. in 1986 for his work in the world of opera.

H.R.H THE DUKE OF KENT

(1902-1942)

The late Duke of Kent, fourth son of King George V, was a glamorous figure, whose life was cut short when his aeroplane crashed in the fog of Scotland, while he was travelling on Air Force business during the war. He was more noted for his artistic interests than for his interest in honours and decorations, though he acquired a number of these in his short life.

The Duke was appointed a Knight of the Garter in 1923, on his 21st birthday, a Knight of the Thistle in 1935 in the year of his father's silver jubilee, and perhaps more significantly the year he became Lord High Commissioner to the General Assembly of the Church of Scotland, G.C.M.G. in 1934, the year of his marriage and G.C.V.O. in

The Princess Royal (Princess Mary), in 1937, wearing the riband of the G.B.E., the George V Royal Family Order, and the C.I.

*The Duke and
Duchess of Kent in
the Silver Jubilee
procession 1935.
The Duke wears
the Garter collar,
Thistle riband and
other decorations.*

1924. He was also Bailiff Grand Cross of the Order of St John of Jerusalem (1930) and Prior for Wales from 1936. He was given the Royal Victorian Chain by his brother, King Edward VIII, in 1936.

Interestingly the Duke was never a Knight of St Patrick, nor did he hold any level of the Order of the Bath, despite being a Rear Admiral, a Major-General and an Air Vice Marshal. The Duke held certain foreign Orders:

Knight of the Order of the Chrysanthemum Japan
Knight of the Order of Seraphim Sweden
The Grand Cross of the Order of the Lion Netherlands
The Grand Cross of the Order of Merit (1931) Chile
The Order of the Sun (1931) Peru
The Order of Christ and Aviz (1931) Portugal
The Order of the Southern Cross (1933) Brazil
The Grand Cross of the Order of the Redeemer Greece

Of these, he acquired the Chilean and Peruvian Orders when travelling with his brother, the Prince of Wales, and the Greek Order when he married a Greek Princess.

H.R.H. Princess Marina, Duchess of Kent
(1906-1968)

Princess Marina, Duchess of Kent, was born a Princess of Greece and Denmark, and after a troubled early life of near poverty, married Prince George, Duke of Kent in 1934. She was known for her great beauty and elegance, and wore clothes considerably more fashionable than those of the family into which she married. In the eight years of her marriage, she produced three children, the present Duke of Kent, Princess Alexandra and Prince Michael. She was widowed in 1942, but continued to live in London and at Coppins until her early death at the age of 61 from an inoperable brain tumour.

In the years of her widowhood, she undertook a large number of royal engagements, including several important Commonwealth tours. She represented the Queen at the independence celebrations in Ghana in 1957, and in Botswana and Lesotho in 1966.

Princess Marina was given several British Orders. She received the C.I. (1937), and the G.B.E. (Civil) in the same year to mark the coronation of King George VI. She was given the G.C.V.O. in 1948, the year of the King's Silver Wedding. She was also a Dame Grand Cross of the Order of St John of Jerusalem (1935) and held the Defence Medal.

Princess Marina had several foreign Orders:

Grand Cross of the Order of St Olga and St Sophia, Greece
Order of the Aztec Eagle, 1st class (1959) Mexico
Grand Cross of the Order of the Sun (1959) Peru
Grand Cross of the Order of Merit (1959) Chile
Grand Cross of the Order of the Southern Cross (1959) Brazil

The Greek Order is one given to ladies of the Greek Royal House. The South American Orders were given to her on her tour of Latin America with Princess Alexandra between 11 February and 19 March 1959.

THE DAUGHTERS OF KING EDWARD VII

The daughters of King Edward VII came from a generation of royalty whose ladies were not given great ribbons to wear. They had to be satisfied with Orders such as the V.A., given by their grandmother, Queen Victoria, the C.I., also given to most British princesses, and the Order of St John. Of the three sisters, only Queen Maud of Norway lived long enough to profit from a wider distribution of more glamorous Orders.

H.R.H. THE PRINCESS ROYAL

(1867-1931)

Princess Louise was the eldest daughter of King Edward VII and she married the Duke of Fife, a wealthy landowner, whose family had originally leased the land of Balmoral to Queen Victoria. She was a shy and retiring Princess, not well known to the British public. On a voyage to Egypt in 1911 to improve her health, their ship was wrecked in a gale, hastening the death of the Duke of Fife. In later life, the Princess spent much of her time in seclusion, fishing for salmon on the Dee from her home at Mar Lodge. She was the mother of Princess Arthur of Connaught and Lady Maud Carnegie (later Countess of Southesk).

The Princess Royal was a V.A., a C.I. (1887) and a Lady of Justice of the Order of St John of Jerusalem (1888). She also held the Royal Family Orders of Edward VII and George V.

*Queen Alexandra
with her three
daughters, Princess
Louise (later
Duchess of Fife),
Princess Victoria
and Princess Maud
(later Queen of
Norway).*

H.R.H. THE PRINCESS VICTORIA
(1868-1935)

Princess Victoria was the second daughter of Edward VII and Queen Alexandra, and the daughter that was kept at home by her mother. She could have married Lord Rosebery but this was not allowed. Thereafter she lived an embittered life, and her nephews, particularly the Duke of Windsor, called her 'The Snipe' because she never omitted to pass on any of their misdemeanours to her brother, George V, to whom she spoke every day on the telephone. She died in December 1935, bequeathing Coppins to the Duke of Kent, and precipitating the King's demise the next January.

Princess Victoria, like her elder sister, was a V.A., a C.I. (1887), and a Lady of Justice of the Order of St John Jerusalem (1888), promoted Dame Grand Cross (1928). She also held the Royal Family Orders of Edward VII and George V.

H.M. Queen Maud of Norway
(1869-1938)

Queen Maud of Norway was the youngest of the three sisters. She married Prince Charles of Denmark, who was elected King Haakon of Norway in 1905. Thereafter she divided her time between Oslo and Appleton House, King's Lynn, near Sandringham.

As a child, Queen Maud was a country-loving girl and something of a tomboy. When she went to live in Norway, she greatly encouraged her son, Crown Prince Olaf* in his love of yachting and skiing. But she never really liked Norway while she loved England and returned to Norfolk every year except during the Great War. Queen Mary's great-aunt, the Grand Duchess of Mecklenburg-Strelitz, gave her opinion that it was 'too horrible for an English princess to sit upon a Revolutionary Throne'!

Queen Maud was a close friend of her sister-in-law, Queen Mary, and after the abdication confided to her some less than charitable hopes as to the fate of Mrs Simpson.

Queen Maud outlived her brother, King George V, and she was present at the coronation of King George VI in 1937. She travelled in the carriage with Queen Mary, who created a new precedent by being the first Queen Dowager to attend a Coronation. Queen Maud died in London in 1938.

Like her sisters, Queen Maud was a V.A., a C.I. (1887) and a Lady of Justice of the Order of St John of Jerusalem (1888), promoted Dame Grand Cross (1928). And she had the Royal Family Orders of Edward VII and George V. These she wore at George VI's Coronation, along with the riband and star of the G.C.V.O. given to her by her nephew to celebrate the great event.

Being the wife of a foreign King, Queen Maud also had numerous foreign Orders.

Queen Maud of Norway.

H.R.H. The Duke of Connaught
(1850-1942)

Prince Arthur, Duke of Connaught, was Queen Victoria's third son. Arguably the Queen's favourite son, he was involved in military matters from an early age. At one time he was stationed in Canada and he held a command in the Egyptian War. Later he lived at Clarence House, and learned hindustani when in India, but his wish to be Commander-in-Chief in India was sadly unfulfilled. He did serve as Commander-in-Chief in Ireland, and he represented King Edward VII at the 1902 Delhi Durbar. In 1911 he was appointed Governor-General of Canada, serving there throughout the First World War. In his later years he often spent the winter at his villa in the South of France.

The Duke provides an interesting link in history. He was the godson of the great Duke of Wellington, and lived to be the godfather of the present Queen.

The Duke came from the generation of royalty who received every decoration possible.[†] He was a Field Marshal in the Army, and K.G. (1867), K.T. (1869), K.P. (1869),

---

* He ruled as King Olav of Norway from 1957-1991.

† As a professional soldier, the Duke worked his way up the Order of the Bath, earning his C.B. (1882), K.C.B. (1890) and then G.C.B. (1898). When King Edward VII came to the throne, he appointed the Duke of Connaught to succeed him as Great Master. The Duke's other brother, Alfred, Duke of Edinburgh (who died in 1900) was only given a G.C.B. when he commanded the Mediterranean Station in 1889.

*The Duke of
Connaught with his
brothers, King
Edward VII and
Alfred, Duke of
Edinburgh in 1893.
All three brothers
wear the Garter
collar.*

G.C.B. (1898) and Great Master (1901), G.C.S.I. (1877), G.C.M.G. (1870), G.C.I.E. (1887), G.C.V.O. (1896), G.B.E. (1917) (on its inauguration), and had the Royal Victorian Chain (1902). The Duke was Bailiff of the Order of St John (before the 1888 charter). He became a Knight of Justice (1905), Bailiff Grand Cross (1926) and served as Grand Prior from 1910 to 1939. He held numerous foreign orders too.

His Garter was given to him by his mother on her birthday when he was a mere 17. The Star of India was conferred on him on New Year's Day 1877, the first day on which Queen Victoria signed herself 'V.R. & I.'. At dessert, the Duke gave the toast: 'Queen and Empress of India'[6]. In the 1880s the Duke served as Commander-in-Chief in the Presidency of Bombay, returning briefly for his mother's golden jubilee in 1887, on which occasion he was created Knight Grand Commander of the Order of the Indian Empire.

His wife, H.R.H. the Duchess of Connaught, was a V.A., C.I., and R.R.C.. She is interesting as far as honours are concerned because she was unique in wearing the Order of the Victoria and Albert on a long riband from the left shoulder, as depicted in her portrait by Sargent.

The Duke's son, H.R.H. Prince Arthur of Connaught, was also well honoured. He was K.G. (1902), K.T. (1913), G.C.M.G. (1918), G.C.V.O. (1899) and curiously C.B., a rare example of a minor grade of an honour being given to a Prince of the Blood. Yet when he received it, his father, the Duke of Connaught, told him that he was most fortunate to get it. He was appointed Kinght of Justice of the Order of St John of Jerusalem (1905), and Bailiff Grand Cross (1926).

Prince Arthur was given the Royal Victorian Chain in 1906 (for the Garter Mission to Japan). He was sent to Japan on various occasions, and he served as Governor-General and Commander-in-Chief of the Union of South Africa from 1920 to 1924. Like many royal princes, Prince Arthur held several foreign Orders. While he was in South Africa, Great Britain was involved in the renewal of the Selborne Agreement. During the negotiations in 1922, relations between Portugal and the Union became strained whereas between Britain and Portugal everything was very friendly. The Portugese Governor-General stayed in Capetown for a while, and when everything was settled, he proposed to bestow the Order of Jesus Christ (first class) on Prince Arthur, and a lesser degree of the Order on his secretary, Captain Bede Clifford. But after consultations with the Dominions Office, it was agreed that these 'celestial' decorations should not be accepted. Clifford was disappointed.

'It's alright for Your Royal Highness,' he said to the Prince, 'because you belong to the Swedish Order of the Seraphin and your place in Heaven is therefore assured.'

'That may be,' Prince Arthur replied, 'but I am also a White Elephant – at any rate in Siam if not yet in South Africa!'

He married his cousin, H.H. Princess Alexandra, Duchess of Fife in her own right, who had the R.R.C. She was a Lady of Justice of the Order of St John of Jerusalem (1913), and promoted Dame Grand Cross (1926). Prince Arthur died of cancer in his father's lifetime, in September 1938, aged 55. Princess Arthur, who was matron of her own nursing home in Bentinck Street for many years, suffered from crippling rheumatoid arthritis in later life and took no part in royal engagements from 1946 onwards. She died in 1959.

The photograph that shows Prince Arthur most adorned with Orders is the balcony group following the Silver Jubilee of King George V in 1935.

The Duke of Connaught's daughter, Lady Patricia Ramsay, formerly Princess Patricia of Connaught (1886-1974), was a V.A. (1902), and a Lady of Justice of the Order of St John (1910), promoted Dame Grand Cross (1934).

THE DAUGHTERS OF QUEEN VICTORIA

Two of Queen Victoria's daughters lived into the reign of King George VI and interestingly they fared better than the daughters of Edward VII as far as honours were concerned. The first of these was Princess Louise, lately the subject of several biographical studies.

H.R.H. THE PRINCESS LOUISE, DUCHESS OF ARGYLL
(1848-1939)

Princess Louise was a sculptress whose large sculpture of Queen Victoria adorns Kensington Gardens to this day. She was the most intelligent, most artistic and most interesting of the daughters of Queen Victoria. She was also the least conventional and in recent years her reputation has been re-appraised by several biographers. In 1871 Princess Louise married Lord Lorne (later 9th Duke of Argyll), but they had no children.

Between 1878 and 1883, Princess Louise lived in Canada where her husband was Governor-General. During her stay she was involved in a tobogganing accident, losing part of her ear. Back in England, she led as bohemian a life as possible, entertaining artists and sculptors such as Sir J.E. Boehm, Sir Alfred Gilbert and Sir Lawrence Alma-Tadema. She gave strong encouragement to the education of women, founding the National Union for the Higher Education of Women in 1872. Amongst her own works of sculpture is the memorial in St Paul's Cathedral to Canadian soldiers who fell in the South African War.

Princess Louise was a V.A. (1st class) (1865), C.I. (1878), an R.R.C. and a Lady of Justice of the Order of St John of Jerusalem (1884), and promoted Dame Grand Cross (1926). In 1918 she was appointed a civil G.B.E., one of the first ladies so appointed, and then in 1937, George VI gave her the G.C.V.O. which it is unlikely she ever wore as she was by then too old to take part in state occasions and did not attend the coronation.

Princess Louise died at Kensington Palace on 3 December 1939, at the age of 91.

H.R.H. THE PRINCESS BEATRICE
(1857-1944)

Princess Beatrice was the youngest daughter of Queen Victoria, and the one who was meant to stay at home with her mother. However, in 1885, she was permitted to marry Prince Henry of Battenberg, on condition that they remained with the Queen. Her early life was thus occupied in fulfilling the difficult role of being Queen Victoria's closest confidante.

Princess Beatrice was the mother of two sons who died young, Prince Maurice of Battenburg and Lord Leopold Mountbatten, as well as of the Marquess of Carisbrooke, the last surviving grandson of Queen Victoria. Her daughter was Queen Ena of Spain. Princess Beatrice's husband died on the return from the Ashanti expedition in 1896.

Queen Victoria bequeathed her private journals to Princess Beatrice who then spent forty years transcribing these by hand, excising any material that was considered harmful, and then destroying the originals as her mother had ordained. She was the last surviving daughter, dying at Brantridge Park, Sussex, on 26 October 1944, at the age of 87.

Princess Beatrice was a V.A., a C.I. (1878), R.R.C. and promoted from Lady of Justice to Dame Grand Cross of the Order of St John of Jerusalem (1926). She was appointed a civil G.B.E. in 1919, and given a G.C.V.O. in 1937 as a coronation gift from George VI. Like her sister, it is unlikely that she ever wore it.

Princess Beatrice was also appointed to the Russian Order of St Catherine in 1874, which would seem to be a rare occasion for a British princess in those days.

Of the other daughters of Queen Victoria, it is worth noting that H.R.H. Princess Christian held all the usual orders as well as a G.B.E. (1918), and had the Russian Order of St Catherine (1874). She was appointed Lady of Justice in the Order of St John (1881). Both her daughters, Princess Helena Victoria and Princess Marie Louise received G.B.E.s at about the same time as their mother (*see below*).

H.R.H. PRINCESS ALICE, COUNTESS OF ATHLONE
(1883-1981)

Princess Alice, Countess of Athlone, was the last surviving grand-daughter of Queen Victoria, living 97 years and 315 days, and dying shortly before the engagement and marriage of the present Prince of Wales. A sprightly figure, she was still taking part in royal ceremonies until 1978, and on the occasion of the Queen's silver jubilee, she received and wore a Silver Jubilee Medal, the more remarkable since she had witnessed all jubilees and coronations back to Queen Victoria's Golden Jubilee in 1887 (some ninety years earlier).

Princess Alice was a V.A., G.C.V.O., G.B.E. and G.C.St.J.. She received the Order of Victoria and Albert from her grandmother, Queen Victoria, in 1898, when she was 15. George VI gave her the Grand Cross of the Order of the British Empire at the time of his coronation in 1937, and made her a Dame Grand Cross of the Royal Victorian Order in 1948. These two Orders she wore according to the whim of the moment, regardless of the seniority of the latter. Indeed the famous photograph taken of her by Lord Snowdon for her 95th birthday shows her adorned with the G.B.E. and her Order of Victoria and Albert (of which she was the last survivor by nearly seven years).

The Princess was made a Dame of Justice of the Order of St John of Jerusalem in 1904, and promoted Dame Grand Cross in 1926. She held two foreign Orders:

Dame Grand Cross of the Order of Christ (1918) Portugal
Dame Grand Cross of the Legion of Honour (1945) France

Princess Alice, Countess of Athlone, wearing the G.C.V.O., the George V Royal Family Order, and the V.A.

H.H. PRINCESS HELENA VICTORIA
(1870-1948) and

H.H. PRINCESS MARIE LOUISE
(1872-1956)

Princess Helena Victoria and Princess Marie Louise were the spinster daughters of Queen Victoria's third daughter, Princess Helena (H.R.H. Princess Christian – see above). The elder sister never married, though Princess Marie Louise made a brief, unfortunate match with Prince Aribert of Anhalt, which was widely considered to have been unconsumated. King Edward VII, her uncle, was attributed the cruel line: 'Poor Marie Lou, she came home just as she *vent*.'

Both Princesses were a part of royal life for many decades, always attending ceremonies such as the distribution of the Royal Maundy. Princess Helena Victoria can be seen in her wheelchair in the Queen's wedding group, with her devoted sister beside her.

Princess Marie Louise was the author of two books, *My Memories of Six Reigns*, and *Letters from the Gold Coast*. Princess Marie Louise was interested in honours. When travelling in the Gold Coast in 1925 she met a veteran soldier from the Gold Coast Regiment who was wearing Queen Victoria's 1887 Jubilee medal with a badly faded and stained ribbon. She offered to obtain another ribbon for him, but warned that it might take a long

Princess Marie Louise

time. Her interpreter assured her that the soldier would happily wait years for it, confident that 'the Great White Queen's grandchild' would not forget. Nor did she.[7]

While Princess Helena Victoria died in 1948, Princess Marie Louise lived on into the present reign and died in 1956.

Princess Helena Victoria was a V.A., a C.I. (1889), G.B.E. (1918), and R.R.C. She was appointed Lady of Justice of the Order of St John (1892) and Dame Grand Cross (1928).

Princess Marie Louise fared better as she lived longer. Like her sister, she was a V.A., a C.I. (1893), G.B.E. (1919), and R.R.C. She was appointed a Lady of Justice of the Order of St John and promoted Dame Grand Cross. The present Queen gave her the G.C.V.O. in 1953, which she wore at her coronation.

ADMIRAL OF THE FLEET EARL MOUNTBATTEN OF BURMA

(1900-1979)

No study of honours, royal or otherwise, would be complete without a detailed survey of the honour-seeking career of the late Earl Mountbatten of Burma. No man took such an interest in his own progress through life, no man acquired so many decorations or adorned himself with such a wide variety of them. When others appeared in morning dress, he thought nothing of appearing bedecked as an admiral, for example at the wedding of Princess Margaret in 1960.

On a cruise with Prince Philip in 1971 Mountbatten was caught out in Samoa, when the Samoans suddenly inisted on a full-dress arrival. Mountbatten therefore borrowed a set of Prince Philip's medals − ('I found I was entitled to every one, including the Greek War Cross and the French Croix de Guerre'[8]) − his Order of Merit, and a spare Garter ribbon without the Lesser George or Star. 'With all this borrowed plumage I felt somewhat embarrassed,' wrote the sea-dog 'but Patricia assured me I looked all right.'[9] He was extraordinarily bedecked with honours when he attended the coronation of the King of Nepal with Prince Charles in 1975, but from his own account, it was at the wedding of the present King of Spain to Princess Sophia of Greece in 1962, that he particularly excelled himself:

Earl Mountbatten of Burma, wearing the Garter riband and star, and stars of G.C.B., G.C.S.I., and G.C.V.O. and the neck badge of the O.M.

> After only five hours' sleep I had to get ready for eight hours of full dress. It was everything and the kitchen stove today. Five British stars, Greek and Spanish stars, the collar of the Garter and three neck decorations!* [10]

Lord Mountbatten's career was an extraordinary one. In his early days he accompanied his cousin, the Prince of Wales, on some of his successful world tours. He married a rich and glamorous heiress, whom he met at the Viceroy's house in India. He rose through the Navy to become First Sea Lord, serving on the way as Supreme Commander in South East Asia, and both as last Viceroy of India and first Governor-General after the transfer of power. In his later career he was Chief of the Defence Staff.

---

* Lord Mountbatten was disobeying all regulations about the wearing of stars. For some years now, the maximum has been four, whether British or otherwise.

'Lord Mountbatten loved honours and medals and jewels – not just for himself but for others too,' wrote his secretary John Barratt.[11]   According to Barratt, he was involved in a campaign to acquire a field marshal's baton for his 80th birthday, and had made many overtures to the Queen about this. He felt that the Queen might be resist-ing the appointment as she would have to pay for the baton, and even hatched a scheme whereby his daughters would pay for the baton. Nothing came of this as Mullaghmore intervened. Barratt wrote of the campaigns that Mountbatten waged to get knighthoods for Charlie Chaplin and Noel Coward, and when he obtained one for Jimmy Carreras, of Variety Club International, he cabled his congratulations: 'Once a knight is enough',[12] The one name he failed over was Barbara Cartland. He wanted her to be made a Dame. This only happened under John Major in 1991.

Mountbatten spoke openly of his love of honours:

> Ambition is a very funny thing. I only had one conscious clearly formed ambi-
> tion and that was to rise to the top of my profession, and obviously to succeed
> my father as First Sea Lord. I had a lot of idle sort of day-dreams lying in bed
> before going to sleep . . . I had a romantic feeling about the glamour of the
> Garter. I never thought I could get that. I thought the most worthwhile Order
> was the O.M.. I knew that was out of my reach . . .
>
> I think I've inherited a certain weakness about dressing-up. I come from a long
> line of dressers-up . . . I must confess it entertains me vastly to be dressed up and
> to have Orders and decorations. Except this: I want to have earned the uniform.
> I want to have earned the decoration. And then I'm very pleased to have it.[13]

There had been a fracas in December 1945 when Mountbatten was offered a barony. He played for time and eventually received a Viscountcy, but to his wife Edwina, he confided his true wishes: 'I would gladly have the Garter instead if deemed worthy of it. For God's sake be tactful about that. The Order of Merit would be the next best.'[14] The Garter came at the end of 1946.

Lord Mountbatten was very proud to be a Knight of the Garter, created along with the other war leaders, and he had a special Garter star made glistening with diamonds.* He was a Privy Councillor (1947), and held the G.C.S.I. (1947) and G.C.I.E. (also 1947), both Orders being automatically his as Viceroy of India†. Earlier, at the time of George VI's coronation, he was appointed G.C.V.O. and wore the robes of that Order at the 1937 coronation§. He became a G.C.B. in 1955¶, a year before being promoted

---

* This is now in the Mountbatten exhibition at Broadlands, along with most of Lord Mountbatten's robes and Orders, including the splendid robes of the Grand Master of the Order of the Star of India, and Grand Master of the Order of the Indian Empire.

† Lord Mountbatten continued to wear the Grand Master's Badge of the Order of the Star of India. He wore it at the Silver Jubilee celebrations of the Queen in 1977, below the Order of Merit.

§ Mountbatten was appointed M.V.O. in 1920 after serving on the Staff of the Prince of Wales on his New Zealand trip, and promoted K.C.V.O. in 1922, the star of which he wore on his naval uniform at his wedding to Hon. Edwina Ashley.

¶ Lord Mountbatten worked his way up through the Order of the Bath. In 1943 he was made a C.B. and in 1945 a K.C.B. When he met General Sir Kaiser Shumshere in Nepal in 1946, the General asked if he could examine his 'salad bowl'. He then scrutinised Mountbatten's medal ribbons which included the K.C.B. and the D.S.O. He said to him: 'Insufficient recognition, as I thought. I suppose a mixture of the King's fear of being accused of nepotism and the jealousy of the Commanders older than you.' [Philip Ziegler, *Personal Diary of Admiral the Lord Louis Mountbatten, 1943-1946* (Collins, 1989) pp.17-18]

from Admiral to Admiral of the Fleet, and received the Order of Merit in 1965 on his retirement as Chief of the Defence Staff and Chairman of the Chiefs of Staff Committee. He was also a Knight of St John (1943).

Lord Mountbatten's foreign Orders were numerous, and would have been more so had the Foreign Office not caused him to refuse so many. As his biographer, Philip Ziegler put it: 'Mountbatten collected decorations as others collect stamps.'[15]

Grand Cross of the Order of Louis of Hesse
The Order of the Rising Sun, 4th class (1922) Japan*
The Order of the Nile, 4th class, (1922) Egypt
Grand Cross of the Order of Isabella Catolica
   (1922) Spain
Grand Cross of the Order of Crown (1924) Roumania
Grand Cross of the Order of the Star (1937) Roumania
Greek Military Cross (1941) Crete
Legion of Merit (1943) U.S.A.
Distinguished Service Medal (1945) U.S.A.
Special Grand Cordon of the Cloud and Banner
   (1945) China
The Order of the White Elephant (1946), Siam[†]
Grand Cross of the Most Refulgent Order of the Star
   (1946) Nepal[§]
Grand Cross of the Legion of Honour (1946) France[¶]
Grand Cross of Order of George I (1946) Greece
Grand Cross of the Order of the Lion (1947) Netherlands
Grand Cross of the Military Order of Aviz (1951) Portugal
The Order of Seraphim (1952) Sweden

* This was given to Mountbatten on his trip to Japan with the Prince of Wales in 1922. He was never given any other Japanese Orders, and he refused to attend the state banquet for Emperor Hirohito at Buckingham Palace in October 1971. Had he done so, it would have been interesting to see if this lowly Order, given to an A.D.C. years before, would have got an outing.

† Lord Louis received this from the King of Siam at an investiture ceremony at the Boromphiman Palace, along with the Santi Mala Medal. The Foreign Office were grudging about his acceptance of these, saying they could only be worn on this occasion and thereafter were to be treated as war souvenirs. In his diary, Mountbatten wrote: 'I shall ask the Foreign Office to provide me with an explanation that I can hand to the King of Siam if ever I meet him at a State occasion in London and am not wearing his precious White Elephant. It is certainly quite the most expensive-looking order I have seen, and outshines any European order in magnificence.' [Philip Ziegler, *Personal Diary of Admiral the Lord Mountbatten, 1943-1946* (Collins, 1988), p.286] The star contains three white elephants, is backed with fabulous enamel and o'ertopped by a golden temple.

§ The investiture in May 1946 was a muddled occasion. The King began to invest Mountbatten, who thought the speech should come first. The speech was read by a general. Then the King pinned 'the biggest star' Mountbatten had ever seen on to him, hung the broad ribbon over his right shoulder and then put the collar round his neck. There was a salute of seventeen guns, after which Mountbatten made a speech. The star has sixteen spikey silver points and is indeed no small or discreet thing.

¶ Lord Mountbatten was invested with the Grand Cross and the Croix de Guerre by General Juin of France, at a ceremony at Les Invalides in Paris. Mountbatten wrote that his future son-in-law, Lord Brabourne, 'let the side down by smirking visibly when the General was kissing me on both cheeks'. [*Personal Diary 1943-1946*, p.341] Receiving this embrace, Mountbatten clutched the General round the waist.[18]

Agga Maha Thiri Thuddhamma (1956) Burma*
Grand Cross of the Order of Dannebrog (1962) Denmark
Grand Cross of the Order of the Seal of Solomon (1965) Ethiopia[†]
The Most Esteemed Family Order (1972) Brunei[§]

In later life, Mountbatten wore these Orders whenever he could find the appropriate excuse. He was also inclined to offer to show a particular decoration to friends. Somehow it would always be at the bottom of the case, and so all the others would come out first. There is no doubt that more than any other men (with the possible exception of Field Marshal Lord Montgomery), he derived the greatest pleasure from his extensive collections of honours.

He also wore a great number of medals, including the medals of several Orders, the D.S.O., two First World War medals, seven Second World War medals, five relating to coronations and jubilees, and five other miscellaneous ones (mainly foreign).

Lord Mountbatten arranged that the various Orders and decorations were borne in his funeral procession through the streets of London, a colourful adornment of an already impressive display.

COUNTESS MOUNTBATTEN OF BURMA
(1901-1960)

Edwina Mountbatten was highly decorated for a woman. This was partly because she worked very hard in the St John Ambulance Brigade, rising to be Superintendent-in-Chief in 1942, in which capacity she served until her death. It is also normal that the Vicereine of India be given honours commensurate with the position. When Lady Mountbatten appeared in her uniform with stars and Orders and particularly with medals, she must have seemed (to the uninitiated eye) as well decorated as a general. Though something of a Twenties party-goer when young, travelling widely and avail-

---

* The Order when translated meant: Highest, Great, Glorious, True and Law. As Mountbatten wrote in his diary: 'Put it literally, it means The Highest and the Great Glorious Commander of the Most Exalted Order of true Law; but put it liberally, it means The Highest and the Most Glorious Commander of the Most Exalted Order of Truth.' The Order is solid gold and platinum and includes a gold plate angled to go over the left shoulder, from each side of which twelve gold chains hang, joining it up and suspending the star at the front. When the President of Burma attempted to invest Mountbatten, he put it on the wrong way round, holding it over his head for him to put the wrong arm through. Mountbatten took control, as so often, and after much difficulty, the ceremony was concluded. The President pronounced a citation wholly pleasing to the Earl. [Philip Ziegler, *From Shore to Shore* (Collins, 1989), pp.17-18]

[†] Mountbatten visited Ethiopia in 1953, but was forbidden by the Foreign Office to accept a splendid diamond encrusted Order from Emperor Haile Selassie. This was on account of Field Marshal Montgomery having accepted one some years before. The Emperor invested Mountbatten with the broad ribbon, the solid gold star and badge in the Throne Room in the Palace at Addis Abba in front of a large groupf of nobles. The Crown Prince told Mountbatten that the Order was only given to the Imperial Family and to crowned heads. The Queen had it, as did President de Gaulle and President Eisenhower. Mountbatten enquired anxiously about Prince Philip. The satisfying reply came that Prince Philip was given the Order of Sheba, Ethiopia's second Order.

[§] Mountbatten thought he might have to decline this as he did not have permission to accept it. But as he was travelling on *Britannia* with the Queen, Prince Philip and Princess Anne, all of whom had the Order, he asked the Queen's permission to accept. She said he could do so as the Order was given during one of her official visits.

ing herself of the many delights of her considerable Cassel fortune, in later life Lady Mountbatten was a tireless charity worker. She died while on a tour for the St John Ambulance Brigade, at Jesselton, North Borneo, in 1960.

Countess Mountbatten held the C.I. (1947) as Vicereine of India, and was given the G.B.E. at the same time (she had been appointed C.B.E. in 1943). She was made a D.C.V.O. by George VI (1946), and she was a G.C.St.J. (1945).

Lady Mountbatten also had the following foreign Orders:

The American Red Cross Silver Medal (1946), 1st class (despatches)
The Belgian Red Cross, 1st class (1946) (despatches 1946)
The Order of the Brilliant Star (China) (1947)
The Netherlands Red Cross Medal (1947)
The Princess' Cross of the Order 'Pour le Merite', Roumania
The Grand Cordon of the Three Divine Powers (Nepal), which was awarded to her posthumously in 1960.

OTHER MINOR MEMBERS OF THE ROYAL FAMILY

Two royal Knights Grand Cross of the Order of Hanover survived into this century: Field Marshal H.R.H. the Duke of Cambridge (1819-1904), son of Prince Adolphus, Duke of Cambridge, and a grandson of King George III; and H.R.H. the Duke of Cumberland and Teviotdale, 3rd Duke of Brunswick (1845-1923), grandson of Prince Ernest, Duke of Cumberland, and therefore a great-grandson of King George III.

As good a way as any to get an honour was to be a minor member of the Royal Family or to marry into the Royal Family. One of the most interesting cases was the 1st Marquess of Milford Haven, who was given a civil G.C.B. in 1887 and a military one in 1921*. In 1932 George V gave the G.C.V.O. to the 2nd Marquess of Milford Haven, son of Princess Victoria (of Hesse) (a grand-daughter of Queen Victoria). And his younger brother Lord Louis Mountbatten got the G.C.V.O. in 1937 entirely for reasons of birth, though he earned many other honours for genuine reasons (*see above*).

Prince Christian Victor (1867-1900) was given the G.C.B. and the G.C.V.O. by Queen Victoria, though all he achieved was to serve in the South African War as Captain in K.R.R.C., and indeed he died in Pretoria. His wholly unmemorable bachelor brother, Prince Albert (1969-1931), also picked up a G.C.V.O. for nothing.

Princess Beatrice's son, the Marquess of Carisbrooke, an aesthetic figure who lived at Kensington Palace until his death in 1960, was made a G.C.V.O. at the time of George V's coronation (1911) and a G.C.B. in 1927. His wife, who undertook good works, was awarded the G.B.E. in 1938. Carisbrooke's younger brother, Lord Leopold Mountbatten (1889-1927), a haemophiliac, was another G.C.V.O.. Their other brother, Prince Maurice, who died of wounds received at Mons in 1914, was merely a K.C.V.O..

---

* He wore the military star and the civil star when in uniform. He was also G.C.V.O., K.C.M.G., and a Privy Councillor.

Honours were by no means in short supply amongst Queen Mary's immediate family. Her eldest brother, the Marquess of Cambridge was a G.C.B. (1911), G.C.V.O. and C.M.G*. Her second brother, Prince Francis of Teck, a delightful ne'er-do-well, was a G.C.V.O., who did at least earn himself a D.S.O.. The other brother, the Earl of Athlone, took a more important part in public life, serving as both Governor-General of South Africa and later of Canada. He was therefore a K.G. (1928), G.C.B.(1911), G.C.M.G. (1923), and G.C.V.O (1904). Interestingly he was first made K.C.V.O. as early as 1898, when he was 24, and advanced to G.C.V.O. on his marriage to Princess Alice of Albany. He was a member of the Privy Council (1931), appointed Knight of Justice of the Order of St John (1904) and promoted Bailiff Grand Cross (1929).

Queen Mary's nephew, the 2nd Marquess of Cambridge, became a K.C.V.O. (1927) and G.C.V.O. (1935) at the time of the Silver Jubilee. And the husbands of several minor royals fared well from this source, the Duke of Beaufort (husband of Lady Mary Cambridge) receiving his G.C.V.O. in 1930, and the Garter in 1937, Colonel Sir Henry Abel Smith receiving a K.C.V.O. in 1950 (on his retirement as Colonel, Corps of the Household Cavalry), while Lord Carnegie (later Earl of Southesk and a man who lived to be 98) received a K.C.V.O. in 1926 merely for being married to the asthmatic Princess Maud of Fife[†].

Therefore the Queen's attitude to honours is admirable in comparison with the ease of earning enjoyed by these cousins in the early years of the century.

[†]   Lord Cambridge and Lord Athlone were made G.C.B.s at the time of George V's Coronation.
[†]   The Earl was present at all the Royal Victorian Order services in St George's Chapel, including the one in 1991, by which time he was 97.

EPILOGUE

The Queen, speaking of the honours system, in the documentary film *Elizabeth R*:

'The system does discover people who do unsung things. And I think that's very satisfactory. And I think people need pats on the back sometimes. It's a very dingy world otherwise.'

SOURCES

Introduction
1 *The Times*, 6 March 1993.
2 Hugo Vickers, Unpublished Diary, 13 April 1983.
3 Sir Sidney Lee, *King Edward VII, Volume Two, His Reign* (Macmillan, 1927), p.101.

Chapter One: The Present Royal Family
1 Edward Mirzoeff film, *Elizabeth R.*
2 *Ibid.*
3 *From Shore to Shore*, edited by Philip Ziegler, (Collins, 1989), p.290.

Chapter Two: The Order of the Garter
Some of the historical material derives from a lecture the present author gave to the Eton College Heraldic and Genealogical Society in 1969. Fortunately he retained his notes from that occasion.
1 N.H. Nicholas, *History of the Orders of Knighthood of the British Empire* (1842), Introduction I, p.xlvii.
2 Elias Ashmole, *Institution, Laws and Ceremonies of the Most Noble Order of the Garter* (1672), p.183.
3 G.F. Beltz, *Memorials of the Garter* (1841).
4 Sir Sidney Lee, *King Edward VII, A Biography* (Macmillan, 1927), pp.452-53.
5 James Pope-Hennessy, *Lord Crewe* (Constable, 1955), p.62.
6 Philip Magnus, *King Edward VII* (John Murray, 1964), p.303.
7 Lord Hardinge of Penshurst, *Old Diplomacy* (John Murray, 1947), p.143.
8 Lord Redesdale, *The Garter Mission to Japan* (Macmillan, 1906), pp.16-17.
9 *Ibid*, pp.17-18.
10 *Ibid*, pp.20-21.
11 Noble Frankland, *Prince Henry, Duke of Gloucester* (Weidenfeld, 1980), p.94.
12 *Ibid*, p.95.
13 Philip Ziegler, *Edward VIII* (Collins, 1990), p.26.
14 Private notes.
15 Kenneth Rose, *George V* (Weidenfeld, 1969), p.173.
16 *Ibid.*
17 Kenneth Rose, *Superior Person* (Weidenfeld, 1969), p.335.
18 Rose, *op. cit.*, p.256.
19 Ponsonby, *op. cit.*, pp.352-53.
20 *Ibid.*
21 The Marquess of Reading, *Rufus Isaacs, 1914-1935* (Hutchinson, 1945), p.344.
22 Gravestone of the 7th Earl Stanhope, Chevening Churchyard.
23 Earl Stanhope, *Chevening* booklet, July 1966.
24 *Report of the Friends of St George's*, 1936.
25 Duchess of Sermoneta, *Sparkle Distant Worlds* (Hutchinson, 1947), p.139.
26 Sarah Bradford, *King George VI* (Weidenfeld, 1989), p.249.
27 Martin Gilbert, *Winston S. Churchill 1939-1945, Vol.III* (Heinemann, 1988), p.109.

28 *Ibid*, p.111.
29 James Pope-Hennessy, *Lord Crewe* (Constable, 1955), p.174.
30 Sir John Wheeler-Bennett, *King George VI: His Life and Reign* (Macmillan, 1958), pp.758-59.
31 Wheeler-Bennett, *op. cit.*, p.753.
32 *The Times* 24 April 1948.
33 Lord Moran, *Winston Churchill, The Struggle for Survival 1940-1965* (Constable, 1966), p.404.
34 Lord Moran, *op. cit.*, p.555.
35 Lord Moran, *op. cit.*, p.556.
36 Lord Moran, *op. cit.*, p.666.
37 *The Times*, 7 April 1956.
38 Lord Moran, *op. cit.*, p.699.
39 Christopher Hibbert, *The Court at Windsor* (Longmans, 1964), p.285.
40 John Cloake, *Templer - Tiger of Malaya* (Harrap, 1985), p.1.
41 Alastair Horne, *Macmillan, Volume 2* (Macmillan, 1989), p.572.
42 Private information.
43 Lord Drogheda, *Double Harness* (Weidenfeld, 1978), p.361.
44 Lord Longford, *Diary of a Year* (Weidenfeld, 1982), p.127.
45 Philip Ziegler, *Mountbatten* (Collins, 1985), p.528.
46 *From Shore to Shore*, edited by Philip Ziegler (Collins, 1989), pp.340-41.
47 *Ibid*, p.341.
48 John Brooke-Little, *Royal Ceremonies of State* (Country Life), p.99.
49 Lord Drogheda, *Double Harness* (Weidenfeld, 1978), p.361.
50 Private information.
51 Philip Howard to author, June 1976.
52 Lt-Gen. Sir Brian Horrocks, *A Full Life* (Fontana Books), p.259.
53 Lord Drogheda, *Double Harness*, p.361.

Chapter Three: The Order of the Thistle
1 Sir Ivan de la Bere, *The Queen's Orders of Chivalry* (Spring Books, 1964), p.97.
2 De la Bere, *op. cit.*, p.99.
3 Duff Cooper, *Haig - Volume 2* (Faber & Faber, 1936), p.129.
4 Lord Home, *The Way the Wind Blows* (Collins, 1976), p.99.
5 William Douglas-Home, *Sins of Commission* (Michael Russell, 1985), p.95.
6 Sir Thomas Innes of Learney, *The Queen's Coronation Visit to Scotland* (Pitkins, 1953), p.32.

Chapter Four: The Order of St Patrick
The author has drawn much of the present chapter from Peter Galloway's excellent, informative and amusing book, *The Most Illustrious Order of St Patrick 1783-1983* (Phillimore, 1983), copies of which are obtainable in Dublin, but harder to find in London.

1 Sir Ivan de la Bere, *The Queen's Orders of Chivalry* (Spring Books, 1964), p.174.
2 *The Order of St Patrick, 1783-1983* (Phillimore, 1983), p.1.
3 *Ibid*, p.6.
4 *Ibid*, p.24.
5 Hugh Shearman, *Northern Ireland 1921-1971* (H.M.S.O., 1971), p.18.

Chapter Five: The Order of Merit
1 Philip Magnus, *King Edward VII* (E.P. Dutton, N.Y. 1964), p.305.
2 Kenneth Rose, *King George V* (Weidenfeld, 1983), p.257.
3 Sir Sidney Lee, *King Edward VII - Volume Two - The Reign* (Macmillan, 1927), p.98. [Letter from the King to Lord Salisbury, the Prime Minister]
4 *Ibid*, p.98.
5 *The Statutes of the Order of Merit*, p.2.
6 *Ibid*.
7 Kenneth Rose, *King George VI*, p.258.
8 Cecil Woodham-Smith, *Florence Nightingale* (Constable, 1950), p.592.
9 *Ibid*.
10 Kenneth Rose, *King George V*, p.260.
11 *Ibid*.
12 *Ibid*. p.261.
13 James Lees-Milne, *The Enigmatic Edwardian* (Sidgwick & Jackson, 1986), p.349.
14 *The Statutes of the Order of Merit*, additional statute, dated 16 December 1935.
15 Private notes by Lord Hardinge of Penshurst (Private Collection).
16 Martin Gilbert, *Winston S. Churchill, Volume VII* (Heinemann, 1986), p.524.
17 Martin Gilbert, *Winston S. Churchill, Volume VIII, Never Despair, 1945-1965* (Heinemann, 1988), p.178.
18 David Dilks, *The Diaries of Sir Alexander Cadogan* (Cassell, 1971), p.791.
19 John Wheeler-Bennett, *John Anderson, Viscount Waverley* (Macmillan, 1962), p.403.
20 *From Shore to Shore*, edited by Philip Ziegler (Collins, 1989), p.131.
21 *Ibid*, p.131.

Chapter Six: The Order of the Bath
1 James Risk, *The History of the Order of the Bath* (Spink & Son, 1972), p.xi.
2 *Ibid*, p.3.
3 *Ibid*, p.19.
4 *Ibid*, p.11.
5 *Ibid*, p.92.
6 *The Order of Service, Ceremony of the Installation of Knights of the Most Honourable Order of the Bath*, 10 May 1928.
7 Sir Ivan de la Bere, *The Queen's Orders of Chivalry* (Spring Books, 1964), p.130.

Chapter Seven: The Order of St Michael and St George
1 Sacheverell Sitwell, *Great Palaces* (Spring Books, 1964), article by Nigel Nicolson, p.281.
2 Sir Charles Johnston, Unpublished Diary 17 July 1979.

3 *Ibid*, 18 July 1981.
4 *Ibid*, 20 July 1983.
5 *Ibid*, 12 July 1984.
6 The *Independent*, April 1992.

Chapter Eight: The Royal Victorian Order
1 Sir Frederick Ponsonby, *Recollections of Three Reigns* (Eyre & Spottiswode, 1951), p.210.
2 Lord Hardinge of Penshurst, *Old Diplomacy* (John Murray, 1947), p.179.
3 *Ibid*.
4 Sir Ivan de la Bere, *The Queen's Orders of Chivalry* (Spring Books, 1964), p.146.
5 Hugo Vickers, Unpublished Diary, 7 December 1978.
6 The late Audrey Russell to author, April 1983.
7 Hugo Vickers Diary, April 1991.

Chapter Ten: The Companions of Honour
1 The Statutes of the Order of the Companions of Honour (1919), p.3.
2 Sarah Bradford, *Sacheverell Sitwell* (Sinclair-Stevenson, 1993), pp.433-34.
3 Alastair Horne, *Macmillan Volume II* (Macmillan, 1989), p.343.
4 *Ibid*, p.345.
5 *Ibid*, p.348.
6 Arnold Goodman, *Tell Them I'm On My Way* (Chapmans, 1993), p.229.
7 *Ibid*.

Chapter Eleven: The Order of The British Empire
1 Kenneth Rose, *King George V* (Weidenfeld, 1983), p.257.
2 *Ibid*, p.258.
3 Frederic Hood, *The Chapel of the Most Excellent Order of the British Empire* (Oxford University Press, 1967), p.6.

Chapter Twelve: The Imperial Service Order
1 *The Statutes of the Imperial Service Order*, 1954.

Chapter Thirteen: The Indian Orders
1 Lord Hardinge of Penshurst, *My Indian Years* (John Murray, 1948), pp.54-55.
2 *Burke's Peerage*, 1938, p.2966.
3 Charles Allen, *Lives of the Indian Princes* (Century, 1984), p.317.
4 *The Times*, 9 August 1924.
5 Charles Allen, *Lives of the Indian Princes* (Century, 1984), p.180.
6 *Ibid*.

Chapter Fifteen: The Order of St John of Jerusalem
1 *The Royal Encyclopedia*, p.499.

Chapter Sixteen: The Commonwealth Orders and Decorations
1 *Spectator*, 21 November 1992.
2 Much of the above is drawn from: Gough Whitlam, *The Whitlam Government 1972-1975* (Penguin Books, Australia, 1985), pp. 138-141.
3 Governor-General's Message, *The Australian Honours System* (AGPS Press, Canberra, 1991).
4 Letters Patent of the Order of Australia, given under

SOURCES

the Great Seal of Australia at the Court of St James's 14 February 1975. (*Order of Australia*, pub. Govt House, Canberra 1992).

5 *Order of Australia*, p.3.
6 *Ibid*, p.5.
7 *Ibid*, p.6.
8 *Ibid*, p.4.
9 *Ibid*, p.6.
10 *Ibid*, p.6.
11 *Ibid*, p.5.
12 *Ibid*, p.6.
13 *The Royal Encyclopedia*, p.353.
14 *The Order of Canada*, 1983, p.1.
15 *Ibid*, p.3.
16 Private information.
17 *The Govenor-General of Canada*, (Rideau Hall, July 1990), Canadian Honours System.
18 *Decorations for Bravery* (Rideau Hall, August 1990), pp.11-13.
19 Gough Whitlam, *The Whitlam Government 1972-1975* (Penguin Books, Australia, 1985), p.99.
20 Ibid, p.99.

Chapter Seventeen: Other Royals of the Past
1 H.H. Princess Marie Louise, *My Memories of Six Reigns* (Evans Brothers, 1956), p.173.

2 Sir Ivan de la Bere, *The Queen's Orders of Chivalry* (Spring Books, 1964), pp.86-87.
3 H.R.H. the Duke of Windsor, *A King's Story* (Cassell, 1951), p.117. [Letter from H.M. King George V, dated 19 September 1915]
4 *Ibid*, pp.117-18.
5 Michael Maclagan to author, 1976, recalling a story told to him by Sir Alan Lascelles.
6 Sir George Aston, *H.R.H. The Duke of Connaught and Strathearn* (Harrap, 1929), p.87.
7 Hon. Sir Bede Clifford, *Proconsul* (Evans, 1964), pp.113-14.
8 H.H. Princess Marie Louise, *Letters from the Gold Coast* (Methuen, 1926), p.106.
9 *From Shore to Shore* edited by Philip Ziegler, (Collins, 1989), p.214.
10 *Ibid*.
11 *Ibid*, p.69.
12 John Barratt, *With the Greatest Respect* (Sidgwick & Jackson, 1991), p.106.
13 *Ibid*, p.109.
14 John Terraine film, *The Life and Times of Admiral of the Fleet Earl Mountbatten of Burma*, Episode 12.
15 Philip Ziegler, *Mountbatten*, (Collins, 1985) p.310.
16 *From Shore to Shore* edited by Philip Ziegler, (Collins, 1989), p.13n.

PICTURE CREDITS

half-title: Hugo Vickers
6: Photographers International
10: Hulton-Deutsch
11: Hulton-Deutsch
14: Royal Collection
18: Photographers International
19: Photographers International
20: Hugo Vickers
23: Camera Press
25: Photographers International
26: Photographers International
27: Photographers International
28: Photographers International
29: Hugo Vickers
31: Hugo Vickers
32: Hugo Vickers
33: Photographers International
34: Photographers International
36: Press Association
38: Popperfoto
39: Popperfoto
40: A F Kersting
44: Hugo Vickers
46: Hugo Vickers
49: Hulton-Deutsch
55: Hugo Vickers
58: Hulton-Deutsch
60: Photographers International
62: Photographers International
65: Hugo Vickers

68: Royal Collection
69: Hugo Vickers
70: Popperfoto
72: Camera Press
77: Photographers International
78: Hulton-Deutsch
82: courtesy of Spink and Son Ltd
84: Popperfoto
85: Hugo Vickers
86: Hugo Vickers
87: Hugo Vickers
88: Royal Collection
97: Royal Collection
98: Royal Collection
100-1: Press Association
102: Photographers International
105: A F Kersting
108: Popperfoto
110: Hugo Vickers
112: Popperfoto
113: Hugo Vickers
116: Hulton-Deutsch
119: courtesy of Spink and Son Ltd
122: courtesy of Spink and Son Ltd
124: Camera Press
125: Hugo Vickers
126: courtesy of Spink and Son Ltd
128: Hulton-Duetsch
129: Hulton-Deutsch
130: Hugo Vickers

133: Photographers International
136: Hugo Vickers
138: British Library
140: Hulton-Deutsch
141: Hugo Vickers
143: Hulton-Deutsch
144: Camera Press
146: Hugo Vickers
147: courtesy of Spink and Son Ltd
149: Photographic Records Limited
150: Photographers International
156: Hugo Vickers
159: Camera Press
160: Hugo Vickers
164: Hugo Vickers
166: Hulton-Deutsch
167: (left) Royal Collection
     (right) Hugo Vickers
168: Hugo Vickers
172: Hugo Vickers
175: Hugo Vickers
176: Hugo Vickers
178: Hulton-Deutsch
179: Hugo Vickers
180: Royal Archives
183: Hugo Vickers
184: Hulton-Deutsch